Democracy, Dictatorship, and Default

The International Monetary Fund (IMF) predicts that, in the coming years, more than fifty countries are at risk of default. Yet we understand little about the political determinants of this decision to renege on promises to international creditors. This book develops and tests a unified theory of how domestic politics explains sovereign default across dictatorships and democracies. Professor Ballard-Rosa argues that both democratic and autocratic governments will choose to default when it is necessary for political survival; however, regime type has a significant impact on what specific kinds of threats leaders face. While dictatorships are concerned with avoiding urban riots, democratic governments are concerned with losing elections, in particular the support of rural voting blocs. Using cross-national data and historical case studies, Ballard-Rosa shows that leaders under each regime type are more likely to default when doing so allows them to keep funding costly policies supporting critical bases of support.

CAMERON BALLARD-ROSA is an Assistant Professor of Political Science at the University of North Carolina at Chapel Hill. He is a recipient of the David A. Lake award for best paper from the International Political Economy Society.

Democracy, Dictatorship, and Default

Urban–Rural Bias and Economic Crises across Regimes

CAMERON BALLARD-ROSA
University of North Carolina at Chapel Hill

CAMBRIDGE
UNIVERSITY PRESS

University Printing House, Cambridge CB2 8BS, United Kingdom

One Liberty Plaza, 20th Floor, New York, NY 10006, USA

477 Williamstown Road, Port Melbourne, VIC 3207, Australia

314–321, 3rd Floor, Plot 3, Splendor Forum, Jasola District Centre, New Delhi – 110025, India

79 Anson Road, #06–04/06, Singapore 079906

Cambridge University Press is part of the University of Cambridge.

It furthers the University's mission by disseminating knowledge in the pursuit of education, learning, and research at the highest international levels of excellence.

www.cambridge.org
Information on this title: www.cambridge.org/9781108836494
DOI: 10.1017/9781108871310

© Cameron Ballard-Rosa 2020

This publication is in copyright. Subject to statutory exception and to the provisions of relevant collective licensing agreements, no reproduction of any part may take place without the written permission of Cambridge University Press.

First published 2020

A catalogue record for this publication is available from the British Library.

Library of Congress Cataloging-in-Publication Data
NAMES: Ballard-Rosa, Cameron, 1982– author.
TITLE: Democracy, dictatorship, and default : urban–rural bias and economic crises across regimes / Cameron Ballard-Rosa, University of North Carolina at Chapel Hill.
DESCRIPTION: Cambridge, United Kingdom ; New York, NY : Cambridge University Press, [2020] | Includes bibliographical references and index.
IDENTIFIERS: LCCN 2019057513 (print) | LCCN 2019057514 (ebook) | ISBN 9781108836494 (hardback) | ISBN 9781108819138 (paperback) | ISBN 9781108871310 (epub)
SUBJECTS: LCSH: Debts, Public–Political aspects. | Financial crises–Political aspects. | Rural-urban relations–Political aspects. | Democracy–Economic aspects. | Dictatorship–Economic aspects.
CLASSIFICATION: LCC HJ8015 .B35 2020 (print) | LCC HJ8015 (ebook) | DDC 336.3/4–dc23
LC record available at https://lccn.loc.gov/2019057513
LC ebook record available at https://lccn.loc.gov/2019057514

ISBN 978-1-108-83649-4 Hardback

Cambridge University Press has no responsibility for the persistence or accuracy of URLs for external or third-party internet websites referred to in this publication and does not guarantee that any content on such websites is, or will remain, accurate or appropriate.

Contents

List of Figures		*page* vii
List of Tables		ix
Acknowledgments		xi
1	Introduction	1
	1.1 *Economic Crisis and Political Reform*	4
	1.2 *My Argument in Brief*	10
	1.3 *Outline of the Book*	13
2	Political Survival, Mass Politics, and Sovereign Default	16
	2.1 *Political Survival and Sovereign Default*	16
	2.2 *Mass Politics and Political Survival*	17
	2.3 *Rural Bias and Democratic Default*	32
3	Regime-Contingent Biases and Sovereign Default, 1960–2009	55
	3.1 *Motivation*	55
	3.2 *Data and Estimation*	59
	3.3 *Results*	65
	3.4 *Alternate Accounts*	67
	3.5 *Temporal/Systemic Factors*	70
	3.6 *Subsidy Costs*	74
	3.7 *Discussion*	78
4	Default Pressures in Closed versus Electoral Autocracy: Zambia and Malaysia	80
	4.1 *Introduction*	80
	4.2 *Zambia*	82
	4.3 *Malaysia*	94
	4.4 *Discussion*	115

5	Default Pressures in Consolidated versus Contentious Democracy: Costa Rica and Jamaica	116
	5.1 Theoretical Predictions for Democratic Default	116
	5.2 Costa Rica	119
	5.3 Default in Contentious Democracy	137
	5.4 Jamaica	138
	5.5 Discussion	155
6	Urban–Rural Pressures across Regime Types: The Case of Turkey	157
	6.1 Introduction	157
	6.2 Case Selection	159
	6.3 Initial Transition to Democracy	159
	6.4 Build-Up to the First Crisis	160
	6.5 The Crisis of 1978–1979	162
	6.6 Rural Electoral Advantages	164
	6.7 Military Intervention, 1980–1985	167
	6.8 Discussion	169
7	Conclusion	171
	7.1 Interrelationship between Domestic Politics and International Markets	172
	7.2 Urban–Rural Politics	173
	7.3 Looming Fiscal Crises in the Developed World	174
	7.4 Concluding Remarks	175
Bibliography		177
Index		191

Figures

1.1	Proportion of countries in default, 1800–2009.	*page* 3
2.1	Optimal electoral subsidy, as a function of the urban population share (α).	39
3.1	Proportion of years spent in default in autocracies, by urbanization.	56
3.2	Proportion of years spent in default in democracies, by urbanization.	57
3.3	Relative Rate of Assistance (RRA) to agriculture, by regime type.	77

Tables

3.1	Autocratic sovereign defaults, 1960–2009	*page* 60
3.2	Democratic sovereign defaults, 1960–2009	61
3.3	Food imports, urbanization, and debt default, 1960–2009	66
3.4	Systemic effects and debt default, 1960–2009	72
3.5	Food export status and democratic default, 1960–2009	75
3.6	High subsidies and debt default, 1960–2009	79
4.1	Malaysia: Compliance with lending guidelines, selected sectors	105

Acknowledgments

For a book about the failure to honor one's debts, it is crucial to acknowledge the incredible array of support that made this work possible. The book is an outgrowth and refinement of a dissertation written in the Department of Political Science at Yale University, where my first set of intellectual debts were accrued. To this end, no single individual has been more influential in shaping my academic career than Ken Scheve, who was an incredible chair, both from across the hall and from across the country. Ken was a fantastic and selflessly devoted mentor and role model – a successful scholar, teacher, and colleague. I thank him for his (sometimes searing) intellectual honesty and incredible practical guidance. I also wish to thank Alex Debs, whose class on political economy first allowed me to get my hands dirty digging into important formal models in the literature. Throughout graduate school, Alex provided unyielding support, always treated me like a colleague, and delved deeper into the appendix of my formal theory than any person should have to do. Rounding out my stellar committee was Thad Dunning, whose astounding diversity of research talents has improved every aspect of my own work. I am extremely grateful to Thad for advice and direction, and for emphasizing the importance of each prong of multimethod approaches.

Beyond members of my dissertation committee, the origins of this book also benefitted tremendously from a rich set of conversations with other scholars. Peter Aronow, Rob Blair, Quintin Beazer, Allison Carnegie, Gary Cox, Allan Dafoe, Madhavi Devasher, Shawn Fraistat, Nikhar Gaikwad, Petr Gocev, Lucy Goodhart, James Hollyer, Greg Huber, Susan Hyde, Sigrun Kahl, Malte Lierl, Nuno Monteiro, Tatiana Neumann, Celia Paris, Maggie Peters, Luis Schiumerini, Rachel Silbermann, Pia Raffler, John Roemer, Nick Sambanis, Sue Stokes, Rory Truex, Jeremy Wallace, Steven Wilkinson, and Libby Wood all provided invaluable feedback and suggestions at various stages of the project. I am also thankful to audience participants at Yale's Comparative Politics

Workshop and International Relations Workshop, the Leitner Political Economy Seminar, the Midwestern Political Science Association, and the International Political Economy Society for additional sources of critique and new directions for refinement.

Once the original dissertation had been expanded into a full book, I was lucky to be able to host a book conference supported financially by the Institute for Arts and Humanities at the University of North Carolina at Chapel Hill (UNC). This day-long workshop helped refine literally every single section of the work that sits before the reader today; it is no stretch of hyperbole to suggest that the current manuscript is publishable only due to the incredible attention to detail and support of the attendees of this conference. Extra special thanks goes to those readers who were given the arduous task of reading and providing comments on the entire document: I cannot express sufficiently my gratitude to Pablo Beramendi, Mark Copelovitch, Layna Mosley, Tom Pepinsky, and Mike Tomz for the dedication of time and collective brainpower represented at the conference. I also benefitted from feedback on sections of the manuscript from several of my colleagues at UNC who attended the book workshop, including Tim McKeown, Jason Roberts, and Graeme Robertson.

Parts of this manuscript were written while I was a research fellow at Princeton University's Niehaus Center for the Study of Globalization and Governance. The time afforded by this fantastic fellowship to dig deeply into primary archival material for several of my cases was an invaluable contributor to the richness of historical detail this book presents. As I expanded my historical material to include additional cases, Kai Stern and Michelle Smoler provided fantastic research support in identifying relevant secondary source material.

Finally, while the academic debts incurred in the progress of completing this book are legion, I would be remiss in not also acknowledging the personal debts I have accrued to important individuals in my private life. First, I would like to express my gratitude to Ryan Marenger and Eric Bourne, for lifelong friendship and intellectual stimulation of widely varying ambit. Next, I wish to thank Garett and Kate Ballard-Rosa, for making home my favorite place to be and providing a much-needed shelter and escape from the stresses and pressures of academic life. I am tremendously grateful to my parents, Michael and Maurine Ballard-Rosa – whose academic experiences were an inspiration for my own – for creating a family environment in which education was valued above all other pursuits, and for unending love. Dad, I wish you were here today. Mom, I'm so thankful you are.

Finally, my deepest debts are to my brilliant and loving wife. This book is dedicated to Lucy Martin, for everything. You are the base of my support, my truest critic, fiercest champion, and best friend.

1

Introduction

> A national bankruptcy is by no means illegal, and whether it is immoral or unwise depends altogether upon circumstances. One can hardly ask of the present generation that it alone suffer for the folly and waste of its predecessors, for otherwise in the end a country could hardly be inhabited because of the mass of its public debts.
>
> Gustav Hugo (1819), *Textbook of Natural Law*

> "It really is irresponsible of the president to try to scare the markets," said Senator Rand Paul, Republican of Kentucky. "If you don't raise your debt ceiling, all you're saying is, 'We're going to be balancing our budget.' So if you put it in those terms, all these scary terms of, 'Oh my goodness, the world's going to end' – if we balance the budget, the world's going to end? Why don't we spend what comes in?"
>
> "If you propose it that way," he said of not raising the debt limit, "The American public will say that sounds like a pretty reasonable idea."
>
> *New York Times*, October 8, 2013

Seeking to cover a large and growing budgetary imbalance, in late 1976 the president of Egypt, Anwar Sadat, turned to the World Bank for loans. As is customary in cases of borrowing from international financial institutions, the World Bank responded by demanding that – in exchange for new lending – the Egyptian government would need to reform several policies that were viewed as detrimental to the budget. Of particular importance was an emphasis on the need to do away with costly food subsidies, especially on bread. Under external pressure to reform cheap food policies, in January 1977 Sadat announced the end of government subsidies on several basic commodities, including flour, rice, and cooking oil. As prices for food skyrocketed by nearly

50 percent over the next few weeks, the response by a struggling population lacking other channels of government influence was predictable: widespread rioting and unrest in which dozens died and hundreds were injured. Echoing calls by rioters for bread as a mobilizing cry, the "bread riots" of 1977 represented a large-scale outpouring of antiregime protest that was seen as a critical threat to the stability of Sadat's rule. In response, by month's end, the government backpedaled on the economic reforms and reinstated the food subsidies. Yet having failed at the reforms called for by the World Bank, Egypt has subsequently struggled periodically to raise foreign capital, particularly during times of budgetary crisis. This tension between politically popular (and regime-stabilizing) subsidies for the population, and demands for their reform in order to secure international loans, has persisted up to this day: As recently as February 2018, *The Economist* ran an article identifying food subsidies as a constant source of fiscal trouble for Egypt.[1]

Internal demands on government finances are a crucial component of politics. Yet, in the quest to identify additional sources of revenue, states may sometimes run up against external demands for reform in exchange for more money. This dilemma puts incumbent leaders in an exceedingly difficult bind, as fiscal politics is the lifeblood of the state. Without sufficient government revenue, armies go unlevied, granaries are emptied, and bridges fall into disrepair. Regardless of a politician's particular aims for staying in power, these goals will almost certainly require funding to be achieved – and so, before it is anything else, politics is inherently fiscal. This is particularly true in redistributive regimes, where battles over spending and taxation occupy the center of the political spectrum. Whom to tax, and how heavily? Whom to benefit, and how much? If budgets must be balanced between revenue brought in, and spending going out, then every policy choice comes at the expense of some (potentially politically relevant) group, and the delicate balancing act between competing interests will be the source of bitter political struggle.

And yet, as most countries have discovered, the presupposition that fiscal politics occurs under the constraint of a binding budget need not necessarily be true, at least in the short to medium term. If maintaining power requires pleasing multiple groups beyond the normal budgetary capacity of the state, there exists a means of smoothing over this discrepancy: debt. When cash is flush, politics is relatively easy; if you can afford to give everyone what they want, why not do so? By borrowing the difference between what states are capable of coaxing out of taxes, and the spending they wish to pursue in order to please important constituencies, leaders can secure safe tenure in office – until these funds run dry.

---

[1] www.economist.com/news/middle-east-and-africa/21736552-egyptians-are-addicted-subsidies-make-them-poorer-what-fuel-bread-and

Introduction

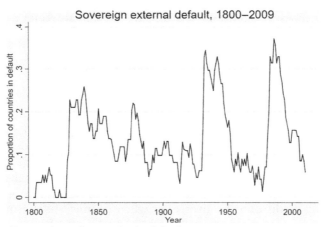

FIGURE 1.1. Proportion of countries in default, 1800–2009.

It is during times of fiscal crisis, when outside borrowing no longer suffices to bridge the gap between what a state spends and what it earns, that politicians are forced to engage in difficult political calculus and identify those groups in society whose support is truly crucial. During these difficult times, some countries manage to successfully engage in structural reforms in order to remain current on their international debt payments. Others, however, ultimately decide that the costs of austerity are politically unpalatable, and thus default on their sovereign debt. What determines the capacity of countries to successfully reform? Conversely, what characterizes the political dynamics of countries that fail to do so, and are forced to default instead?

Figure 1.1, drawn from pathbreaking work on the history of economic crises by Reinhart and Rogoff (2009), shows the yearly proportion of countries that have been in default on debt owed to external creditors, beginning in 1800. As can be seen, default is far from a rare occurrence: there are years when a third of all countries have been in default on their international financial obligations. Additionally, since the 1830s, there has never been a year in which no country was in default. Looking over the entire period, the average proportion of countries in default for the entire sample is just under 15 percent, which suggests that in any given year, we should expect to find one out of every seven countries in the world to be in default. Sovereign default is a historically prevalent, periodically recurrent, and potentially catastrophic form of economic crisis. And yet – despite the right to renege on international debt obligations generally being held by politicians themselves or politically-appointed bureaucrats – our understanding of the political determinants of sovereign default is largely undeveloped. This work fills the gap, deriving a regime-contingent theory linking dynamics of political survival to specific fiscally burdensome policies that, during times of budgetary crisis, prove difficult to remove, and thereby increase the likelihood of sovereign default.

1.1 ECONOMIC CRISIS AND POLITICAL REFORM

1.1.1 The Politics of Economic Reform

While there exists little work on the politics of sovereign default in particular,[2] there is a long-standing literature in political science on the politics of economic reform more generally that helps inform my own theorizing. For instance, Gourevitch (1986) usefully linked the material interests of the owners of different factors of production (such as laborers and farmers) to specific policy conflicts that could only be overcome when seismic shifts from economic crisis created opportunities for new political coalitions of support. Relatedly, Simmons's (1997) account of which countries were better able to implement the economic changes necessary to preserve their commitments to the Gold Standard in the interwar years relied in large part on the credibility that such reforms would be feasible to domestic political audiences. To the extent that there existed greater domestic political instability, the implied shortening of time horizons for sitting incumbents was expected to reduce concerns over the long-run costs of reneging on currency obligations. Frieden's (1991, 8) assertion that, during times of fiscal crisis, "policymakers provided more resources to those who exerted more pressure on them, and that economic interest groups exerted pressure on policymakers in direct proportion to what they had to gain or lose from policy and the ease with which they could mobilize" is a close parallel to the broad theoretical approach I employ in this work.

In focusing on the apparent failure of many African countries to successfully reform their economies – despite decades of economic distress – Van de Walle (2001) emphasizes that the reform process has generally taken a back seat to political considerations, such that burdensome but politically influential programs like state employment and agricultural price control have remained stubbornly resistant to change. And while some governments have had success in cutting expenditures for public programs while under the guidance of international institutions like the IMF, work by Nooruddin and Simmons (2006) demonstrates that these effects often vary across regime types, presumably due to differential political pressure from groups under different kinds of institutional settings. While it might seem that authoritarian regimes ought to enjoy advantages in implementing unpopular economic reforms through greater repressive capacity and limited need for popular support, more careful work on the political limits of autocratic rulers has emphasized that there are

---

[2] While work along such lines remains limited, I am certainly not the first to recognize the need to disaggregate the domestic politics of debt default – over 20 years ago Eichengreen and Lindert (1992, 6) had already noted that "different domestic interest groups may attach very different priority to the maintenance of debt service [and so] understanding either the domestic politics of debt or the course of international negotiations requires disaggregating domestic interest groups."

still significant constraints on what people in nonelectoral regimes can be asked to bear before turning to protest, particularly in regimes without access to large rents from oil or other natural resources (Haggard 1985). In addition, Pepinsky (2008, 2009) demonstrates that understanding the response of autocratic regimes to economic crisis requires more careful consideration of the precise constellation of societal groups that form the core of its political support.

More recently, Walter (2013, 2016) has developed a useful typology of "vulnerability profiles" for countries facing the need for reforms due to financial crises. This work identifies that, in most cases of macroeconomic disequilibrium that lead to subsequent trouble, countries can usually engage in either "external adjustment" by allowing the currency to depreciate, or "internal adjustment" via austerity measures meant to reduce aggregate demand and thereby affect domestic prices. Walter (2016) emphasizes that countries will generally adjust along the margin which is least politically painful for incumbents; for example, when importers are not a politically-salient constituency, currency devaluation may be more palatable than, say, cutting government expenditures. Alternately, when maintaining a fixed exchange rate is of paramount importance, but domestic expenditure programs to be reformed do not benefit core regime supporters, economic reform via internal adjustment is more likely to occur.

While extremely useful as a guiding typology, I note that, for developing countries facing external debt troubles, neither reform path is likely to be easy. Walter's (2013) focus is primarily on the responses of various developed European countries during the European debt crisis; in such settings, the emphasis on internal versus external margins of adjustment is of central concern. However, as noted by Mosley (2000, 2003) and reaffirmed by Reinhart and Rogoff (2009), concern over sovereign default is much more pronounced among low- to middle-income countries,[3] where the sets of relevant domestic and international pressures during crisis may be somewhat distinct from those faced in the OECD. To begin, much borrowing from foreign lenders by developing countries is denominated in foreign currency – this serves as a means of lessening risks to lenders from currency fluctuation. While this "original sin" of sovereign borrowing by developing countries may have helped reduce risk premia in the short run (Eichengreen, Hausmann, and Panizza 2007), once countries find themselves in financial trouble, this can have the effect of radically increasing the costs associated with the external adjustment path. That is, for countries with foreign-denominated debt, the consequence of currency devaluation is likely to be a dramatic increase in the real cost of debt-servicing, making this adjustment option much less palatable. In addition, my work helps highlight precisely those domestic groups that benefit from

---

[3] Mosley (2000, 2003) demonstrates that bond traders generally do not fear default risk in developed countries, but do take the threat of default more seriously when investing in developing sovereign debt. Additionally, Reinhart and Rogoff (2009) note that, as a matter of empirical observation, countries above a certain income threshold appear to "graduate" from sovereign debt defaults – for example, while France defaulted on loans to the Crown repeatedly throughout the eighteenth and nineteenth century, after attaining "developed" country income levels, it has yet to do so again.

government spending programs, and whose support is likely to prove crucial to the continued survival of incumbent rulers. Thus, sovereign debt crises should generally fall into the dreaded "Type II" set of country conditions, which Walter (2016) emphasizes are likely to be characterized by sustained delays in adjustment success, and continued reliance on external financing to make ends meet. When pushed to an extreme, of course, the market tolerance for such delays is not likely to be infinite – it is under these general conditions that I expect sovereign default to be most likely to occur.

1.1.2 Economic Causes and Consequences of Default

While work on the politics of default is limited, there is a well-developed literature on the economic causes and consequences of reneging on international borrowing commitments.[4] This literature takes an anarchic international environment as a starting point: Given the lack of any supranational governing agency, the existence of sovereign debt appears at first as a puzzle. While domestic loans between businesses can ultimately rely on national courts to adjudicate cases in which an agent has defected from its responsibilities, with the exception of the use of force (which is now generally viewed as unacceptable), if a sovereign state chooses to default on repaying its loans, there are no institutional consequences for doing so. Given this lack of a supranational debtors court, rational financial actors should be able to predict that a government with time-inconsistent preferences will eventually find it in its best interests to renege on repayment obligations, and as such, should never make such loans in the first place.

Eaton and Gersovitz's (1981) seminal paper was the first to point to the market itself as an enforcer of international promises. The centerpiece of their argument rested on the assumption that future loans to governments could be conditioned on past behavior, presenting a game in which financial agents punished countries that defected in previous rounds by excluding them from borrowing forever. Given this strategy, it might no longer necessarily be in the best interests of a government to default on its debt, even without an international institution that would hold it accountable. So long as incumbent rulers valued access to future lending, they would internalize the consequences of breaking their word to lenders today, thereby establishing a rational basis for sovereign loans.

However, subsequent work by Bulow and Rogoff (1989) points out that this explanation for sovereign loans replaces one cooperation problem with another: in a world of tens of thousands of individual investors in sovereign bonds, it should be difficult to maintain the exclusion of countries from access to capital markets even in the case of default. Even if lenders who were defaulted upon decided to deny future loans to a defaulting country, that country would

---

[4] For the definitive summary of recent work in this field, see Tomz and Wright (2013).

1.1 Economic Crisis and Political Reform

be willing to offer better terms on loans to other investors, who would find it in their best interest to cooperate, thereby undermining the exclusion mechanism which was supposed to make sovereign borrowing rationally possible in the first place. It has been subsequently demonstrated that,[5] especially in the middle to late twentieth century, countries that defaulted on foreign loans were able to return to capital markets at roughly the same rate as those that had remained faithful in repayment,[6] although more recent work by Cruces and Trebesch (2013) recovers a significant linkage between size of the "haircut" associated with debt restructuring and subsequent terms of financial market access.

Rather than relying on market exclusion, Bulow and Rogoff (1989) propose the importance of "issue-linkage" – particularly the connection between sovereign loans and international trade – as the driving force behind sovereign lending. According to their argument, countries do not fear to default because of restricted access to future borrowing. Instead, debtor countries often find that trade with partners from whom they have borrowed is tied, either explicitly or implicitly, to remaining current on interest payments, and that foreign financing for trade may also depend on faithful debt servicing. Subsequent empirical work by Rose (2005) demonstrates a significant reduction in trade levels between lender–debtor country pairs following a default, a finding replicated by Borensztein and Panizza (2009).[7]

A third school of thought resuscitates the original linkage between default and future borrowing originally suggested by Eaton and Gersovitz (1981) by focusing more specifically on reputation-based arguments. Most prominent among these accounts is Tomz's (2007) book tracing the rise of sovereign lending in Europe and its spread to New World nations which emphasizes the importance of a reputational mechanism in affecting market rates of loans to different countries at the time, and especially the interest rate spreads that followed default instances during the nineteenth and early twentieth century. At the center of this account is a recognition of the need to consider bondholder behavior in a world of incomplete information – with perfect understanding of borrowers and their interests, Tomz notes, reputation would have little effect at all. Conversely, in the more realistic world of incomplete information, investors inform their view of the likelihood of being repaid as a function of updating beliefs about a borrower's type, as determined by their record of repayment under good times and bad. Rather than replacing one cooperation

---

[5] See, for example, studies found in Eichengreen and Lindert (1992) or Sturzenegger and Zettelmeyer (2006).

[6] One of the most egregious examples of this is found in Jorgensen and Sachs's (1988) account of the Latin American debt crisis of the 1930s, in which Argentina was essentially the sole major Latin American country which did not default on its debt obligations at the time. While this did apparently earn Argentina slightly lower interest rates on continued borrowing to repay its existing loans through the end of the 1930s, "having conscientiously retained its creditworthiness by honoring its debt service obligations, [Argentina] did not receive noticeably better treatment in the 1950s in return for its admirable behavior in the previous two decades" (78).

[7] However, see Tomz (2007) for evidence against this account.

problem among lenders with another among enforcers of issue-linked policies, a reputation-based theory of sovereign lending allows self-interested lenders to best protect their own expected profitability by internalizing the past play of different debtors. Knowing this, governments should place great weight on their international reputation, as the economic consequences of damaging this reputation can include costly risk premia or even complete credit rationing by the private market.

Yet, despite presenting a wealth of evidence to demonstrate the preeminence of a reputational theory of sovereign borrowing over others based on sanctions or the use of force, the data from Figure 1.1 still point to an important puzzle: Given these reputational consequences, why do so many countries still choose to default? As noted by Tomz (2007, 16–17), "many factors could affect how governments balance the costs and benefits of debt repayment. The political strength of incumbents, the willingness of citizens to tolerate austerity, and the power of contending interest groups could all come in to play. So, too, could the time horizons of leaders – their patience for reputational rewards that might not materialize for months or years." Tomz continues by noting that "the exact sources of heterogeneity [in government preferences for default] are interesting in their own right, but are not the focus of this book." Tomz takes the political calculations over default as given, and develops a theory of international reputation to explain why countries might still remain current on international obligations, even in an anarchic environment. Contrarily, this work looks at the other side of the coin: I take the reputational costs of default as given, and develop a theory linking citizen influence over political survival to incentives for leaders to renege on their sovereign debt.

Finally, a current avenue of research is focused on determining what domestic-level factors impact the sustainability of debt, in the hopes of generating predictive models to indicate early warning signs that countries are headed into dangerous waters. For example, Kraay and Nehru's (2006) investigation of developing country debt defaults finds that, while standard economic factors such as the size of the debt burden and economic shocks explain a decent fraction of the variation in default cases, the predictive power of their models is substantially improved by the inclusion of broad measures of institutional quality as well. In a finding that echoes that of Reinhart, Rogoff, and Savastano (2003), the authors point out that while a standard "rule of thumb" for evaluating the sustainability of borrowing is to look at debt to export ratios, in fact the level of debt to exports at which countries have defaulted appears to be contingent upon the underlying institutional structures in the country. It is with these sorts of results in mind that recent summaries of the literature in economics on sovereign debt default have suggested that "there also needs to be more work on the private incentives of policymakers to default or fight a crisis as opposed to the incentives of a social planner ... [and] to our knowledge, a systematic analysis of the relationship between sovereign debt, defaults, and political career concerns has not been undertaken and is an interesting area for future research" (Panizza, Sturzenegger, and Zettelmeyer 2009, 682, 692).

1.1.3 The Politics of Sovereign Debt Default

In the past several years, a limited literature has developed that looks at default explicitly as a political problem. Tomz's (2002, 2004) work on the political dynamics of default in Argentina's crisis at the turn of the millennium spearheaded empirical investigation of the topic, as did Stasavage's (2003) investigation of the role that domestic political dynamics played in making credible the commitment to honor economic obligations by the English government following the Glorious Revolution. A series of empirical papers by Van Rijckeghem and Weder (2009), Saiegh (2009), and Kohlscheen (2010) have produced a new "stylized fact" of defaults in developing democracies, finding that countries with parliamentary political systems and with coalition governments tend to be less likely to default than presidential systems. This is argued to result from the inclusion in the ruling coalition of holders of a country's sovereign debt, who clearly favor faithful repayment. As these individuals tend to be found within the relatively wealthy minority of citizens, it is argued that they are most likely to have influence over decisions to default in political environments that encourage the representation of small electoral groups – this should be most likely under parliamentary systems, particularly when no single party can secure executive control without a broader coalition of support.[8]

While laudable for their efforts to begin to unpack the politics of default, these empirical findings do not fully explain politicians' priority to represent bondholders over other groups, and ignore the political dynamics of default in autocracies entirely. On the first point: despite arguing that default is prevented when bondholders are included in the ruling coalition, these works do not explain why bondholders (as opposed to some other voter group) would necessarily become an electorally salient coalition member during fiscal crises; this seems particularly problematic given the tiny number of voters likely to be represented by such a party. This is not to argue that wealthy investors lack political influence – they almost certainly do – and yet it is uncommon to view their primary source of power as linked to their electoral strength. Instead, they are likely to influence democratic outcomes through access to vast lobbying resources; yet, if true, it is unclear why these resources could only be deployed in proportional representation systems or under coalition governments.

---

[8] While not directly studying the decision of a government to default or not, there is closely-related recent work on the preferences for default among the public in democracies by Curtis, Jupille, and Leblang (2014) and Nelson and Steinberg (2018); one of the most consistent findings in this literature is the effect of partisan orientation in driving support for repayment of international loans.

Additionally, these works ignore the politics of autocratic default entirely. If sovereign default is primarily an economic phenomenon, then perhaps this omission is understandable. Alternately, if the survival dynamics of incumbent politicians are the same across autocracies and democracies, then focus on the particularities of autocratic systems may be redundant.[9] However, casual observation suggests that both these claims are untrue, and in this work I provide evidence demonstrating not only that politics is a critical driver of default outcomes, but that the specific political processes by which citizens link incumbent survival to fiscal politics vary widely across democratic and autocratic regimes.

1.2 MY ARGUMENT IN BRIEF

1.2.1 Closed Autocracy and Urban Bias

Politicians enjoy the perquisites of power, whether they rule in democracies or dictatorships. Yet the specific ways in which citizens may threaten an incumbent's tenure vary across these regime types. In *closed autocracies* that lack multiparty elections, the will of the people is of little importance to the ruling elite, except when the masses can threaten their hold on power. This is most likely, I argue, when citizens can credibly threaten revolt if their basic demands go unmet. While there are a host of factors that may improve the collective action capacity of the masses, it is easier to get more people out to protest when there are more people nearby. This suggests that unrest should be more common in urban areas than in rural ones, given simple facts of demographic density (Bates 1982; Wallace 2014). If a rural farmer needs to walk several miles to reach her nearest neighbor, and if government offices are far away in distant towns, mobilizing rural actors will be particularly difficult. Contrast this with the situation facing an urban worker, who may be able to reach hundreds of potential coconspirators in his apartment building or on the workfloor at his factory. In addition, a walk across town to government offices or central squares is likely to prove much less arduous than a trek from rural hinterlands to the center of political power. With urban consumers often literally at the doorstep of government, autocrats wary of unrest will place much greater weight on the needs of potentially restive city dwellers.

This suggests that we should observe an *urban bias* in autocratic policies – one of the most common forms of such urban bias comes from the quest to provide food cheaply. Following Engel's Law, food comprises a large and important proportion of total expenditure by the poor, particularly the urban

---

[9] If autocracies are also likely to suffer from credit rationing, as suggested by Beaulieu, Cox, and Saiegh (2012), then the issue of autocratic default may be even worse. Note, however, that Oatley (2010) finds that autocracies appear to have taken on more foreign debt than democracies. See also the discussion of borrowing rates across regimes in Cox (2011).

poor, and autocratic rulers seeking support of the masses have often gone to great lengths to keep food prices low in cities. Yet these cheap food policies can prove fiscally burdensome, particularly in food importing autocracies, and such government interventions in food markets are therefore a common target of reform during times of fiscal crisis. When removing food subsidies is a precondition for successful maintenance of debt repayment, this puts urban-biased autocrats in a difficult political dilemma: If they renege on their international financial obligations, they may lose access to future foreign loans, thereby reducing the expected value of holding office. Yet, to avoid default, they may face massive unrest that could threaten their hold on power today. Thus, I expect that *more urbanized* and more *food importing* autocracies will be willing to face the long-run economic consequences of sovereign default, rather than a short-run threat to their survival in office.

1.2.2 Competitive Autocracy and Limits to Urban Bias

However, while the "pure" dictatorship that many imagine is likely to lack any semblance of electoral competition, more recent work on authoritarian politics has noted that a growing number of nondemocratic regimes not only engage in the act of voting, but also actually allow opposition candidates to run in such elections (Levitsky and Way 2010). For example, Svolik (2012, 36) notes this recent increase in "competitive authoritarian" regimes: From 1946–2008, nearly 30 percent of autocracies have permitted legislative elections in which multiple political parties have actually won seats in the legislature. At first glance, the presence of multiparty elections would seem to contradict the classification of such countries as nondemocracies. Closer evaluation of these elections suggests a degree of electoral manipulation beyond the pale of what would be tolerated in a truly democratic society. Given this high degree of regime interference with the electoral process, the outcomes of such elections are usually perceived to be a foregone conclusion. But, if multiparty elections are not held to actually assess who should govern the country, then what is the point of such exercises?

Magaloni's (2006) work on the stability of the PRI in Mexico, despite running elections against an opposition party for nearly 75 years, clarifies that the actual function of elections is to prove the omnipotence of the regime. By demonstrating overwhelming levels of popular support, even when the opportunity to vote for an opposition exists, *competitive autocracies* are able to discourage potential elite schisms while also binding the public to the clientalist transfers that often follow from electoral largesse. While such elections are not meant to truly lead to a changeover in power, the presence of such elections does have systematic effects on the relative importance of different social groups. In particular, as many developing countries are characterized by large fractions of the population that live in rural areas, the ability to capture huge blocs of rural votes by providing some transfers to the agricultural hinterlands suggests that, unlike in closed autocracies that pay no mind to rural agents at all, electoral autocracies will be characterized by less single-minded focus on the cost of urban living. As such, I predict that the advantages for urban collective mobilization may be undercut in those autocracies that also rely on rural voters to demonstrate their overall political dominance.[10]

1.2.3 Consolidated Democracy and Agricultural Electoral Biases

While democratically elected incumbents certainly do not like the prospect of massive rallies by opponents, *consolidated democracies* are characterized by the internalization of elections as the sole means of replacing leaders. In this regard, I argue that the collective mobilization advantages of urban areas do not translate into the same political influence in consolidated democracies that they enjoy in non-democratic regimes. While protests are still likely to occur under democratic rule, when all actors recognize that electoral competition is the only legitimate means of establishing political control, the nature of such protests is likely to lack the sort of violence that poses an immediate threat to regime stability.[11] Instead of focusing on urban protesters, in many developing democracies the majority of the population lives in rural areas, which suggests that, if politicians pursue policies that will win them the greatest number of votes, focus on rural priorities will be greatly improved. This should be particularly true for agricultural support policies – like government-guaranteed prices for farm produce – that are favored by a large swath of the rural community, and that serve as an organizational rallying cry for rural economic interests.

Recent research has documented that democracies do indeed engage in *rural-biased* agricultural programs (Cole 2009; Golden and Min 2012); removing these policies has proven a consistent hurdle in negotiations over international exchange (Davis 2003; Naoi and Kume 2011; Barari, Kim, and Wong 2019). And, like the cheap food policies pursued by autocrats, these farm subsidization programs often become fiscally burdensome – particularly in food-exporting democracies – and are therefore common targets of reform during times of fiscal crisis (Varshney 1998). This can put incumbents into a political pickle, especially when the electoral environment is unstable or fragmented: Default on sovereign debt can have severe long-run consequences for a country's ability to regain access to foreign finance. But if removing agricultural subsidies results in the loss of crucial rural voters, engaging in structural reform may result in certain losses at the polls. I therefore expect *more rural* and *food exporting*

---

[10] This lessening of the relative dominance of urban interests to affect political survival through protest is likely to be complemented as well by recent scholarship by Robertson (2007, 2010) that details the ways in which hybrid regimes have often captured the protest process, and turned it towards regime-strengthening ends.

[11] Using McAdam, Tarrow, and Tilly (2003)'s terminology, protest in stable democracies tends towards acts of "contained" rather than "transgressive" contention.

1.3 Outline of the Book 13

democracies to default on their sovereign debt, rather than engage in electoral suicide in the face of external demands for reform.

1.2.4 Contentious Democracy and Limits to Agricultural Biases

Limits on the political impact of urban revolt in consolidated democracies rests on the shared social belief that unrest holds no part in driving political stability. Unfortunately, however, not all democracies have been successful in completely eliminating the role of mass violence in politics. In these *contentious democracies*, competitive elections can and do still lead to replacement of governing politicians. Yet standard electoral strategies by political parties in such systems are often complemented by more violent approaches; this can include the mobilization of political "gangs" that can selectively target regime opponents during elections in order to discourage turnout, as well as efforts by outsiders to delegitimize incumbent rulers by creating a more general environment of violence (Wilkinson 2006). The use of mass violence for electoral ends suggests that politicians must give greater consideration to those groups that possess advantages in mobilization for violence – as suggested earlier in the chapter, among other factors, a dense concentration of city dwellers is likely to prove a critical source of violent unrest.

This can become particularly problematic if the application of force for political ends during elections leads to greater societal instability subsequently. Recent work by Hafner-Burton, Hyde, and Jablonski (2014) demonstrates, for example, that the threat of citizen revolt is greater following elections where parties used violence as a political tool. This suggests that the type of "pure electoral" influence accorded citizens by their capacity to generate votes discussed above may be tempered by additional considerations towards appeasing urban actors, which may limit the rural biases demonstrated in the general democratic case. Indeed, to the extent that unrest becomes systemic, and regime stability is called into question, I expect to observe that some contentious democracies may look much closer to the sorts of urban-biased dictatorships discussed initially.

1.3 OUTLINE OF THE BOOK

By focusing on the specific survival dynamics particular to each regime, I arrive at two distinct and essentially symmetric sets of predictions regarding factors likely to increase sovereign default in democracies versus autocracies. Absent attention to the particular mechanisms of executive replacement I identify, it would be difficult to account for such wildly different expectations; indeed, if sovereign default were only a matter of economics, we would not expect to find any variation in these factors across the two regime types. My regime-contingent theory of sovereign default provides several novel and counter-intuitive predictions ignored by extant research; these hypotheses are substantiated and validated with a wealth of subsequent quantitative and qualitative evidence.

The rest of the book is structured as follows. Having argued that the ability of citizens to affect political survival is likely to vary by regime type, I begin in Chapter 2 by detailing two specific strategies of mass politics: *voting* and *revolt*. After identifying that urban and rural divisions of society serve as an important and systemic division of preferences over particular policies related to food pricing, I formalize my general theory linking citizen interests to the political survival of politicians under different institutional settings, and generate specific hypotheses over factors likely to drive default across varying regime constellations. In Chapter 3, I provide a wealth of empirical tests employing cross-national quantitative data to support my primary predictions, even after accounting for a host of alternative domestic and systemic explanations.

Having demonstrated strongly robust support on average for my key predictions about the varying effects of urbanization and food trade status on sovereign default, in Chapter 4 I describe (drawing on hundreds of primary archival source documents) historical cases of fiscal crises in authoritarian regimes to clarify the intervening role of competitive elections in affecting the relative importance of urban or rural citizens to regime support. The case of Zambia, in which no major political opposition was tolerated, provides clear evidence of the centrality of food pricing concerns for urban dwellers as at the core of the survival strategy of the incumbent regime, and also details that worries about unrest in the face of economic reforms ultimately drove Zambian external default in 1986. Conversely, however, the Malaysian case helps document that, when autocrats rely on rural electoral mobilization to generate supermajorities, bias toward urban dwellers is significantly attenuated; greater flexibility in approaches to economic reform helped Malaysia avoid external default despite facing serious budgetary troubles in the 1980s.

Chapter 5 delves into greater historical detail surrounding two cases of sovereign default in democratic regimes that varied crucially in the role of political violence as an electoral tool. The chapter begins by discussing the case of Costa Rica, a country renowned for its peaceful political culture. The Costa Rican case is one where the electoral role of rural agriculturalists is crucial, and as expected, this political centrality of farmers corresponded to heavy (and costly) farm support programs by the Costa Rican government that became targets of reform once the country ran into fiscal issues. However, despite success in doing away with a host of other government programs, the inability of Costa Rican politicians to successfully reform farm subsidies was specifically identified as one of the main issues that drove Costa Rican default in the 1980s. The chapter concludes with a discussion of the Jamaican case, which broadly mirrored initial conditions in Costa Rica but varied significantly in the role that political violence was accorded in elections. Following the rise of politically-mobilized urban gangs and a concomitant eruption of broader political violence, Jamaica is a case where the needs for stability in the capital

1.3 Outline of the Book

city took clear precedence over winning votes from the rural electorate. This corresponded to food subsidy policies more reminiscent of the closed autocracies I described earlier in the chapter; this similarity included the fact that, when faced with large-scale protests as a result of attempted economic reforms, Jamaica defaulted on its international loans multiple times instead of successfully doing away with cheap food policies.

While Chapters 4 and 5 discuss the effects on urban–rural biases of differing institutional arrangements, as is generally true with historical comparisons across different countries, it is possible that these cases varied along other dimensions than the ones I emphasize as important. Chapter 6 traces changing pressures historically for agricultural support prices within a particular country – Turkey – and shows that while democratically elected governments repeatedly proved incapable of reforming farm subsidies, a military interlude had no trouble doing away with such rural-biased programs. Yet, the same individual who opposed farm support policies when serving in the military government, following the resumption of competitive elections completely reversed his position to advocate expansion of agricultural subsidies in order to fend off electoral challenges from political opponents. The Turkish case helps make clear, holding nearly all features of a country constant, that providing citizens a channel for electoral influence can have systematic consequences on the attentiveness of government to urban or rural groups, with crucial consequences for the fiscal health of the state subsequently. Finally, in Chapter 7 I conclude the book by highlighting important scope limits on the generalizability of my emphasis on food policies as a politically central issue of contention, while also discussing extensions of my more general argument over the difficulty of removing costly policies for crucial regimes supporters as a political theory of sovereign default moving forward.

2

Political Survival, Mass Politics, and Sovereign Default

> Give us this day our daily bread.
> And forgive us our debts,
> As we forgive our debtors.
>
> Matthew 6:11–13, *King James Holy Bible*

2.1 POLITICAL SURVIVAL AND SOVEREIGN DEFAULT

Sovereign debt is a puzzling affair. In the anarchic international system that sovereigns inhabit, lenders should always worry about the likelihood of being repaid, since states that break their promises cannot be punished by some suprastate with authority to enforce contracts. This lack of direct enforceability implies that states would want to default all the time. Of course, many sovereigns repay their debts faithfully, even at times when it can be difficult to do so, particularly when they seek to maintain their reputation in international markets due to the costly consequences of reneging on international obligations. Yet, while political leaders are clearly aware of the importance of reputation in international affairs, we nonetheless observe instances of default frequently. Given the reputational damage done by sovereign default, which is likely to raise future borrowing costs substantially – even to the point of complete market exclusion for particularly egregious cases – why would any country ever choose to renege on its international financial obligations?

This book develops an answer to this question by focusing on an important but sometimes overlooked fact: Sovereign default is a *political* decision. To understand why politicians might sometimes choose not to repay the money they owe international creditors, it is critical to start by understanding what it is that politicians want. While different rulers value a panoply of particular things – ranging from personal wealth to fame to influence to a benevolent sense of duty to country – one of the most undisputed tenets of modern political science is that, before all else, politicians want to stay in power. The belief that politicians take actions to increase their likelihood of surviving in office is a core assumption of nearly all work in the discipline; as a starting point, this suggests that governments would consider defaulting on sovereign debt when it increases their likelihood of remaining in office.

Of course, how precisely incumbents stay in power varies enormously across different political systems. What, then, are the main threats to political survival that incumbents are likely to face? There exist many, but this book focuses on one particular form: threats from "the people." Concerns from disgruntled citizens are certainly not the only threats that leaders can face, nor will they necessarily always be the most imminent or important. However, as I argue in this chapter, focusing on the potential for mass citizen action to affect incumbent survival has the advantage of providing both parsimony in theory as well as high likelihood of generalizing to many countries. Recognizing that any event as complex as sovereign default will likely be the result of multiple competing interests, I start my account by focusing on survival concerns I expect to hold across a wide set of cases, then progressively add additional nuance and layers of complexity to the core argument where relevant.

In order to hone my expectations about the role of political survival incentives in driving the decision to default on sovereign debt, I develop in this chapter a series of formal models that expose the core assumptions I make about which political actors matter, how they form their preferences, and how these preferences translate into political action. Like all theories, this is a simplification of a much more complicated world. The value of the model comes from generating clear hypotheses, which are evaluated empirically – both quantitatively and qualitatively – throughout the rest of the book. As a result of an explicit focus on a specific set of policies, my theory also highlights the importance of the interplay between domestic policy choices and the potentially unintended consequences they can have in an interconnected global economy. The core of the model's predictions hinge around domestic political pressures for survival as a function of existing political institutions and the fiscal ramifications of pricing policies. In a world where goods can flow across borders, the relative trade status of a given country is revealed to be a crucial intervening variable.[1] Formalizing my theory helps make explicit how these different realms interact.

2.2 MASS POLITICS AND POLITICAL SURVIVAL

This book seeks to understand the influence of common citizens on incumbent survival. The political force of any one individual is likely to be essentially zero – no single vote can sway an election, nor can a single protester topple a

---

[1] Rogowski (1989) similarly demonstrates how urban–rural political conflict relates to international economic integration.

dictatorship. When the will of common citizens has been expressed in politics, it has been large blocs of votes, or teeming masses of revolutionaries, that have leaned on the wheel of history to overturn incumbent rulers. To the extent that everyday citizens may capture the attention of politicians, it is likely to be only when they are engaged in what we may term *mass politics*, or activities in which citizen preferences are aggregated and expressed not as single units but as unified and mobilized multitudes (Frieden 1991).

This emphasis on mass mobilization of common citizens betrays immediately something of a paradox: As made clear in Olson's (1965) famous work on the logic of collective action, the difficulties inherent in achieving mass mobilization are most likely to inhere in large and diverse groups. Given all the known difficulties of the collective action problem, we might wonder if citizens are ever able to translate their preferences into power. While throngs of revolutionaries marching through the streets or large swaths of voters casting their ballots in a unified front both represent forms of potential political influence, there is no guarantee that all groups in society will be successful in actualizing this political energy (Acemoglu and Robinson 2006). How, exactly, do citizens affect political survival of incumbent leaders?

I focus in this book on two central strategies citizens may employ to make their voices heard to sitting politicians: via *voting* or *revolt*. While there exist other forms of attracting politicians' attention – such as financing electoral campaigns or threatening a military coup – I argue that average citizens generally lack access to the material resources (either economic, military, or otherwise) that would be required to make such strategies viable. As noted earlier in the chapter, neither a single voter nor a solitary protester is likely to affect the outcome of political struggles for power. However, the weakness of voting or revolting as an isolated individual belies an enormous potency when joined together with a host of other citizens. Given the need to aggregate individual citizens into a collective body, I argue that voting and rioting represent the two primary means via which the latent political force of mass movements is actuated in politics.

2.2.1 Citizens: The Urban–Rural Divide

Different groups of citizens may vary in their capacity to mobilize in elections or in rebellion. Yet how, precisely, are we to identify different social groups? Certain cleavages among social agents may be salient in particular settings; for example, in some parts of the world ethnic identities serve as an important division of political attention. In others, religious beliefs may condition political support. And, in still others, economic class or ideology may form the basis of dominant electoral cleavages. However, few of these divisions are likely to hold true across all societies. While undoubtedly useful in investigating the political dynamics of certain countries or regions, these particular divisions may prove somewhat ill-fitting when transported to other parts of the globe.

2.2 Mass Politics and Political Survival

In this work, I identify instead a common geographic source of differentiation among citizen groups by focusing on those differences that arise between *urban* as opposed to *rural* citizens. This approach has the advantage, firstly, of applying to all countries. Unlike divisions based on ethnic identity, for example, which may simply not be a dominant feature of political identification in some places, all societies have urban centers and rural hinterlands, and so focus on the concentration of differences in preferences of urban as opposed to rural agents is likely to be more generally applicable cross-nationally. In addition, this focus on geographic distributions of a population also has the advantage of overlapping well with a defined set of economic preferences (Beramendi 2012): At a basic level, most rural agents engage in some form of agricultural production, and so their economic well-being is generally tied to the profitability of the farming sector.

Yet, to the extent that many farms produce food, this identifies a source of tension with the second group of urban citizens. Insofar as rural agents want to improve their well being, they should favor higher costs for the food products they produce. Urban workers, on the other hand, generally focus on the strength of their purchasing power; for a set level of nominal wages, higher prices of food erode the real value of urban incomes, and thus make city dwellers worse off. Gourevitch's (1986, 24) classic account of policymaking during times of crisis focuses on the role of land and labor – as the two factors of production owned by common citizens – in responding to economic downturns; in this account, he notes that "unionized labor tended to be concerned with keeping down the cost of food ... Nearly everywhere agriculture and labor found it difficult to cooperate."[2] This geographic division of economic interests, as crystallized around the price of food, is also captured in Bates (1982, 35), who notes that "[agricultural] pricing policy finds its origins in the struggle between urban interests and their governments ... it is the rural producers who bear the costs: they are the ones who bear the burden of policies designed to lower the price of food." By pursuing a geographic partition of citizens into urban and rural agents, the theory developed in this chapter specifies a relatively universal division of social groups with easily identified and potentially opposed economic preferences over specific government policies.

Beyond this appeal of wide applicability, the focus on urban versus rural citizens also dovetails nicely with preexisting work that identifies agents that enjoy advantages in mobilization for protest and for voting. In the case of political mobilization for revolt, a broad collection of work has previously noted that the collective action advantages of densely populated areas means that urban settings play host to the vast majority of actual protest movements (Lipton 1977; Schultz 1978; Bates 1982; Wallace 2014). And, while there

---

[2] Gourevitch also considers the role of business interests ("capital") in shaping response to crises; given my focus on mass politics, I elide this part of the discussion here.

have been many determinants of urban unrest, times of food scarcity and high pricing have consistently been linked to instances of mass unrest. In addition, as regards the capacity to influence political outcomes by casting votes, past studies of dominant voter cleavages have frequently highlighted that rural farm votes are common targets of electoral favoritism in democratic regimes (Dixit and Londregan 1996; Persson and Tabellini 2000; Davis 2003; Naoi and Kume 2011; Chen and Rodden 2013). In electoral regimes as diverse as Japan, Kenya, and Turkey, the translation of agricultural price supports into consistent electoral gains has proved a durable strategy of solving the difficult calculus required to win elections. This book's focus on urban and rural citizens' views over government intervention into the price of food products maps nicely not only onto clear economic preferences for two widely recognized societal groupings but also onto varying capacities in the two dominant strategies of mass politics identified earlier in the chapter.

Yet, of course, the feasibility of either strategy – and therefore the attentiveness of politicians to certain groups – is likely to depend critically on existing institutions (Nooruddin and Vreeland 2010). In the next two sections I focus specifically on "pure" institutional types, in which citizens possess only one of the two potential sources of influence over incumbent survival, to detail the biases that arise either toward urban citizens in autocracies or rural citizens in democracies. Importantly, these theories describe two ends of a spectrum of regime characteristics. While I expect the pressures I describe to hold on average across democracies or autocracies, more recent work in political science has emphasized the diversity of sub-regime characteristics across autocratic or democratic systems, which I consider more explicitly after describing the two polar cases.

Finally, it is important to emphasize potential limits to the scope of my theoretical focus on food price policies as a crucial political strategy to win urban or rural support. As citizen incomes rise, the proportion of their income dedicated to food consumption is likely to fall – a property sometimes referred to as "Engel's Law." This suggests that, while citizens of all countries must eat, the relative salience of food pricing policies may be reduced in wealthier countries, limiting the applicability of my core issue of interest. However, these developed countries are the least likely to default in the first place (Mosley 2003); a theory with greatest validity in the developing world is still well suited to explaining sovereign default.[3] Moreover, while I focus on conflict over food pricing policy, the implications of my theory can be generalized to any zero-sum policy that divides the preferences of two important social groups, particularly those that vary in their capacity to mobilize for revolt or as voters (as discussed in greater detail in the Conclusion).

---

[3] For excellent recent work considering the political importance of subsidy policies in economically developed democracies, see Rickard (2018).

2.2 Mass Politics and Political Survival

2.2.2 Formalization of Citizen Preferences

I consider a country with two groups of citizens divided between urban and rural areas. Urban citizens (U) make up a fraction α of the population, while rural citizens (R) make up the remaining ($1 - \alpha$) of the population. Each group is engaged in a particular economic activity; each rural agent produces $\bar{b}$ units of "bread," and each urban agent produces $\bar{x}$ units of some additional consumption good.[4] While it is common to assume that citizens have consumption preferences over different types of products, I follow work in development economics that notes that food consumption exhibits demand patterns that are somewhat unique. In basic terms, food is different from most other types of products in that some baseline level of food consumption is required for individuals to actually stay alive. Given the centrality of food to physical survival, individuals cannot simply substitute their consumption to other goods if the price of food becomes too high.

The most standard formal approach for dealing with this need for a baseline level of food consumption is the adoption of the Stone–Geary utility function, which includes a term that captures baseline consumption. Taking this baseline level of food to be β, consumption utility for citizen i of type $j \in \{U, R\}$ is given by

$$w_{ij}(b,x) = (b - \beta)^{\gamma}(x)^{(1-\gamma)} \qquad (2.1)$$

where γ captures the relative preference of consumers for food as opposed to other goods. In what follows, I assume that rural farmers produce at least enough food that they could keep themselves above this basic subsistence threshold; formally, I assume that $\bar{b} > \beta$.[5]

Without loss of generality, I normalize the price of x to unity. With sufficient integration into the world economy, the domestic price of food (p) should, without any intervention, be equal to the world food price (π). However, given the centrality of government food price policies to urban–rural political conflict, I assume that the government can affect the domestic price of food by implementing a price subsidy $\phi \in \{\underline{\phi}, \bar{\phi}\}$, such that the domestic price is given by $p = \pi + \phi$. Note that with $\underline{\phi} < 0$ and $\bar{\phi} > 0$, the government can either raise or lower the domestic price of food in order to appease particular political constituencies; specifically, when the government selects a negative ϕ, this reduces the domestic price of food below the international price, whereas

---

[4] Note that, following common practice, agents here are modeled as supply inelastic: They always produce a fixed amount of a given good, irrespective of the price of that good. This assumption is made to facilitate analysis of equilibrium dynamics, but relaxing this assumption would only further exacerbate the fiscal dilemmas that arise from either subsidizing urban consumption or providing support prices for rural production.

[5] This assumes that, were farmers to engage solely in subsistence farming, they would still have enough food to at least avoid "starvation." This is likely to be violated only under severe cases of natural disaster; I restrict my analysis to the more general case.

when the government selects a positive ϕ this increases the domestic price above the world price. Taking this policy intervention by the government, citizens will maximize their consumption utility $w_{ij}(\cdot)$ subject to their budget constraint as defined by personal income y_j. For urban workers, individual income is given simply by $y_U = \bar{x}$, while for rural farmers individual income is $y_R = (\pi + \phi)\bar{b}$.

2.2.3 Citizen Strategy in Closed Autocracy: Revolt

As highlighted in the introduction to this chapter, I argue that citizen preferences are likely to be taken into consideration by incumbent politicians only when such preferences are successfully aggregated into mass politics via voting or violence. Of course, the effectiveness of either potential strategy is likely to be affected by existing institutions – without elections, an advantage in vote mobilization will be of little use. I begin by considering a world in which citizens do not possess electoral influence, which I refer to as a *closed autocracy*.

When lacking the opportunity to vote, citizens have but one option available to them to vent their discontent at existing policies: protest. Formally, I assume that citizens choose whether or not to engage in unrest, captured as $\omega_j \in \{0, 1\}$. While the literature on collective mobilization is massive and complex, I focus here on food crises as a historically prevalent and consistent trigger of mass revolt. As noted by Walton and Seddon (2008, 25), from the mid-sixteenth to the mid-nineteenth century, "[R]iot was the most common form of popular protest and uprisings related to food were the most common form of riot." The removal of food subsidies was a consistent trigger of urban revolt during the 1970s and 1980s, and a number of studies show the same holds true today (Walton and Seddon 2008; Lee and Ndulo 2011; Weinberg and Bakker 2014). Accounts of the French Revolution note that in addition to demands for equality and freedom, rioting peasants called for bread; a similar refrain was taken up during the Russian Revolution. More recently, uprisings during the Arab Spring included a linkage between high food prices and societal unrest; for example, Gelvin (2015, 10) notes that "protests in Algeria ... began as an old-fashioned 'bread riot' – protesters initially shouted 'We want sugar!' – before shifting their focus to include political demands." Yet why should there be such a tight link between food crises and societal unrest?

When rising food prices put subsistence consumption out of reach, citizens are likely to experience a large and discontinuous drop in their utility. Such a discontinuity may explain why food shortages (or, an inability to acquire existing food due to high prices) have so frequently led to mass unrest historically – given the necessity of food for survival, when subsistence levels of consumption become infeasible, this does not merely decrease overall consumption utility in a smooth way, as is the case for more general products. Instead, by pushing citizens up against the bounds of subsistence, the outcome of doing nothing becomes suddenly much worse, incentivizing citizens to partake in mass violence. In addition, there is reason to suspect that as individuals

2.2 Mass Politics and Political Survival

become hungrier, they experience physiological effects that trigger increasing aggressiveness and more easily rise to anger, precisely the sorts of responses that may lead to greater willingness to engage in the risky activity of rebellion or revolt. Finally, beyond these physiological motivations, basic food such as bread or rice hold an almost hallowed position in many cultures, as captured in such expressions as "to break bread" with someone or prayers that ask to "give us this day our daily bread." I remain agnostic below as to the precise emotional and physiological pathways by which food shortages lead to rebellion, instead taking as given this general relationship that has been observed across regions and over time. Within the context of the model, I assume that citizens always choose to riot when their consumption of food falls below the subsistence threshold.[6]

When unrest occurs, I assume that it leads to the ouster of the incumbent government with probability v_j. Many factors may affect the likelihood of revolt leading to the overthrow of a government; at a basic level, easy access to the seat of power and greater concentration of social actors are both likely to increase the chances that rebellions bring down an incumbent. In particular, I follow the literature on urban bias in arguing that, in many developing autocracies, a prominent potential threat to continued autocratic rule comes from the concentration of citizens in densely populated urban capitals.[7] This threat is due to the relative collective action benefits enjoyed by people in urban areas vis-à-vis their rural compatriots: By definition, urban areas are those with greater density of population, which implies that there are simply more opportunities for opponents of the regime to locate and mobilize other citizens. In addition, city dwellers are much closer to the actual seat of political power and are also frequently much more visible when acting in central political spaces (Wallace 2014). All of these factors suggest that, when politicians worry about the effects of mass unrest, they should focus primarily on the needs of urban areas.

Food typically forms a central part of an urban worker's consumption bundle, and a legacy of large-scale "bread riots" has made ruling autocrats wary of high food prices (Wallace 2010; Hendrix and Haggard 2014). While clearly not all riots are the result of food crises, I make an additional simplifying assumption about the costs of collective action, such that citizens will never choose to revolt if their basic food needs are met ($\omega_j^* = 0$ whenever $b_j^* \geq \beta$). This is not to suggest that all rebellions can be quelled by simply keeping a population fed; however, within the conceptual context of this work, it does grant governments a relatively straightforward policy option for limiting mass unrest that both maps cleanly onto the economic interests of the geographic

---

[6] Formally, citizens of group j will engage in mass unrest (choose $\omega_j^* = 1$) whenever $b_j^* < \beta$.

[7] On the threat to autocratic survival from mass unrest, see Boix (2003) and Acemoglu and Robinson (2006). For works emphasizing urban political biases, see Lipton (1977), Schultz (1978), and especially Bates (1982).

division of citizens I consider, while also tracking quite closely a historically prevalent government strategy for establishing social stability.[8]

2.2.4 The Autocrat

While political leaders under different institutional settings have varying priorities, in what follows I assume that the preferences of politicians are identical, regardless of regime type. This is surely a simplification – even taking as given that both democratic and autocratic leaders want to stay in power, the means they would consider to do so, and the genuine concern they might hold for societal welfare, are likely to diverge. However, as an empirical matter, it is quite difficult to identify convincingly what the precise "values" of a given leader are. Instead, I seek to identify systematic patterns of ruler concern for particular groups of citizens as a function of the institutional settings of a given regime. Thus, I argue that the particular survival incentives generated by a given regime, rather than the differing nature of politicians across political settings, are the key determinant of which societal actors will be privileged.

At a basic level, I assume that all politicians seek to hold office, and attach to the possession of political power a value of χ. Regardless of a leader's personal aims, without hold on the strings of government and access to the resources that the budget provides, it is generally not possible to achieve a particular set of policy goals. Beyond this basic valuation of maintaining power, I also assume that leaders care about their access to financial resources (Levi 1989). Some of these resources come from continued functioning of the government; many, however, can also be drawn from abroad. More precisely, I assume that politicians care about some stock of future expected loans (l), to be drawn from international financial markets; as is standard I assume that these future benefits are "present discounted" by a politician's discount rate (ρ).

As discussed in the introductory chapter, many countries mask the redistributive struggles at the core of their political economy by simply borrowing the difference between government tax revenue and expenditures on government policies. To the extent that this "easy money" allows incumbents to appease all politically relevant agents, this should help secure the stability of a given government's tenure (DiGiuseppe and Shea 2015). In addition, beyond this stabilizing effect on political rule, leaders in more corrupt systems may also value access to future borrowing for selfish reasons: If leaders can channel government borrowing toward projects or investments in which they hold a personal share, this can be a strategy for incredible enrichment through access to the public purse. As sovereign borrowing heightens the scale of resources available to government, I expect that politicians will be concerned with retaining access to these funds in the future. Yet, as both past history and

---

[8] Note that this treatment of unrest does not address directly the findings of recent work on the strategic control of protest in "hybrid regimes" as a means of strengthening political control, rather than threatening it (Robertson 2007, 2010; Weiss 2013, 2014).

recent events in the international financial system have made clear, future access to cheap government lending is by no means guaranteed for all regimes. While a host of particular features may affect access to sovereign credit, the most obvious way in which a government may jeopardize its future borrowing is by failing to make payments on its existing stock of debt today (Eaton and Gersovitz 1981; Bulow and Rogoff 1989; Tomz 2007).

Thus, while defaulting on sovereign debt may open additional budgetary space for short-term priorities, it is likely to result in long-term consequences for a country's reputation, leading to much higher credit costs or even complete credit rationing by the private market (Tomz 2007). Taking this reputational cost as given, I therefore make access to future loans explicitly conditional on the default decision of the government. Combining these elements, the government's (G) utility, so long as it remains in power, is as follows:

$$u_G(\delta) = \chi + (1 - \delta)\rho l \qquad (2.2)$$

where χ captures the (economic or psychic) benefits from being in power, $\delta \in \{0, 1\}$ is a binary default decision, l is a set of future international loans the leader expects to enjoy if $\delta = 0$, and ρ captures the leader's present-discounting of expected future benefits.[9] Following standard accounts of the reputational costs associated with defaulting on a country's sovereign debt, I assume that default results in the government being excluded from capital markets in the future, and so politicians can expect to benefit from foreign loans in future periods only when the country has managed to avoid defaulting in the past. For any nonzero set of future loans l, the government should generally prefer not to default, as so doing guarantees this flow of subsequent resources.

Yet why should governments need to default at all? When faced with insufficient fiscal resources, politicians might also be able to respond either by raising taxes or decreasing expenditures in other areas. Work on crises in developing countries has emphasized a frequent inability to increase government tax extraction, particularly in those countries with already weak bureaucratic capacity, and so I focus particularly on the importance of lending in these times of crisis as a means to plug gaps in normal government revenue (Wibbels 2006). In fact, even existing revenue collection may become more difficult during times of crisis, such as when rising unemployment leads to a fall in income taxes, or when collapsing asset prices reduce the tax take from capital gains or property taxes.

Conditional loan programs often involve the need for government to reduce expenditure on a number of fronts, such as for military investments or public works (Kahler 1989; Nooruddin and Simmons 2006). However, if reducing spending on these other policies is unlikely to trigger the loss of support of

---

[9] Where I assume $\rho \in (0, 1)$. The comparative statics that follow are akin to those from an infinitely-repeated game with Markovian equilibria in which the leader's future borrowing costs depend on its default decision today.

critical social groups, I argue that leaders should be more willing to make these cuts first. Indeed, as made clear in the historical cases of default in subsequent chapters, it is striking the degree to which governments are unwilling to forgo food subsidies even when they are successful in cutting funding for a host of other programs (Haggard 1985; Van de Walle 2001). More generally, I follow the approach of other works on governmental response to crises in arguing that, particularly during difficult economic times, incumbents will be most resistant to removing those policies that benefit the core groups of their support coalition (Frieden 1991; Pepinsky 2008, 2009; Walter 2013, 2016).

In addition to choosing whether to default, the government sets a per-unit food subsidy (ϕ), where the total cost of this subsidy program must be feasible given the government's existing budgetary resources (μ), less any debt repayments it must make (d). Letting $C(\phi)$ represent the costliness of a given food subsidy policy,[10] the government's *budget constraint* is given by the following restriction:

$$C(\phi) + (1 - \delta)d \leq \mu \qquad (2.3)$$

So long as this budget constraint holds without need for default, there should be little pressure for fiscal reform. It is precisely when honoring existing debt obligations presses against the capacity to provide costly social programs, however, that politicians may begin to consider failing to repay.

2.2.5 Urban Bias and Autocratic Default

Even when autocrats do not need to win votes to stay in power, this does not mean that people are completely powerless, as they can still engage in mass revolt when sufficiently displeased. In these *closed autocracies*, the ability of autocrats to retain power depends heavily on their capacity to assuage unrest; given the collective action advantages in urban areas, this is especially likely to result in pricing policies to keep food cheap.[11] Urban bias often results in significant food subsidies for urban consumers – from Roman emperors distributing bread to cheering crowds in the capital, to modern Egyptian government-run bakeries that provide bread at pennies on the loaf, this strategy of preventing unrest by keeping the masses fed cheaply has a long historical pedigree.

Of course, state-mandated low prices for food come at the expense of rural agricultural producers. When the autocrat enjoys monopsonist marketing

---

[10] I derive this cost function explicitly and endogenously in Section 2.2.6 later in this chapter.
[11] Apart from "buying off" important segments of the population, there may exist another strategy for some autocratic regimes which is to simply repress any unrest if and when it occurs. While not denying the importance of such a strategy, I argue that such acts of repression should be more difficult the larger is the urban population that must be kept down. Thus, while some regimes may have greater repressive capacity, I expect the dynamics I identify to exist *on average* across autocratic regimes.

power for domestically produced food, all rural goods must be sold to the government initially, which then resells these food products to urban consumers (Bates 1982). As the autocrat controls completely the marketing of domestic agricultural production, this gives it price-setting power: If rural producers wish to sell their surplus production on the market, there is only one avenue to do so, and thus farmers cannot sell to buyers willing to pay higher prices for their food.[12]

This identifies a prominant characteristic of mass politics under closed autocracies: When citizen influence over political survival is limited to participation in riot and rebellion, rural agents are likely to (almost) never credibly threaten a dictator with revolt.[13] This work is not the first to identify such an asymmetry in potential political force between urban and rural actors in closed autocracies: Stasavage (2005) develops a similar model in which an autocratic ruler faces the threat of removal by urban citizens only. Such a treatment is equivalent to assuming that the costs of rural collective action are such that the threshold for revolt is never met; see Scott (1985) for the classic treatment of the relative weakness of rural mobilizational capacity.[14]

2.2.6 Cost of Subsidy Program and Food Trade Status

In order to assess the fiscal feasibility of a given set of food policies, I make explicit the costliness to the government of a given subsidy program. I begin by defining this cost as the procurement cost less profits from resales; the degree to which the government either makes or loses money via its agricultural policies will depend on the price it pays for food goods it secures, as well as the price it earns from selling these goods to consumers. Critically, my formal model helps make clear that the fiscal burden of government interference in the agricultural market depends both on whether the government pushes domestic prices above or below the world price and on whether the country is a net importer or exporter of food.

Citizen demand for food in equilibrium is a dynamic function of its price; as the price of food rises, citizens should demand less of it, while conversely

---

[12] This interpretation of government monopsony is a stylization, meant to capture that governments possess some capacity for influencing domestic agricultural prices. See Krueger, Schiff, and Valdes (1988); Krueger, Schiff, Valdes et al. (1991); or Krueger (1996) for ways governments in developing countries have affected the urban–rural terms of trade.
[13] Although see work by Pierskalla (2016) that shows that, in cases where rural insurgencies can credibly threaten violence against the state, urban-biased policies are lessened.
[14] In focusing on threats to autocratic rule from mass unrest, I privilege in this account what Svolik (2012) terms the *problem of authoritarian control*. However, as Svolik's work makes clear, nondemocratic rulers often also face a separate *problem of authoritarian power-sharing*, involving the delicate balancing act of maintaining support among a critical core of regime insiders (see also, e.g., Gandhi [2008]; Pepinsky [2009]). Given my conceptual interest in the political weight of mass politics, I largely leave to the side questions of intraelite competition.

overall demand for food should grow as the price falls. I begin by defining total domestic demand for food as

$$D_b(\phi) = \alpha b_U^* + (1 - \alpha) b_R^* \qquad (2.4)$$

While rural agents do engage in some production of food (given by $(1 - \alpha)\bar{b}$), it is not necessarily the case that – particularly when food demand is high – this domestic production will be sufficient to feed everyone in the country. When domestic food production is less than total food demand, this requires the purchase of additional food distributed on the world market – that is, food imports. Alternately, when domestic demand falls below domestic production, this will lead to the sale of excess production to other countries – that is, food exports. Formalization of my argument helps make clear that the fiscal burden of engaging in price manipulation of food products turns critically on whether governments must rely on international markets to satisfy hungry consumers, or instead offload additional production not consumed by domestic agents. Interaction of these two factors reveals four possible cost regimes that are treated in detail in the following subsection.

Regime A: Rural-Biased Export Regime

In the case where the government raises the domestic price above the world price (sets $\phi > 0$) and the country is a net exporter of food $((1 - \alpha)\bar{b} > D_b(\phi))$, any increase in subsidies creates greater fiscal strain on the budget. When domestic agricultural production exceeds domestic demand, the government must purchase food from farmers at an inflated domestic price, but then sell the excess on the international market at a lower world price. An increase in the subsidy, all else equal, will increase the wedge between the domestic and world prices, thus increasing the loss the government must take on a given level of purchases. In addition, any increase in the domestic price will also reduce domestic demand for food – for a fixed level of agricultural production, this will result in an increasing quantity of food that must be sold at a loss. In such a regime, increased agricultural subsidies may pose a serious threat to the government's fiscal position.

Regime B: Rural-Biased Import Regime

However, the fiscal cost of providing above-market price subsidies to agriculture ($\phi > 0$) should be significantly reduced in countries that are net food importers $((1 - \alpha)\bar{b} < D_b(\phi))$. The logic behind this is relatively straightforward: assuming that the government can sell the entirety of domestic agricultural production to domestic consumers at the going market rate, there will be no fiscal cost for intervention. In fact, if the country is able to import additional food at the lower world price, and then resell it to domestic consumers at the higher domestic price, this may actually represent a net fiscal boon for government.

2.2 Mass Politics and Political Survival

Observe, however, that in a dynamic setting, this regime is less likely to remain stable. With government offering supra-market prices for food goods, this should incentivize private actors to increase their production of such products. Over time, as farmers become accustomed to producing products with downside price risk guarantees by the government, this should increase domestic production of food to the point that imports may no longer be necessary. In addition, there is reason to suspect that such a scheme would be electorally dangerous for government should the public become aware that they are paying higher prices for imported foods essentially as an indirect form of taxation. Thus, while food-importing rural-biased regimes are likely to face few fiscal costs, they are also unlikely to be pervasive and long-lived.

Regime C: Urban-Biased Export Regime

Turning to cases where the government chooses instead to subsidize food consumption (sets $\phi < 0$) and is a net food exporter ($(1 - \alpha)\bar{b} > D_b(\phi)$), it again becomes clear that government agricultural interference need not be a drain on state coffers. In this case, the government is able to completely satisfy domestic demand with domestic production, and thus incurs no cost from this transfer. In fact, if the government then sells excess production procured at a lower domestic price at the higher world price, this may actually help the government's fiscal standing. Perhaps the most tragic historical example of this came during the disastrous Great Leap Forward in China, when local rural political leaders delivered exaggerated reports of agricultural production to Communist Party elites, who after securing enough food for urban citizens offloaded "excess" production on international markets to generate funds (Wallace 2014). That this occurred in a period in which tens of millions of rural Chinese farmers are estimated to have starved to death speaks both to the overriding concern with urban consumers in closed autocracies, along with the general political weakness of rural agents when unrest is the only true strategy of mass politics that citizens possess.

This dynamic is also reminiscent of a number of African cases identified by Bates (1982) in which urban-biased governments suppressed domestic agricultural prices in order both to appease domestic consumers as well as to capture foreign reserves. However, this type of regime is not likely to be stable in a dynamic environment. Bates (1982) argues explicitly that antiagricultural bias drove rural producers either to diversify into other crops or instead to move to urban areas – the effect of this dynamic was to turn several previous "breadbaskets" of the region into net food importers. Thus, while urban-biased food exporting regimes need not experience a fiscal impact of food subsidies in the short run, in the longer term this type of policy may push them to import food for a growing urban population with less agricultural domestic production, a phenomenon Wallace (2014) describes as the "Faustian Bargain" of urban-biased policies.

Regime D: Urban-Biased Import Regime

Finally, in cases where the government subsidizes food consumption ($\phi < 0$) but is forced to turn to world markets to fulfill domestic food demand $((1-\alpha)\bar{b} < D_b(\phi))$, the fiscal costs of government agricultural interference again increase in the size of the price distortion. Most obviously, when governments must buy food at a higher world price that is resold at a lower domestic price, a greater consumer subsidy generates a larger fiscal loss for any given amount of imported food. In addition, as the price of food falls at greater levels of subsidization, the demand for food will increase as well, which increases the quantity of food which must be imported. That is, when domestic food production does not suffice to keep urban bellies full, the strategy of repressing food prices becomes more fiscally onerous for a government that needs to purchase food at the world price and then resell these goods at a lower rate.

2.2.7 Equilibrium Behavior: The Autocrat's Default Dilemma

I now consider equilibrium behavior, which I solve via backwards induction.[15] In the final stage of the game, if the autocrat has set a subsidy such that $b_U^*(\phi) \geq \beta$, urban citizens do not revolt, whereas if $b_U^*(\phi) < \beta$, then regime opposition takes place and is successful in removing the autocrat from power with probability v_U. Thus, the dictator should generally prefer to set $\tilde{\phi}$ such that $b_U^*(\tilde{\phi}) = \beta$. However, whether this is feasible depends on the assets available to government in austerity or default. In cases where default would be necessary to afford urban demands, the autocrat's decision will depend as well on how much it values staying in power, its expected future benefits for continued repayment, and the threat posed to its rule by urban unrest.

Comparative Statics

When considering the budget constraint, it is clear that governments with greater resources (higher μ) and less debt (lower d) should be more able to afford subsidies while still remaining constant on debt repayments, which reproduces two standard predictions from economic models of default. In addition, increases in the costs of a given subsidy program make it less likely to be feasible without default. Intuitively, as the number of mouths to feed in urban areas grows, which concomitantly reduces the number of rural farmers producing food domestically, the amount of imports required to ensure stability increases as well. The cost of providing the quiescence subsidy ($C(\tilde{\phi})$) is strictly increasing in the size of the urban population so long as the subsidy remains below the world price, and as long as some amount of food demand is satisfied by international imports.

As the fiscal burden of food subsidy programs increases with food imports, those autocracies more reliant on imported food should be more likely, all else

---

[15] Complete solution provided in the Appendix.

2.2 Mass Politics and Political Survival

equal, to face the trade-off between continued maintenance of international loans, or instead defaulting on these loans in order to maintain subsidies. In addition, larger urban populations drive up the costs of food subsidy policies, generating more mouths to feed as well as fewer farmers to generate domestic food production. The model predicts that both increased food imports as well as larger urban populations will be associated with greater fiscal burdens of urban-biased food policies, thereby increasing the possibility that the government's budget constraint may be exceeded if it attempts to repay its loans while retaining food subsidies. In these cases, default becomes necessary to retain such programs and avoid mass unrest.

Turning now to the autocrat's incentive compatibility constraint (described in Equation 2.16), I find that the probability of autocratic default should increase in the threat that urban unrest poses (higher v_j). While there are a host of factors that may affect the likelihood of successful revolt, the threat of rebellion should be greater as the proportion of the population taking part increases. This reinforces the comparative static on urbanization discussed earlier in the chapter: as countries with greater urban populations face larger and more threatening riots during times of unrest, I again expect that more urbanized autocracies will fear the possibility of mass revolt if they remove food subsidies. Despite the long-term reputational consequences of default, this option may prove preferable to severe short-term threats to political survival. This suggests that, even controlling for the indirect effect of larger urban populations on increased food costs, urbanization should still be related to autocratic default through a "collective action" channel.

My theory linking cheap food policies to pressures for autocratic default provides two main testable hypotheses. Given the collective action advantages of urban areas in facilitating mass mobilization, I expect that more urban autocracies should be less willing to make structural adjustments necessary for reform in the face of fiscal crisis, especially when enacting such policies can lead to riots or rebellion. This suggests that, all else equal,

Hypothesis 1 *Autocracies that are* more urbanized *will be more likely to default on their sovereign debt, due to urban collective mobilization advantages.*

While autocrats may be unwilling to remove urban-biased policies generally, my theory suggests that cheap food policies will be particularly fiscally burdensome for those autocracies that are heavily reliant on imports of food to satisfy domestic demand, as these countries are forced to buy food at a higher international price and then re-sell it at reduced prices to domestic consumers. Thus, I also expect that, all else equal,

Hypothesis 2 *Autocracies that* import more food *will be more likely to default on their sovereign debt, due to the heavy fiscal burden of cheap food policies for such regimes.*

2.3 RURAL BIAS AND DEMOCRATIC DEFAULT

It may seem reasonable to assume that democratic incumbents would wish to provide citizens with access to cheap food. Indeed, a central premise in Sen (1999) is that democratic rulers should seek to avoid famines because of electoral losses that would ensue, whereas autocrats need not fear being removed from power when food shortages occur. Yet previous work suggests that, contrary to the urban bias that often arises in autocracies, many democracies exhibit a *rural bias* in their policymaking, especially in agricultural policy. Why should there exist regime-contingent differences in urban–rural biases?

The primary means of differentiating democracies from autocracies rests on identifying the presence of competitive electoral turnover: at its core, the difference between a democratic and nondemocratic country is the existence of institutionalized mechanisms of executive replacement (Przeworski 1991). These institutions, in turn, can have a profound impact on the potential political influence of citizens. Unlike in closed autocracies, where citizens can only make themselves heard by taking to the streets, in democracies every citizen is equipped with a new capacity for political influence: the vote. This is not to say that protests lose all meaning in democracies – they can often act as a rallying call to focus voter attention on particular issues. Yet the number of democratically-elected rulers who have lost power due to protesters storming the capital is small, especially in comparison to the number of incumbents who have left office due to unsuccessful management of electoral dynamics.[16] Thus, in democracies, citizen political influence is first and foremost an issue of *electoral* influence. While mass unrest may on rare occasion affect political survival dynamics, its relative importance – particularly in comparison to the autocratic case – is greatly diminished. As such, what matters most for democratically elected incumbents is identifying crucial components of successful electoral calculus – put simply, finding those groups of voters whose support is critical for winning an election.

At a basic level, it is intuitive to think that democratic elections should privilege larger groups in society. There exists a simple mathematical advantage to larger groups, all else equal, as they contribute more overall ballots than smaller groups do. A limited literature on the geographical distribution of political power across regime types has identified that many developing democracies exhibit a *rural bias* in their policymaking. When a substantial majority of the population lives in rural areas – as is the case in nearly all developing countries – rural voters are more likely to be favored by politicians seeking to curry favor among a large swath of the electorate (Stasavage 2005; Harding 2012). Work by Varshney (1998), for example, found evidence for substantial rural bias in Indian politics following the rise of Charan Singh and his movement to empower farmers, particularly in the form of farm price supports. The tendency

---

[16] For recent work on the differential survival threats faced by dictators versus democrats, see Hollyer, Rosendorff, and Vreeland (2015, 2018).

2.3 Rural Bias and Democratic Default

for Indian politicians to favor agricultural producers, especially during close elections, has been reconfirmed by findings in Golden and Min (2012) on abuse of electricity provision by rural actors in the Indian state of Uttar Pradesh, who use nearly 17 percent of all electoral supply but pay for less than 5 percent of it.

In work considering explicitly the differential mobilization advantages of urban or rural groups across regimes in Africa, Bates and Block (2011, 322) find that, while larger rural population shares are associated with greater anti-agricultural discrimination in autocracies, "electoral competition transforms high values of rural population share from a political liability into a political asset [and thus] the institution of competitive elections has transformed rural producers in Africa from a disadvantaged lobby into a potent electoral influence." In striking support for a regime-contingent theory of urban–rural political influence, these authors find that rural groups in African autocracies face government discrimination via low agricultural prices, whereas large farming populations in democracies experience exactly the opposite sort of support in price policy; the finding that agricultural taxes are reduced under democratic competition is reinforced in Kasara (2007). Relatedly, Cole (2009) finds pronounced evidence of increased lending by public banks to rural farmers in the lead up to elections, as well as higher rates of delinquent loans by politically-important agricultural producers; these effects are most pronounced in regions of India with larger rural population shares. Perhaps most relevant for the current argument, Hendrix and Haggard (2015) demonstrates that, in contrast to autocracies, democracies intervene systematically in food prices in ways favorable to rural farmers, as opposed to urban consumers.

Beyond simple advantages of group size, rural actors may also be rewarded in democratic politics because of their "swingness" – the capacity of rural groups to mobilize large blocs of votes over a single issue can make rural voters a critical component of successful electoral calculus by competing parties. Within the formal literature on electoral swingness, two of the standard references both explicitly highlight rural agricultural voters as examples of groups that tend to be favored due to their ability to swing close elections. Dixit and Londregan (1996, 1134) motivate their discussion of disproportionate electoral influence by noting that, "[i]n this setting, largesse for some minority interest groups enjoys bipartisan support – both parties compete for the title of *'farmers' best friend.'*" Persson and Tabellini's (2000, 159) consideration of special interest politics additionally argues that a "classical example of this systematic bias is agricultural policy. Virtually all democracies provide generous support for their farmers through trade policies, direct subsidies, and various other programs." Empirical and historical work on agricultural trade policy in democracies more generally has consistently argued for the "special place" of rural voters, arguing that this arises from a disproportionate ability to mobilize rural voters over agricultural policies (Davis 2003; Naoi and Kume 2011; Barari, Kim, and Wong 2019).

Mobilizational advantages in rural areas derive from at least three related factors. Frieden (1991) argues that more concentrated industries will be more motivated to lobby for political protection; agricultural producers are generally more similar economically than are urban groups. In countries with large agricultural workforces, a sizable proportion of the population is engaged in the production of only a handful of key food products, and may therefore be affected by government price policies on a very small number of goods. Contrast this with the diversification of urban economies, where factories may produce widely differentiated products, greatly fragmenting the ability of the government to secure large groups of urban voters with a few simple price policies. This allows politicians to "buy" large numbers of agricultural votes by focusing on relatively simple policies – government guaranteed high prices for agricultural products (Gourevitch 1986).

Additionally, due to infrastructural difficulties of marketing rural production, a common component of rural communities is the presence of an agricultural marketing board responsible for securing goods grown in rural areas and transporting them to urban markets. While these boards are the source of abuse in many autocracies intent on squeezing agricultural producers in order to provide food cheaply to urban consumers, in democracies these marketing agencies instead often become the locus of electoral political activity. That is, these production agencies bind together the electoral and economic interests of rural farmers quite explicitly – in Japan, for example, Mulgan (1997, 885) notes that "at the local level, each farming community has formed the core of agricultural cooperative membership, with strong bonds of community interest reinforced by loyalty to a common group. These organizational factors have meant that the Nokyo [farmer cooperative] vote has been relatively cohesive and thus able to be moved in blocs by agricultural cooperative leaders." Mulgan (1997, 888) continues by arguing that, as a result, "Nokyo has been described as the LDP's biggest vote-gathering machine." Nor is this type of organization unique to Japan. For example, following independence in Kenya there developed strong local rural political groups (*harambee*) that served as effective conduits of rural votes in exchange for government transfers; it is not surprising that Kenya was a country in which farmers enjoyed some of the highest producer prices in Africa (Widner 1994).

Finally, as noted by Harding (2012), traditional social structures often promote the ability of local rural leaders to guarantee the votes of hundreds of their "subordinates," allowing local leaders to deliver large blocs of votes to the highest bidder. Early democratic competition in post-independence India, for example, seems to have followed this logic: Frankel (1978, 386) notes that, at least until the 1969 elections, "[a]t the district level, political mobilization occurred in a vertical pattern: leaders of the elite landed communities constructed multicaste political factions … to create 'an organization based upon the ties between a leader and his followers.'" The ability of landlords to deliver critical votes in exchange for elevated agricultural producer prices

2.3 Rural Bias and Democratic Default

further strengthens the theoretical linkage between rural swingness, agricultural subsidies, and democratic electoral survival.[17] Insofar as democracies exhibit a rural electoral bias due to swingness of rural voters, I expect sitting incumbents to be particularly averse to removing agricultural subsidies in the face of fiscal crisis, even when not doing so may necessitate sovereign debt default.

2.3.1 Citizen Strategy in Consolidated Democracy: Voting

In my general theory of mass politics, I argue that citizens possess two potential sources of influence over incumbent survival: voting and revolt. However, in *consolidated democracies*, elections are recognized as the only legitimate means of establishing political rule – almost by definition, such regimes do not condone the exercise of mass violence in order to drive political outcomes. This is not to say that protest in democracy has no function at all – following discussion of the evolution of "protest societies" in developed democracies as described by Meyer and Tarrow (1998, 2), "rather than calling for comprehensive reforms in the ways political decisions are made ... these marchers are interested less in changing the rules of institutional politics than in exercising greater influence within it." Thus, while opportunities for citizen engagement in mass movements abound in modern democracies, the likelihood that such unrest will lead to an immediate downfall of a sitting regime is minimal. Building on a regime-contingent theory of mass mobilization found in Tilly (2004), recent work by Robertson (2010, 20) similarly identifies the differing roles of protest under liberal democracies as opposed to closed or hybrid authoritarian regimes, arguing that "these effects tend to limit the extent to which protest in liberal democracies threatens either people or property. Consequently ... the vast majority of protests in these regimes tends to be both moderate and public, and more likely to involve making claims, verbalizing challengers, and demonstrating worthiness, unity, numbers and commitment than about taking direct action."

Within the context of the theoretical development of the book, I capture this limited impact of mass unrest in consolidated democracies by removing the ability of citizen groups to threaten political survival by engaging in unrest. That is, I assume that even if citizens choose to protest, the impact of such protests on political outcomes is essentially null; formally, I assume $v_j = 0 \, \forall j \in \{U, R\}$. Given this inefficiency of protest in consolidated democracy, I focus initially only on citizen voting strategies, and suppress any discussion of their incentives to protest.

This assumption is a strong one, but is made to consider the theoretical "pure type" of regimes where citizen influence over incumbents is transmitted entirely via electoral channels. I note, however, that while my work makes this

---

[17] Golden and Min (2012) argues that the ability of local agricultural producers to deliver rural votes en masse to political parties is one of the dominant explanations for their findings on rural bias in distortions to electricity provision.

assumption explicit, a similar expectation about the functioning of democratic politics is implicit in most models of democracy. The lion's share of median voter models, especially with two groups in society, predict that politicians will focus the entirety of their attention on the group that contains the median voter, often to the total exclusion of other voters. Yet, by suggesting that some electorally weak groups will be effectively excluded from politics, these models also must implicitly assume that such excluded groups cannot make their will felt in the political arena in other forms.[18] While I begin my discussion of democratic politics by following a long tradition of excluding civilian violence from the menu of effective actions in consolidated democracy, in subsequent sections I relax this assumption and identify the ways in which consideration of both primary strategies of mass politics may affect political competition in those contentious democracies where civilian violence does carry some sway.

Formally, in systems with multiparty elections, I assume there also exists a political challenger, C, which may be thought of as an opposition party or candidate.[19] In addition to consumption utility, citizens also possess "noneconomic" preferences over the partisan composition of governments with elections. While I remain somewhat agnostic as to the exact content that may drive such views, these additional preferences over which party is in power may be a function of a host of alternative features, such as ethnic identity, economic ideology, or partisan in-group sentiment. Specifically, I assume that all voters receive individual "partisan" utility from the incumbent party remaining in power (σ_{ij}), as well as a common societal "valence" preference for the incumbent party (ϵ). While a particular individual's preference for a given party is not known by politicians, the distributions of such preferences are common knowledge. Following workhorse models of probabilistic voting (Dixit and Londregan 1996; Persson and Tabellini 2000), I assume that these preferences are uniformly distributed and mean zero, such that $\sigma_{ij} \sim U[-\frac{1}{2\psi_j}, \frac{1}{2\psi_j}]$, and $\epsilon \sim U[-\frac{1}{2\eta}, \frac{1}{2\eta}]$. Note that, as these electoral benefits can take positive or negative values, this captures the possibility that some segments of the population may hold the government in ill regard, whereas others may be supporters of the regime even absent material transfers. Thus, in institutional environments in which party competition takes place, citizen full utility is composed of both consumption utility as well as individualized "partisan" preferences for which party is in power, such that an individual's complete utility function is

$$u_{ij}(x,b) = w_{ij}(x,b) + 1\{G = I\}(\sigma_{ij} + \epsilon) \qquad (2.5)$$

---

[18] Ballard-Rosa, Schonfeld and Carnegie (2018) demonstrates that support for democracy falls significantly for urban citizens in rural-biased countries, even to the point of increasing expressed public support for a military coup.
[19] I assume that this challenger's payoff for winning control of the executive is identical to that of the incumbent.

2.3 Rural Bias and Democratic Default

where $1\{G = I\}$ is an indicator function that equals one while the incumbent party G is in office and zero if the challenger C assumes power.

Citizen Views on Default: Forward-Looking?

Before moving to discussion of a democratic government's decision to default, I pause to note an asymmetry of citizen preferences – namely, citizens do not take into account the long-run costs of default in terms of loss of access to future loans, and thus their economic interests are formed entirely over the food price subsidy ϕ. Citizens may have indirect preferences over whether the government defaults or not, especially if so doing frees up more short-term resources to be spent in a preferred subsidy scheme. This lack of citizen consideration of the long-term consequences of default may be defended on a number of grounds, including the belief that voters are more interested in their short-term well-being and will tend to disregard future economic consequences of policies that are beneficial to them in the present. As evidence for this general short-sightedness among voters, consider the lack of strong voter concern in the American political system over clearly looming fiscal crises created by social welfare spending on Medicare or Social Security,[20] which led an editorialist in the *Wall Street Journal* to recently lament that "[t]here is no congressional appetite for spending control because there is no public appetite for it."[21]

Of course, in reality certain individuals may indeed have preferences over whether a country remains constant on its debt servicing payments (Schultz and Weingast 2003; Stasavage 2003; Saiegh 2009). Tomz (2004) originally considered the question within the context of public debate in Argentina in the lead up to that country's historic default; while public employees and unemployed individuals might rationally have recognized that the government's ability to provide continued job insurance and security might be contingent on its behavior in international financial markets, Tomz demonstrates that recognition of this effect is primarily located among the more knowledgeable segment of the voting population. It is argued that this arises due to the relative complexity of the causal chain linking international default to domestic spending priorities.

More recent work by Curtis, Jupille, and Leblang (2014) takes advantage of a public referendum in Iceland on whether the country should honor its foreign debt obligations to further probe individual-level correlates of default preferences. Beyond several "noneconomic" effects for nationalist and cosmopolitan sentiments, the authors found that unemployed individuals were more likely to oppose international repayment. In addition, the authors reconfirmed Tomz's findings on a role for voter sophistication: while in general holders of personal credit debt were no more likely to favor the referendum, among the subset of voters that correctly answered several questions

---

[20] See discussion of this point, for example, in Chinn and Frieden (2011, 168–170).
[21] www.wsj.com/articles/i-love-a-parade-but-not-this-one-1518135401.

reflecting political and economic knowledge, holders of more individual debt were significantly more likely to favor repayment. While there does exist a relationship between sovereign default and domestic borrowing costs more generally, understanding each of the steps in this linkage is likely to be outside the realm of standard understanding to be expected of common citizens.

This lack of average citizen attentiveness to the economic consequences of sovereign default is echoed in recent work by Nelson and Steinberg (2018, 525–526), who study public opinion over honoring Argentina's foreign debts during its most recent spat with foreign creditors in 2015–2016. In contrast to the accounts above, these authors find that "neither sophisticated nor unsophisticated Argentines formulate their preferences over the debt issue on the basis of their economic interests"; instead, preexisting partisan loyalties are found to better explain voter views. In strong support for my expectations over the kinds of issues likely to be salient to voters when considering debt repayment, the authors further reveal that, after including a host of citizen policy preferences, "individuals' views on *price controls* are the only statistically significant correlate of opinions on debt repayment" (Nelson and Steinberg 2018, 528, emphasis added). Thus, without wishing to deny the possibility of more personal preferences on default, I argue that additional consideration of this factor is likely to primarily reinforce the dominant dynamics I present here, and so for sake of analytic clarity I suppress these preferences in subsequent discussion.

2.3.2 The Default Dilemma in Democracy

Given the emphasis in the literature above on rural biases in democracies, and in order to economize on space, I focus here on the conditions that must hold for *rural-biased default* equilibria, noting that discussion of urban-biased equilibria are essentially symmetric. There are, in essence, three main conditions which must hold in any rural-biased default equilibrium: there must be an electoral incentive for favoring rural voters; the country should be a net food exporter; and, the loss in future expected revenues from defaulting must not offset the increased likelihood of winning office that would ensue from higher producer support prices that debt default enables. I now consider each of these conditions in turn.

As discussed earlier in the chapter, I assume that governments value holding office, but also consider the consequences of default on their long-term access to financial resources. In a competitive electoral system, parties must compete to retain the support of voters; in my model, this centers around the choice of food price policy (ϕ). While politicians can always increase their rural vote share by increasing the maximum producer subsidy ($\phi > 0$), or their urban vote share by increasing the consumer subsidy ($\phi < 0$), whether such a policy is fiscally feasible while still maintaining existing debt payments is likely to vary based

2.3 Rural Bias and Democratic Default

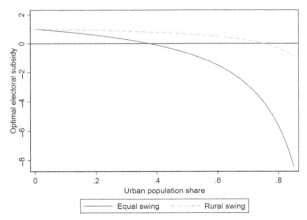

FIGURE 2.1. Optimal electoral subsidy, as a function of the urban population share (α).

on the underlying characteristics of the electorate. As both parties are equally office-motivated, they should always propose the same policy in equilibrium that maximizes the probability of winning the election.

Figure 2.1 demonstrates how this electorally optimal subsidy is affected by changes to the proportion of the population that lives in urban areas (α).[22] As can be seen, the general relationship is the expected negative one: as more citizens live in urban places, the optimal subsidy steadily declines, eventually turning negative for a large enough urban population. However, the severity of this effect is also importantly a function of the relative "swingness" of the two subpopulations. Consider the difference between the solid versus dotted lines, where the solid line tracks the optimal subsidy as a function of urban population shares assuming equal swingness across the two groups ($\psi_U = \psi_R = 1$), whereas the dotted line demonstrates the same graph for a population in which rural blocs of votes are more responsive to changes in agricultural policy ($\psi_U = 1, \psi_R = 5$). As can be seen, when rural voters cluster more tightly around this agricultural policy than do urban workers, the size of urban population over which the government will still intervene by increasing food prices to benefit rural farmers expands considerably. This demonstrates that the optimal electoral subsidy will be increasing both in the size of the population that lives in rural areas, and in the degree to which rural voters are more likely to vote en masse on targeted agricultural policies.

Taking the definition of the government's budget constraint defined in this chapter, the maximum feasible subsidy under "austerity" (that is, when the government successfully repays its debts) can be defined as the $\bar{\phi}_A$ such that

---

[22] Full solution in the Appendix. Figure calculated assuming parameter values of $\bar{x} = 3, \pi = 0.5, \beta = 2, \gamma = 0.1$.

$C(\bar{\phi}_A) = \mu - d$. On the other hand, by not making additional payments on its debt, the government can open additional fiscal space such that it can sustain a higher feasible subsidy under default $\bar{\phi}_D$ such that $C(\bar{\phi}_D) = \mu$. Clearly, if the optimal electoral subsidy can be sustained while still repaying international debts, this is the preferred path for politicians. Thus, when $\phi^* \leq \bar{\phi}_A$, the unique equilibrium of the game is for both parties to select the optimal subsidy while still remaining current on its sovereign debt.

However, politicians are faced with a more difficult dilemma when the electorally optimal subsidy exceeds that which is possible while still maintaining debt repayments. In this world, if parties choose to favor rural voters by setting higher agricultural support prices, it is also important to consider the *food trade* status of the country. As mentioned earlier, setting above-market food prices should create a fiscal burden for government primarily when it is unable to re-sell the entirety of farmers' produce on the domestic market. This will become more costly both as the size of the price distortion increases and as the surplus of domestic agricultural produce grows. This highlights an important testable implication of the model: the government will incur a cost to a positive agricultural subsidy program primarily when it must sell some amount of domestic food production on the world market.[23] As such, pressure to default should result from rural electoral influence only (or especially) in countries that are *exporters of food*.

Finally, in order for default to occur in equilibrium, it must be the case that the increased probability of winning office that results from setting a higher producer support price $\bar{\phi}_D$ outweighs the loss of future revenues from defaulting. In other words, parties must not prefer to split the likelihood of winning office by setting the maximum feasible austerity subsidy $\bar{\phi}_A$ as opposed to defaulting and increasing their odds of winning an office that provides fewer future resources. Formally, this occurs (following substitution and rearrangement of terms) whenever

$$\frac{\rho l}{2\chi} \leq \frac{\eta}{\psi} \left[\alpha \psi_U \left(\gamma ln \left(\frac{\bar{x}}{\pi + \phi_C} - \beta \right) + (1-\gamma) ln(\bar{x} - (\pi + \phi_C)\beta) \right) \right. \\ \left. + (1-\alpha)\psi_R ln(\pi + \phi_C) - \zeta \right]. \quad (2.6)$$

Thus, when Equation 2.6 holds true,[24] parties will favor the rural-biased default equilibrium; factors which make this condition more likely to hold are those that increase the appeal of debt default.

---

[23] Alternately, if the government is unwilling to sell its excess procurement at a lower world price, this may lead to even larger fiscal costs if food exports are uncompetitive on world markets (due to higher prices) and therefore sit rotting in government storage facilities. See the case of Turkey in Chapter 6 for an example of this.

[24] The constant ζ is defined in the appendix.

2.3 Rural Bias and Democratic Default

Comparative Statics
Consideration of Equation 2.6 reveals several key factors that affect the appeal of pursuing austerity as opposed to sovereign debt default in rural-biased democracies. Of greatest theoretical interest for this work is the effect of rural electoral influence. First, the greater the "swingness" of rural voters vis-a-vis urban voters ($\psi_R > \psi_U$), the greater the electoral gains to be had from pandering to agricultural producers. The parameter characterizing the density of the distribution of ideological preferences of different groups ψ_j gives the (marginal) density of voters of a given group that will be swayed by a shift in a given economic policy – if rural agents are often capable of delivering blocs of votes to politicians in exchange for agricultural support, then there may be good reason to expect that this density is higher for rural than for urban voters, suggesting that incumbents in ruralized democracies should favor the farm vote with higher agricultural support prices. While operationalizing the concept of voter "swingness" is difficult, I provide in Chapter 5 historical support for the perceived critical role of rural voters in deciding electoral outcomes in the case of Costa Rica, and in the Turkish case in Chapter 6. In addition, noting that the electorally optimal subsidy level is determined endogenously in the model and is affected by the rural population share, the probability that a party wins office when proposing $\bar\phi_D$ is also a function of the size of the rural electorate $(1 - \alpha)$, such that a larger base of agricultural voters will be a more appealing target for government support. This suggests that, all else equal,

Hypothesis 3 *Democracies that are* more rural *will be more likely to default on their sovereign debt, due to rural electoral advantages.*

As discussed above, when a country is a net food exporter, the costliness of raising the food subsidy increases as the subsidy gets larger. In these cases, the difference between the maximum feasible austerity subsidy and the maximum feasible subsidy under default is increasing in the size of the government's debt (larger *d*), and so the expected electoral gains from default should be greater in countries with more debt to repay. However, in cases where the government is not a net food exporter, increases in the subsidy need not incur additional fiscal costs. Clearly, if there is no additional electoral gain from moving to default (and providing a larger subsidy) in these cases, but there is a direct reduction in the value to holding office for politicians for doing so, default should be unlikely in such regimes.[25] As such, I provide additional tests of my main hypotheses by disaggregating my sample into countries that are net food importers and exporters. This expectation is particularly surprising when one considers that much previous work on sovereign default has argued that, especially in developing countries, the presence of agricultural exports was

---

[25] That is, default due to the fiscal costs of agricultural intervention. Of course, there are a number of other reasons why a country may need to consider default outside of the specific logic I develop here.

actually a critical source of foreign exchange revenue. Under this economic logic, we should expect default to be more likely in democracies that are nonexporters of food, especially if increased reliance on food imports places a severe strain on otherwise scarce foreign currency that may be needed to repay international lenders. As the fiscal burden of agricultural subsidies depends critically on a country's food trade status, this suggests that

Hypothesis 4 *The higher probability of default due to rural electoral biases will be most pronounced in democracies that are* net food exporters.

Finally, the left-hand side of Equation 2.6 reveals the rather intuitive finding that politicians who expect greater resources from financial markets in the future (larger l) should be less likely to favor defaulting on their debt, as should politicians who place lesser relative emphasis on being in office per se (smaller χ). However, politicians with shorter time horizons (smaller ρ) may be more likely to consider default if it increases the likelihood of short-term survival; existing work on political business cycles, for example, argues that this may be particularly likely when parties are unsure of remaining in office given an impending competitive election. While politician-level measures on the value of holding office and expectations over future loan sizes are difficult to operationalize, I provide in the following chapter a test of the effect of politician time horizons on the likelihood of debt default by looking at proximity to impending elections.

Before moving to consider additional variation in citizen influence within regime settings, I pause to admit giving short shrift to analysis of urban-biased democracies so far. As I expect these urban biases to be more pronounced in contentious democracies where the capacity to mobilize for violence is accorded some political sway, more detailed consideration of democratic regimes in which urban interests are accorded particular political attention is found below, where I address these questions more explicitly. However, I note here that, while more detailed consideration of urban-biased default would not change the model's predictions about the value of holding office and expected future loans, my predictions regarding voting population shares and net food trade status would be reversed. That is, if democracies are not rural-biased on average, as has been emphasized in the discussion herein, but instead tend to face urban-biased electoral incentives, I should expect to find exactly the opposite relationship between rural population share, food trade, and democratic debt default of that I have just described. The model helps highlight that, if my theory of regime-contingent urban–rural political influence is wrong, and democracies are characterized primarily by urban electoral biases, the dynamics linking political survival and sovereign default should not differ across different regimes. Having acknowledged that this result does emerge as a possibility from the model under differing assumptions about relative electoral weight across regions, we are left with two equally valid theoretical claims. Resolving this debate requires investigation of the actual empirical relationship between

2.3 Rural Bias and Democratic Default

these factors and sovereign debt default in democracies, to which I turn in the next chapter.

2.3.3 Extensions to the Model

Between these two pure types of institutional arrangements, which I refer to as "consolidated democracies" and "closed autocracies," however, exist a series of more mixed regimes. In conceptualizing this sort of regime variation, I begin by following landmark studies of regime classification that identify that democratic and nondemocratic polities are, first and foremost, a matter of kind (Przeworski, Cheibub, Limongi and Alvarez 2000; Cheibub, Gandhi, and Vreeland 2010; Svolik 2012). While debate still exists over the precise set of features that democracy should entail, the most common identification of democratic rule involves regimes in which "those who govern are selected through contested elections" (Przeworski et al. 2000, 15). When rulers of a country gain and retain power through competitive elections, we recognize that country as a democracy. Of critical importance, of course, is that these elections are actually competitive, in that they provide a credible opportunity for political opposition to acquire power. I conclude this chapter by considering informally how my predictions are affected by considering additional nuance to the starkly simplistic views of autocracy and democracy representing polar cases in terms of the potential influence of citizens through either voting or violence, as well as the role of international geopolitical considerations.

2.3.4 Competitive Autocracy and the Limits to Urban Bias

While my theoretical discussion so far has focused on closed autocratic regimes as those in which citizens lack the capacity to vote entirely, some dictatorships do allow multiparty elections to take place. The outcome of elections in *competitive autocracies* is still largely viewed as preordained; however, the introduction of an opposition vote changes the nature of political survival (Diamond 2002; Pepinsky 2007; Levitsky and Way 2010). In such systems, citizens may consider casting protest votes in favor of the political challenger, while taking into account that the likelihood of electoral manipulation may be high. Yet the lack of true electoral turnover means that the threat of citizens choosing to engage in organized revolt in order to express discontent still remains, suggesting that political leaders will need to counter-balance the electoral demands of rural agents against the cost-of-living considerations of urban workers. To understand these dynamics in greater detail, we must focus more carefully on the role that elections play in non-democratic systems.

To begin, I note that a defining characteristic of electoral autocracy is that tenure in office is not believed to be ultimately driven by elections per se. The function of elections in nondemocratic regimes is not to select a new chief executive, yet it is generally agreed that truly competitive elections, in which the fate of the chief executive is genuinely in doubt, is in many ways the sine qua non of democratic rule. Insofar as we are interested in understanding elections in *nondemocratic* contexts, I begin by observing that the function of such elections is not to determine the survival of incumbent executives. Yet, if elections are not meant to (directly) determine electoral survival, why do so many nondemocracies go to the trouble of hosting nationwide electoral contests?

Demonstration of support for an autocratic elite through the casting of votes, even in cases where such elections are not expected to result in turnover, may still help secure the support of other elites as well as help ensure the quiescence of the masses. Magaloni (2006) provides one of the most elegant accounts of this, starting with the puzzling observation that autocrats often expend serious resources in order to win elections by incredible margins. When considered from the standpoint of democratic elections, in which winning a majority of the vote is the primary motivation, this seems especially puzzling given that the extra resources expended to secure such a dominant margin of votes are "wasted" insofar as they could have gone to some other political project or been kept by the dictator herself (Riker 1962). Magaloni demonstrates that the pursuit of electoral supermajorities allows the regime to project an "aura of invincibility," which helps to reduce the risk of elite defections to the opposition. That is, in a system in which access to power determines access to resources, and in which the outcome of elections are a foregone conclusion, the benefits of defecting to an opposition kept perenially on the fringe is likely to have little personal benefit.[26]

In pursuing these supermajorities, the autocrat also helps bind the interests of the masses to the survival of the regime. Critically, autocratic elections are seen as an important mechanism for the distribution of clientalist support to citizens who espouse loyalty to the party. By tying private benefits to the act of casting a ballot, elections allow dictators to bind the material interests of the masses to their continued rule, while simultaneously sending a signal to the opposition of the strength of their support among "the people." Thus, elections in autocracies – even when not expected to result in losses for the incumbent – do still serve an important role in stabilizing perceptions of power of the regime, which helps explain the resources that states sink into ensuring that these go off without a hitch.[27] One prominent example of this role of elections is the

---

[26] Another prominent explanation for the rise of "pseudo-democratic" elections notes that access to the benefits of the international economy, especially trade, foreign aid, and finance, has become increasingly conditional on the presence of elections (and, often, monitors of such elections) in the developing world (Hyde 2011).

[27] Blaydes (2010) identifies the ways in which, following reduction of state control over economic benefits after neoliberal reforms, the electoral system in Egypt adapted such that clientalist benefits were provided directly by candidates, not by the state. However, this still had the effect of generating citizen support for the regime party, while also tying the economic benefits of elites, garnered through state access provided by legislative seats, to the continued support of Mubarak's rule.

2.3 Rural Bias and Democratic Default

Malaysian case, as summarized in Pepinsky (2009, 64) who notes that "in a political system where elections serve more to legitimate the regime than as true arenas of national electoral contestation, the support of the Malay masses is a critical check against potential opposition movements ... Elections link the regime to ordinary Malays, legitimizing the regime and reproducing its method of rule."

While appealing as a means of securing regime durability, the role of elections in facilitating this exchange between ruler and citizen also likely affects the calculus of autocratic survival in systematic ways (Pepinsky 2009, 80–81). In particular, insofar as a majority of the population of developing countries often lives in rural areas, to the extent that rulers now seek to win a supermajority of votes, this suggests that a large *rural electoral base* is likely to become a critical component of this survival strategy. Note, however, that this suggests an important deviation from the urban biases of nonelectoral autocracies considered earlier in the chapter. While autocrats afraid only of urban revolt have often neglected or even discriminated against rural agriculturalists, the need to secure the appearance of electoral omnipotence suggests that autocrats with large rural populations may be forced to also pay (at least some) attention to the needs of their rural citizens.

This more complex set of supporters has critical implications in particular for the sorts of agricultural policies we expect dictators to pursue. In particular, note that the prior strategy of providing cheap food for urban consumers by exploiting the monopsonist power of rural marketing boards is likely to result in significant opposition from farmers; if these farmers are expected to form an important part of the electoral coalition, we should observe less systematic discrimination against rural producers. In fact, to the extent that autocrats seek to tie farmers to the regime through government transfers, this suggests that electoral autocracies may even be characterized by the sorts of farm support policies I describe above as an important component of the agricultural system that arises in many democratic states seeking to court rural voters. While I follow a tradition in comparative politics that emphasizes a general expectation for urban biases on average across autocratic states, in Chapter 4 I develop this discussion of subregime variation in geographic biases with a detailed historical investigation of the pressures for agricultural support displayed in the Malaysian case after reintroducing multiparty elections.

2.3.5 Contentious Democracy and the Limits to Rural Bias

Symmetrically, while my main discussion of democratic politics above assumes that citizens can affect political survival only through their role as voters, not all democracies have successfully dispelled the specter of violence from the political system. In these settings, electoral outcomes can and do affect the composition of rulers in power. Yet unlike in consolidated democracies in which citizen violence carries no political weight, there are a number of democratic countries where electoral influence is unfortunately complemented at times by the potential for citizen unrest. For example, Wilkinson (2006) identifies the use of ethnically-targeted violence as an electoral strategy by certain parties in Indian elections. In similar fashion, Jamaican politics has been occasionally marred by civil violence stirred up, in part, by gangs organized by political parties (Walton, Shefner, and Seddon 1994, 112). While in consolidated democracies such violence would be considered an illegitimate component of political strategy, not all democracies have successfully eliminated the ability of citizens to express political influence by their capacity for violent action.

When competitive elections do determine incumbent survival, but mass unrest still carries the potential to remove sitting executives from power, the sole focus on groups with electoral advantages detailed in the case of consolidated democracies must be complicated by consideration of the interests of those groups that can credibly threaten mass unrest. To the extent that these instigators tend to find mobilization easier in cities, this suggests a counter-balancing of the electoral needs of rural farmers versus the threat of violence by urban gangs. However, whereas electoral autocrats may be able to provide a minimal level of rural transfers that limits the overall costliness of such programs due to the lack of a truly competitive opposition, *contentious democracies* are characterized by often fiercely competitive elections, and so parties may find that electoral pressures for ever greater farm transfers become increasingly expensive to offset against urban cost of living.

When concerns about minimizing societal unrest become dominant for elected incumbents, this suggests that democracies characterized by extreme electoral violence may give greater weight to the needs of minimizing urban revolt, even at the expense of the interests of rural voters. This is especially likely given findings by Hafner-Burton, Hyde, and Jablonski (2014) that countries with violent elections are more likely to witness antiregime protests following the election. If these pressures lead to cheap food policies combined with imported food, however, this may result in budgetary troubles in contentious democracies that mirror those of the closed autocracies I describe above. Chapter 5 details the historical case of Jamaica, where political parties organized violent urban gangs to deter voter turnout by the opposition, and where food subsidies for consumers in cities became a heavy burden on the budget. Drawing on archival documents, I demonstrate that political unwillingness to face societal unrest due to rising costs of living were at the heart of the Jamaican government's reluctance to engage in economic reforms, ultimately driving the country into default on its international obligations.

2.3.6 International Influences

Finally, while much of my theoretical account privileges the role of domestic political pressures in driving incumbents to default on their sovereign debt, this account notably neglects to consider a broader array of international factors

2.3 Rural Bias and Democratic Default

that are likely to hold sway under certain conditions. Perhaps most glaringly, the strategic actions of creditors for countries is pushed largely to the background in my theory. While I do emphasize that governments that default are likely to face increased costs of accessing international financial markets in the future, in reality there is likely to be variation in the costliness of this market exclusion, particularly insofar as different countries have been able to finance their deficits by relying on different kinds of creditors. For example, whereas modern bond-based financing is usually assumed to be less responsive to the political needs of a given regime, bilateral and institutional lenders may have strategic reasons to provide greater leniency to particular borrowers (Copelovitch 2010). Beyond the source of credit countries pursue, the overall availability of liquidity in the international financial system may also condition the stringency of creditor attentiveness to reform conditions for countries facing trouble, perhaps in part as a function of international capital mobility (Frieden 1991; Kaplan 2013). Of course, so long as these conditions do not vary systematically with my core factors of interest – particularly the role of urban or rural political influence across regimes – omission of these factors should not result in bias. This might be violated if, for example, more urban autocracies were also better able to secure bond financing, which might also leave them more exposed to flighty investment in the face of a downturn (as compared to governments reliant on bilateral or institutional loans, which tend to take a more direct interest in the financial health of a government; e.g., Kaplan and Thomsson [2017]). While I do not develop these theoretical expectations at length in this chapter in the interest of parsimony, I do expect that international financial conditions will play a crucial role in understanding default dynamics more generally, and attempt to account for these conditions robustly in the following empirical chapter.

Beyond the role of different sources of sovereign financing, international financial institutions like the IMF and World Bank have been at the center of demands for fiscal reform across a host of countries over the past half-century (Kahler 1989). In the model, I assume that governments would consider defaulting on their sovereign debt in order to open up additional fiscal space for resources previously dedicated to loan repayment. In reality, the default decision of a government facing fiscal crisis may sometimes take a more complex form: in order to stay current on debt payments, countries usually must rely on conditional loans from the major international financial institutions, primarily the IMF. This interaction with the IMF takes on particular importance when one considers that the IMF has traditionally played a catalytic role in securing additional lending from other entities – obtaining loans from these additional actors during crisis is often contingent upon a country first signing a letter of agreement with the IMF (Copelovitch 2010). The IMF typically makes several demands on countries facing fiscal crisis intended to help remedy either current account or fiscal imbalances – removing government subsidy programs is usually high on the list of changes the

IMF requires.[28] Yet many governments fear removing subsidies for favored constituents will lead to threats to their survival in office, and thus are unwilling to make these changes, which can move them into violation of the terms of their IMF conditional loans and, thus, default. The game presented here abstracts away from this extra institutional step, but is consistent with a framing of the game where the refusal to reduce subsidies to a sustainable level causes removal of IMF support, thereby triggering default.

Yet existing research on the politics of IMF conditionality emphasizes that the terms placed on debtor governments in exchange for access to emergency lending is not always the outcome of apolitical decisions (Vreeland 2006; Copelovitch 2010; Beazer and Woo 2016). This can be especially relevant if geopolitical alignment with a major power translates into systematically different conditions associated with economic reform (Stone 2004, 2008). Combined with the central role of the United States as an exporter on world grain markets, this implies that my focus on the domestic demand for food price policy should be complemented by an attention to international systemic factors. The theory developed above largely suppresses this set of factors to ease explication and development of specific hypotheses; however, it is clear that in the real world of fiscal crises, geopolitical influence is likely to be of importance as well, and so I attempt to account for these alternative accounts systematically in both my quantitative and qualitative empirical work in subsequent chapters, to which I now turn.

APPENDIX

This contains formal proofs of several claims made in the main text of the chapter.

Solution to the Autocratic Game

Having defined player strategies and preferences, I make explicit the timing of the game:

1. The autocrat chooses whether to default or not ($\delta \in \{0, 1\}$) and selects a food subsidy ($\phi \in [\underline{\phi}, \bar{\phi})$).
2. Citizens observe ϕ and decide whether to oppose the regime or not ($\omega_j(\phi) \in \{0, 1\}$).
3. If citizens oppose the regime, the autocrat is successfully overthrown with probability v_j.
4. Payoffs accrue.

I solve for subgame perfect Nash equilibria via backwards induction.

---

[28] For example, Haggard (1985) discusses the difficulty that a host of states faced in reforming food price subsidies under pressure from the IMF during the debt crises of the 1980s.

2.3 Rural Bias and Democratic Default

Citizen Indirect Utility

Given the equations for citizen utility and income in Section 2.2.2, the maximization problem for a citizen of type $j \in \{U, R\}$ can be represented by the following Lagrangian

$$\mathcal{L}_j(\cdot) = \gamma \ln(b - \beta) + (1 - \gamma) \ln(x) - \lambda(x + (\pi + \phi)b - y_j) \quad (2.7)$$

Solving the first order conditions, optimal food consumption for any agent of type j is given by

$$b_j^* = (1 - \gamma)\beta + \frac{\gamma y_j}{\pi + \phi} \quad (2.8)$$

while optimal nonfood consumption is similarly defined as

$$x_j^* = (1 - \gamma)(y_j - (\pi + \phi)\beta) \quad (2.9)$$

Letting y_j represent income for a citizen of type $j \in \{U, R\}$, a citizen's indirect consumption equilibrium utility is

$$v_j(\phi) = \left(\gamma \left(\frac{y_j}{\pi + \phi} - \beta\right)\right)^\gamma ((1 - \gamma)(y_j - (\pi + \phi)\beta))^{1-\gamma} \quad (2.10)$$

Derivation of Food Subsidy Costs in Autocracy

Total food demand is an endogenous function of the subsidy chosen, which can be calculated as simply the sum of total urban and rural demand. Explicitly, this function is

$$D_b(\phi) = \frac{\alpha \gamma \bar{x}}{\pi + \phi} + (1 - \alpha)\gamma \bar{b} + (1 - \gamma)\beta \quad (2.11)$$

For an autocrat seeking to limit instability due to mass unrest, this can be accomplished by choosing the subsidy $\tilde{\phi}$ that ensures that $D_b(\tilde{\phi}) = \beta$. After some rearrangement, this gives the following closed form solution for the optimal "quiescence subsidy" that ensures that no unrest occurs:

$$\tilde{\phi} = \frac{\alpha \bar{x}}{\beta - (1 - \alpha)\bar{b}} - \pi \quad (2.12)$$

As should be expected, as the urban population grows larger, the level of subsidy required to ensure that food remains cheap enough for city dwellers grows as well (in absolute magnitude, as the government must select some $\phi < 0$ in order to reduce prices); formally, $\partial \tilde{\phi}/\partial \alpha < 0$.[29]

Yet, as emphasized earlier, the fiscal cost of subsidizing domestic food prices is likely to depend critically on the food import status of the country. When

---

[29] Under the assumption that $\beta < \bar{b}$.

domestic food production does not suffice to keep urban bellies full, the strategy of repressing food prices becomes more fiscally onerous for a government that needs to purchase food at the world price and then resell these goods at a lower rate. I capture this intuition of the costliness of a given food subsidization program as the "per-unit loss" of a given subsidy, multiplied by the number of units on which the government suffers this loss. The number of units on which the government suffers such a loss is simply the total amount of food that is imported; under the quiescence subsidy, this is given by

$$M_b(\tilde{\phi}) = \beta - (1-\alpha)\bar{b} \qquad (2.13)$$

As the per-unit loss is simply the international purchase price of food, less the domestic resale price, I define the loss associated with providing the quiescence subsidy as $L(\tilde{\phi}) = \pi - (\pi + \tilde{\phi})$, which after substitution and rearrangement gives

$$L(\tilde{\phi}) = \pi - \frac{\alpha \bar{x}}{\beta - (1-\alpha)\bar{b}} \qquad (2.14)$$

Therefore, defining the total cost of the quiescence food subsidy program as the product of the per-unit loss ($L(\tilde{\phi})$) and the number of units of imported food ($M_b(\tilde{\phi})$) gives the following expression for the fiscal burden of such a policy:

$$C(\tilde{\phi}) = L(\tilde{\phi}) \cdot M_b(\tilde{\phi}) = \pi(\beta - (1-\alpha)\bar{b}) - \alpha\bar{x} \qquad (2.15)$$

As should be expected, an increase in the share of the population that is urban leads to an increase in the per-unit loss associated with the quiescence subsidy.[30]

Decision to Default: Autocrat

Recall Equation 2.3, which describes the government's budget constraint. Consider first those cases where the autocrat can afford to appease urban citizens while still repaying its debt (when $C(\tilde{\phi}) \leq \mu - d$). In such cases, the autocrat prefers debt repayment to default so long as $\rho l > 0$; that is, as long as it values any future access to credit, the unique equilibrium is for the autocrat to choose to not default while providing sufficient food subsidies to urban consumers to earn their quiescence.[31] Thus, default should never occur in equilibrium when the government can afford to appease citizens while still making debt payments.

In cases where food subsidies have become expensive enough that they can only be afforded if the autocrat defaults (when $\mu - d < C(\tilde{\phi}) \leq \mu$), the autocrat's strategy is reduced to a choice between defaulting and keeping high food subsidies, or instead imposing austerity and facing the threat of removal

---

[30] $\partial L(\cdot)/\partial \alpha > 0$ always under the assumption that $\beta < \bar{b}$.
[31] Formally, when $C(\tilde{\phi}) < \mu - d$, $\delta^* = 0$, $\phi^* = \tilde{\phi}$, and $\omega_j^*(\phi) = 0 \,\forall j \in \{U, R\}$.

2.3 Rural Bias and Democratic Default

from office for any affordable subsidy.[32] The autocrat will choose default over austerity whenever $u_A(\delta = 0) \geq u_A(\delta = 1)$, which can be rearranged to give the following *incentive compatibility constraint* for the autocrat:

$$\chi \geq \frac{\rho l(1 - v_U)}{v_U} \qquad (2.16)$$

There are thus two conditions which must hold in order for the autocrat to favor defaulting on its sovereign debt: first, the budget constraint under a given quiescence subsidy (given by Equation 2.3) must be infeasible under austerity, and the preferences of the government must be consistent with the incentive compatibility constraint (given in Equation 2.16).[33]

Solution to the Democratic Game

I make explicit the timing of the game:

1. The Incumbent and Challenger simultaneously choose whether to default or not, and select a feasible producer price subsidy ($\delta_k \in \{0, 1\}$, $\phi_k \in [\underline{\phi}, \bar{\phi}]$ for $k \in \{I, C\}$).
2. Nature draws values for ϵ and for all σ_{ij}.
3. Citizens vote either for the Incumbent or the Challenger based on $u_{ij}(\phi_G)$ versus $u_{ij}(\phi_C)$.
4. The winning party assumes (or retains) control of the executive, and payoffs accrue.

I solve for subgame perfect Nash equilibria via backwards induction. Citizens make electoral comparisons between the existing government G, as opposed to an opposition challenger C, based not only by the consumption utility they expect under different proposed policies, but also by the "partisan preferences" defined above for the incumbent government over a potential challenger. Combining these general electoral elements, a citizen i of type j will vote for the political opposition whenever

$$w_{ij}(\phi_G) + \sigma_{ij} + \epsilon < w_{ij}(\phi_C) \qquad (2.17)$$

where ϕ_G and ϕ_C capture the policy proposals of the incumbent government and opposition challenger, respectively.

---

[32] Emphasis on the potential political dangers from urban unrest to economic reforms echoes the argument found in Oatley 2004, who also posits a relationship between urban population shares and opposition to stabilization.

[33] Technically, in cases where $C(\tilde{\phi})$ is so high as to exceed available government resources even if international debts go unpaid (when $\mu < C(\tilde{\phi})$), there exists no feasible subsidy which will prevent urban unrest. In such a case, any strategy by the autocrat can be observed in equilibrium, and this may act as an "upper bound" to the effect of urbanization and food imports on autocratic default I identify below.

It can be shown that $\partial v_U/\partial \phi < 0$ always; that is, urban citizens are always made worse off by an increase in agricultural producer prices, as this simply translates into higher prices for the food they wish to buy. Thus, an urban consumer's ideal subsidy is the minimum feasible subsidy, or $\phi_U^* = \underline{\phi}$. Additionally, rural producers are made better off by an increase in the price of products that they produce ($\partial v_R/\partial \phi > 0$). As such, a rural voter's ideal subsidy is the maximum feasible subsidy, or $\phi_R^* = \bar{\phi}$.

As urban vote share declines while rural vote share increases with an increase in agricultural subsidies, clearly the Challenger will raise its proposed subsidy only when doing so actually increases its overall probability of victory. By taking the first order conditions on the probability of victory function,[34] and defining $\theta = (1-\alpha)\psi_R(1-\gamma) - \alpha\psi_U$ as the relative rural votes won to urban votes lost from increasing food prices, we find that the optimal electoral subsidy is given by

$$\phi_C^* = \frac{\theta(\bar{x} - \pi\beta) - \alpha\psi_U\beta\pi}{\beta(\alpha\psi_U + \theta)} \quad (2.18)$$

Derivation of Subsidy Cost in Democracy

To determine the fiscal burden of a given set of agricultural price supports, I note that this cost can be calculated as the per unit loss multiplied by the number of units on which a loss is taken. More explicitly, under the assumption that all rational agriculturalists would sell the entirety of their produce to the government at a higher guaranteed price, the acquisition cost for the government is simply the domestic price of food multiplied by the entire rural food production, or $(\pi + \phi)(1-\alpha)\bar{b}$. The domestic demand for such food is given by $D_b(\phi)$, which can be resold at the going domestic price $(\pi + \phi)$, whereas any remaining food must be sold at the lower international market rate (π). Combining these three pieces gives the total costs of a farm subsidy program as

$$C(\phi) = \phi((1-\alpha)\bar{b} - D_b(\phi)) \quad (2.19)$$

As can be seen, the costs of agricultural subsidies can be captured as a multiplicative function of two subpieces: the "per-unit loss" accruing from each unit of food exported (as captured by the additional price paid, ϕ), and the number of units that are actually offloaded on the world market (as captured by the difference between domestic production and domestic demand). Clearly, as an increase in the subsidy drives a greater wedge between the domestic buying price and the international selling price, any factor which drives up the subsidy selected will increase the costs of the program along this intensive margin. This is further reinforced by an additional effect that higher food prices have on

---

[34] Technically, $\partial^2 V_C(\cdot)/\partial\phi_C^2 < 0$ whenever $\alpha\psi_U < (1-\alpha)\psi_R(1-\gamma) + \frac{(\pi+\phi_C)^2\alpha\psi_U\beta^2}{(\bar{x}-(\pi+\phi_C)\beta)^2}$. Note that, where the probability of victory function is convex, this would only accentuate the incentives to cater exclusively to one social group, thereby increasing the likelihood that loss of electoral support of that group would lead to political suicide. I follow standard approaches by focusing on the concave portion of the function.

2.3 Rural Bias and Democratic Default

the domestic demand for food – as should be expected, total food demand decreases as the price rises,[35] and so an increase in the agricultural support price also increases the units of excess food that must be sold at a loss on the international market. Given these reinforcing effects, it is clear that any factor that increases the food price selected in equilibrium will also have the effect of increasing the fiscal costliness of such a farm subsidy.

Probability of Electoral Victory Function

Given policy choices by the Incumbent and Challenger of ϕ_G and ϕ_C, an individual i of type j will vote for the Challenger whenever $v_j(\phi_G) + \sigma_{ij} + \epsilon \leq v_j(\phi_C)$. For each citizen group, I define the "critical" voter in that group as the individual who is exactly indifferent between the two party platforms, which means that her incumbent-party bias $\hat{\sigma}_j$ is such that

$$\hat{\sigma}_j = v_j(\phi_C) - v_j(\phi_G) - \epsilon \quad (2.20)$$

That is, all individuals of group j with $\sigma_{ij} < \hat{\sigma}_j$ will vote for C, while the remainder will vote for G. Given this individual voting rule, the total vote share won by the Challenger is captured as

$$V_C = \alpha F_U(\hat{\sigma}_U) + (1-\alpha) F_R(\hat{\sigma}_R) \quad (2.21)$$

where $F_j(\cdot)$ is the distribution of proincumbent party biases in each citizen subgroup. Replacing these distributions with their known functional form and substituting in for each critical citizen's payoff gives the following closed form solution to the vote share won by the Challenger party:[36]

$$v_C(\phi_C|\phi_G) = \alpha \psi_U \left[\gamma \ln \left(\frac{\frac{\bar{x}}{\pi + \phi_C} - \beta}{\frac{\bar{x}}{\pi + \phi_G} - \beta} \right) + (1-\gamma) \ln \left(\frac{\bar{x} - (\pi + \phi_C)\beta}{\bar{x} - (\pi + \phi_G)\beta} \right) \right]$$
$$+ (1-\alpha) \psi_R \left[(1-\gamma) \ln \left(\frac{\pi + \phi_C}{\pi + \phi_G} \right) \right] - \epsilon + \frac{1}{2} \quad (2.22)$$

Finally, assuming majority rule, the probability of victory for the Challenger is simply the probability that $V_C(\cdot) > 0.5$. Given distributional assumptions on ϵ, and defining $\psi = \alpha \psi_U + (1-\alpha) \psi_R$ as the average density of individual pro-incumbent biases across groups, the probability that C wins the election is

$$V_C(\phi_C|\phi_G) = \frac{\eta}{\psi} \left[\alpha \psi_U \left(\gamma \ln \left(\frac{\frac{\bar{x}}{\pi + \phi_C} - \beta}{\frac{\bar{x}}{\pi + \phi_G} - \beta} \right) + (1-\gamma) \ln \left(\frac{\bar{x} - (\pi + \phi_C)\beta}{\bar{x} - (\pi + \phi_G)\beta} \right) \right) \right.$$
$$\left. + (1-\alpha) \psi_R (1-\gamma) \ln \left(\frac{\pi + \phi_C}{\pi + \phi_G} \right) \right] + \frac{1}{2} \quad (2.23)$$

---

[35] $\partial D_b(\cdot)/\partial \phi < 0$.
[36] Of course, the vote share won by the Incumbent is equivalently given by $V_I(\cdot) = 1 - V_C(\cdot)$.

Party Vote Share

While preferences over agricultural subsidies are straightforward, given an individual's type, knowing the subsidy levels chosen by each party does not completely identify voting behavior, as individuals are also driven by their inherent preferences for one party over another. After some algebraic rearrangement to cluster terms of constants outside the control of the Challenger,[37] I represent the simplified version of the probability of victory for the opposition as

$$V_C(\phi_C|\phi_G) = \frac{\eta}{\psi}\left[\alpha\psi_U\left(\gamma ln\left(\frac{\bar{x}}{\pi+\phi_C}-\beta\right)+(1-\gamma)ln(\bar{x}-(\pi+\phi_C)\beta)\right)\right.$$
$$\left.+(1-\alpha)\psi_R ln(\pi+\phi_C)-\zeta\right]+\frac{1}{2}$$

(2.24)

In equilibrium, each party will select its own subsidy proposal so as to maximize its expected probability of victory, taking its opponent's policy choice as given. Interpretation of $V_C(\cdot)$ is therefore reduced to seeing how the function changes with changes to ϕ_C, and is straightforward to interpret. The first two terms inside the square brackets represent votes won from urban voters; as ϕ_C is in the denominator of this first piece and enters negatively in the second piece, an increase in the agricultural subsidy will result in a reduction in urban votes, as should be expected. In addition, this reduction is proportional both to the overall size of the urban population α as well as to the density of the distribution of urban "ideological" preferences for the incumbent party ψ_U. The right-hand term represents votes won from rural voters; with ϕ_C entering additively into this term, we find that rural votes will increase as ϕ_C becomes larger. Additionally, this increase in rural vote share is proportional both to the rural share of the population $(1-\alpha)$ as well as the density of rural "ideological" preferences for the incumbent party ψ_R.

---

[37] Where $\zeta = \alpha\psi_U\left(\gamma ln\left(\frac{\bar{x}}{\pi+\phi_G}-\beta\right)+(1-\gamma)ln(\bar{x}-(\pi+\phi_G)\beta)\right)+(1-\alpha)\psi_R(1-\gamma)ln(\pi+\phi_G)$.

3

Regime-Contingent Biases and Sovereign Default, 1960–2009

> "The only admission I make," President Kaunda asserted, "where I went wrong, is that we subsidized consumption for too long." In essence, his dilemma was that he was now hostage to an urban population he could neither subsidize nor control.
> Thomas Callaghy (1990) *Lost Between State and Market*

> [A]t the same time, weak governments consisting of multiparty coalitions and facing frequent elections also had the incentive to patronize their electoral supporters and abandon fiscal discipline. In particular, the agricultural sector...had to be repeatedly compensated for electoral advantage.
> Reza Moghadam (2005) *Turkey at the Crossroads*

3.1 MOTIVATION

In the previous chapter, I developed a theory of how different political institutions – in affecting which citizen strategies for mass politics are valid under the "rules of the game" – systematically align the survival incentives of sitting politicians with different geographic constellations of citizen groups. At the most basic level, the theory posits that when citizens can only protest, the advantages of collective action in urban centers makes politicians more likely to favor city dwellers with cheap food that will be difficult to undo when faced with fiscal crisis. Alternately, when voting is the only political strategy open to citizens, my theory highlights that rural actors often are mobilized as blocs of crucial votes, especially in the developing world where a large fraction of the population lives in rural areas. This has led many democracies to pursue pro-farmer policies like agricultural support prices that, while electorally popular, can also prove damaging to the budget and difficult to reform. In each case, I link specific mass strategies to particular policies with clear consequences for their effects on urban and rural citizens. This has important implications especially for the capacity of incumbents to successfully reform policies in

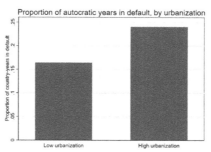

FIGURE 3.1. Proportion of years spent in default in autocracies, by urbanization.

order to remain current on financial obligations during tough times. While no politician relishes the thought of reduced access to international capital in the face of sovereign default, when the alternative requires changing policies that are likely to prove politically suicidal, the model suggests a set of conditions that increase the likelihood that incumbents will be forced to renege on their repayment obligations. Centrally, my theory implies that the effect of urban–rural political dynamics on sovereign default is likely to vary substantially across democratic and nondemocratic settings.

In this chapter, I evaluate the generalizability of these claims in a cross-national quantitative framework, and in subsequent chapters substantiate the specific linkages between urban and rural political influence as channeled through agricultural policy in a series of in-depth historical cases of default across institutional settings. Yet, before turning to more complicated statistical approaches, I begin by demonstrating a strong divergence in the bivariate relationship between urbanization and default across democracies and dictatorships. As shown in Figure 3.1, it does indeed appear that more urbanized autocracies[1] are more likely to have defaulted on their sovereign debt: autocracies with above-average levels of urbanization have been in default approximately 24 percent of the time, whereas less-urbanized autocracies have spent only 17 percent of their time in default.

This finding stands in stark contrast to the relationship between urbanization and default in democratic regimes, presented in Figure 3.2. Here, the raw distribution of defaults across more or less urbanized countries is essentially reversed: democracies with above-average urbanization[2] have been in default a mere 7 percent of the time, as compared to a significantly higher rate of default of 17 percent in more rural democracies. Note that, if the effects of urbanization on sovereign default were purely "economic" in nature, we would have little reason to suspect that these effects should vary across political regimes. Instead, simple descriptions of the data are more in line with my theory linking

---

[1] Specifically, those above the autocratic sample median of 42.7 percent urbanization.
[2] Those above the subsample median of 65.3 percent.

3.1 Motivation

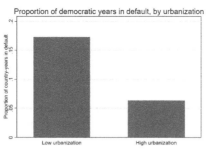

FIGURE 3.2. Proportion of years spent in default in democracies, by urbanization.

regime-contingent survival dynamics – as a function of urban–rural politics – to the decision by incumbents to default on their external debt obligations.

Of course, there may be alternative accounts for these bivariate relationships, as the proportion of the population that lives in urban or rural areas is a correlate of a number of additional factors besides the relative political strength of such groups. For example, if more rural countries are also less wealthy, then the suggestion that more rural democracies are more likely to be in default may represent nothing more than the obvious fact that poorer countries tend to default more frequently than richer ones. Drawing on my theoretical predictions about how the politics of default should vary across democracies and dictatorships, and buttressed by the suggestive differences in the relationship between urbanization and default described immediately in Figures 3.1 and 3.2, I separately analyze default in autocratic and democratic settings. In what follows, I show that the divergent relationship between urban population share and sovereign default across regime types persists even when accounting for several economic correlates of rurality and under more complicated statistical approaches. While the effects of macroeconomic factors remain constant across democracies and autocracies, it is precisely the effect of urban–rural biases that I identify as important drivers of political survival that changes dramatically between the two regimes.

3.1.1 Default under Autocracy: Urban Bias and Imported Food

In closed autocracies, citizen strategy for mass political influence is largely limited to engagement in unrest and rebellion.[3] Lacking any viable means to express their discontent within existing institutional channels, the people have few other options to make themselves heard than to threaten regime stability through revolt. While the potential triggers for unrest are many, a consistent source of mass mobilization in both historical and recent periods has been a sudden unavailabilty of food. Knowing the threat that such food crises can pose to social harmony, many dictators have intervened in domestic food markets to

---

[3] Some results from this section have been previously published; see Ballard-Rosa (2016).

ensure that the price of food, particularly in densely concentrated urban areas where unrest is most likely to arise, has remained low (Bates 1982; Wallace 2014).

Yet such strategies have often proven fiscally burdensome, particularly in those regimes that become reliant on international food imports to satisfy the demands of urban consumers. As such, during times of fiscal crisis, these cheap food policies have been a common target of reform. But succeeding in such reforms presents a serious risk to sitting dictators: If removing food subsidies causes a sudden spike in the price of food, it often leads to mass unrest. If this unrest can subsequently threaten the tenure of a sitting autocrat, I argue that nondemocratic leaders may consider facing the long-run economic consequences of sovereign default rather than face an immediate threat of hungry citizens rebelling throughout the capital.[4]

3.1.2 Rural Bias and Democratic Sovereign Default

I have argued in Chapter 2, however, that due to institutional differences in the survival incentives of incumbent politicians, I do not expect to find that urban bias should help explain sovereign default in democracies on average. Indeed, if anything I expect that *rural biases* in democracies should better help explain cases in which they default. In sharp contrast to urban-biased autocrats fearful of mass unrest, democratically elected leaders often favor rural agricultural producers with costly price supports, and are unwilling to remove these support policies if doing so would lead to losses at the polls. This effect should be most pronounced in democracies with greater rural population shares, as this large mass of voters may prove a critical component of an incumbent's successful political calculus (Varshney 1998). As mentioned in the previous chapter, developing democracies with larger rural populations are more likely to have agricultural price supports in place (Bates and Block 2011), and removal of these politically sensitive subsidies has often proven a significant hurdle in international economic agreements (Davis 2003; Naoi and Kume 2011; Barari, Kim, and Wong 2019). Given that these distortionary policies are a common target of reform during times of fiscal crisis, I therefore expect more rural democracies to be more likely to default on their sovereign debt. In addition, as the fiscal burden of farmer price supports is likely to be greatest for countries that sell excess food production on world markets, I expect the effect of rurality on democratic default to be most pronounced among food exporting countries.

---

[4] Of course, as suggested in Chapter 2, these effects may be attenuated by the presence of electoral competition in autocratic regimes. In this section, I present evidence for the presence of a linkage between food imports, urbanization, and default in autocracies more generally, and then investigate this form of subregime variation more explicitly in the historical case of Malaysia in Chapter 4.

3.2 DATA AND ESTIMATION

My outcome of interest comes from the historical dataset on economic crises presented in Reinhart and Rogoff (2009); in particular, for my main dependent variable I use Reinhart and Rogoff's measure of default to external creditors. As explained in their work, a "sovereign default is defined as the failure of a government to meet a principal or interest payment on the due date (or within the specified grace period). These episodes include instances in which rescheduled debt is ultimately extinguished in terms less favorable than the original obligation" (11).[5] My primary outcome *default* takes a value of one for any country-year that Reinhart and Rogoff code as in default, and zero otherwise. Due to lack of earlier availability of other important covariates, I make use of default data beginning in 1960 and continuing up until 2009. Given my theoretical interest in explaining democratic and autocratic default separately, I first present results after restricting attention to only those country-years which are classified as non-democracies;[6] Table 3.1 lists all nondemocratic country-years that are coded as in default for this period. I subsequently present results from the democratic subsample of country-years;[7] Table 3.2 lists all democratic country-years in default.[8]

3.2.1 Macroeconomic Explanations for Default

The literature on sovereign default has converged on a set of important macroeconomic factors considered significant predictors of debt default.[9] Most obviously, a country's level of existing debt has been repeatedly associated with default crises, as countries without large debt burdens are unlikely to face serious trouble in servicing debt or correcting fiscal imbalances. I therefore

---

[5] For an extended discussion of the evolution of default decisions towards restructuring and away from outright default over the course of the twentieth century, see Roos (2019).
[6] Of the 68 countries covered by Reinhart and Rogoff's data, 43 are coded as nondemocracies at some point. Measures of democracy are taken from the *DD* dataset in Cheibub, Gandhi, and Vreeland (2010). The full list of countries included in Reinhart and Rogoff's dataset is as follows: Algeria, Angola, Argentina, Australia, Austria, Belgium, Bolivia, Brazil, Canada, Central African Republic, Chile, China, Colombia, Costa Rica, Cote d'Ivoire, Denmark, Dominican Republic, Ecuador, Egypt, El Salvador, Finland, France, Germany, Ghana, Greece, Guatemala, Honduras, Hungary, Iceland, India, Indonesia, Ireland, Italy, Japan, Kenya, South Korea, Malaysia, Mauritius, Mexico, Morocco, Netherlands, New Zealand, Nicaragua, Nigeria, Norway, Panama, Paraguay, Peru, Philippines, Poland, Portugal, Romania, Russia, Singapore, South Africa, Spain, Sri Lanka, Sweden, Switzerland, Thailand, Tunisia, Turkey, United Kingdom, United States, Uruguay, Venezuela, Zambia, and Zimbabwe.
[7] There were 55 countries in the Reinhart and Rogoff sample that were coded as democratic at some point.
[8] I found a handful of small discrepancies in the dataset provided versus the codebook from Reinhart and Rogoff, and so there were a very small number of cases where I corrected the dataset to accord with the codebook, which primarily required adding a few cases of "near default" to the data.
[9] See, e.g., Bandiera, Cuaresma, and Vincelette (2010); Tomz and Wright (2013).

TABLE 3.1. *Autocratic sovereign defaults, 1960–2009*

Country	Default years
Algeria	1991–1996
Angola	1985–2003
Argentina	1962, 1982
Bolivia	1980–1981
Brazil	1964, 1983–1984
Central African Republic	1981, 1983–1992, 2003–2008
Chile	1974–1975, 1983–1989
Cote d'Ivoire	1983–1998, 2000–2008
Ecuador	2000
Egypt	1984
Ghana	1966, 1968, 1974, 1987
Honduras	1981
Hungary	1960–1967
Indonesia	1966–1970, 1998
Kenya	1994–1997
Mexico	1982–1990
Morocco	1983, 1986–1990
Nicaragua	1979–1983
Nigeria	1983–1992
Panama	1983–1988
Paraguay	1986–1988
Peru	1969, 1976, 1978, 1990–1997
Phillipines	1983–1985
Poland	1981–1988
Romania	1981–1983, 1986
Russia	1960–1986, 1991–2000
South Africa	1985–1989, 1993
Sri Lanka	1979, 1981–1983
Tunisia	1963, 1979–1982
Turkey	1982
Uruguay	1983–1984
Zambia	1983–1994
Zimbabwe	1965–1974, 2000–2008

All nondemocratic country-years coded as in default by Reinhart and Rogoff (2009).

include in all specifications a measure of *debt-to-GDP*, drawn from Reinhart and Rogoff (2010). As wealthier countries may have more resources to bring to bear during downturns, it is standard to include a measure of *GDP per capita*, which I draw from the World Bank's World Development Indicators (WDI) and which, following normal practice, enters logged into each specification. The importance of this measure of economic development is also emphasized by findings in Mosley (2000, 2003) that market actors tend to be more wary of default risk in less-developed countries. In addition, given concerns raised

3.2 Data and Estimation

TABLE 3.2. *Democratic sovereign defaults, 1960–2009*

Country	Default years
Argentina	1960–1961, 1963–1965, 1983–1993, 2001–2005
Bolivia	1982–1984, 1986–1997
Brazil	1961, 1985–1994
Central African Republic	1993–2002
Chile	1961, 1963, 1965, 1972, 1990
Costa Rica	1962, 1981, 1983–1990
Dominican Republic	1982–1994, 2005
Ecuador	1982–1995, 1999, 2008
Ghana	1970
Greece	1960–1964
Guatemala	1986, 1989
Honduras	1982–2008
India	1969, 1972–1976
Indonesia	1999–2000, 2002
Kenya	1998, 2000–2001
Nicaragua	1984–2008
Nigeria	1982, 2001, 2004–2005
Panama	1989–1996
Paraguay	1989–1992, 2003–2004
Peru	1980, 1984–1989
Philippines	1986–1992
Poland	1989–1994
Turkey	1965, 1978–1979
Uruguay	1965, 1985, 1987, 1990–1991, 2003
Venezuela	1983–1988, 1990, 1995–1997, 2004–2005

All democratic country-years coded as in default by Reinhart and Rogoff (2009).

above about the association between urbanization and economic development more generally, this measure of country wealth is particularly important.

Work by Kraay and Nehru (2006) on predicting default instances in the developing world highlights the importance of "shocks" in triggering debt crises; in their paper, they take *change in GDP* as capturing economic shocks generally, and I follow this approach. Other work on economic crises has suggested that such events tend to be clustered as "twin" or even "triplet" crises, such as when a crashing currency drives up dramatically the costs of servicing foreign-denominated debt, or when the failure of a domestic banking sector leads government to assume massive private debts, thereby endangering the health of sovereign bonds.[10] While including information on changes in GDP may control for crises in somewhat blunt form, one may worry that this measure does not adequately capture the full spectrum of potential economic

[10] De Paoli and Hoggarth (2006); Reinhart and Rogoff (2009).

crises a country may face. If, say, greater food imports result during domestic crises which also make sovereign default more likely, any relationship between food imports and default may be driven by some underlying omitted economic issue. To address this concern, I have constructed an additional measure of whether a country is facing any parallel form of economic crisis in a given year; this measure takes a value of one if Reinhart and Rogoff (2009) code the country as also suffering from any of the following forms of economic crisis: banking, inflation, domestic debt, or currency.[11] In essence, this measure of *crisis year* is intended to capture other parallel crises which may also drive countries to default on their external debt.[12]

Borrowing from international markets – especially by developing countries – is often denominated in foreign currency. This "original sin" of sovereign borrowing can significantly increase the difficulty of repaying outstanding loans when countries lack a substantial base of foreign reserves (Eichengreen, Hausmann, and Panizza 2007). To capture the possibility of threats on foreign currency, I control for a country's *current account balance* (as a share of GDP) to capture instances where significant trade imbalances arise.[13] This set of macroeconomic factors (*debt/GDP, per capita GDP, change in GDP, crisis,* and *current account balance*) has been consistently associated with external sovereign debt crises in the literature, and so I include them as a baseline economic model in predicting years in default.

Beyond these standard controls, given my particular interest in the effects of urban population shares, I also introduce a handful of additional factors to account for alternative linkages between urbanization and default outside of the logic I have specified earlier in the chapter. For example, countries with larger populations are also more likely to have higher rates of urbanization, as well as potentially higher demand for imported food. If the size of a country is correlated with, say, greater likelihood of social divides that impede government's ability to resolve crises (Alesina and Spolaore 2005), then any relationship between urbanization, food imports, and default may simply suffer from omitted variable bias. Alternately, it may be that the effect of urbanization I have identified captures that economies more heavily reliant on agricultural production may be less capable of responding to quickly changing economic conditions such as those induced by international shocks, given the relatively

[11] For precise definitions of each type of crisis, see Reinhart and Rogoff (2009). In unreported further results, in order to address concerns of mis-specification of this measure of parallel economic crises, I have instead added each of the component elements of the crisis measure individually, or with an additive tally of the number of such crises that have occurred, as well as a principal component calculated via factor analysis. In none of these regressions were my main results of interest substantively changed.
[12] There were some country years for which the currency crisis measure was missing in the original dataset; I supplemented this measure using data on exchange rates from the Penn World Tables following the methodology in Reinhart and Rogoff (2009) of classifying currency crises as years in which change in the relative value of the currency exceeded a 15 percent threshold.
[13] Trade data, and data on current account balances, are drawn from the WDI.

long delay between planting, growing, and final harvests. To help control for these concerns, I introduce measures of (logged) *population*[14] as well as *agricultural share of GDP* in a given country.[15]

For those countries facing crisis, work on the politics of conditional loan packages has suggested that not all countries are treated equally by the large international financial institutions, especially the IMF (Stone 2004, 2008; Vreeland 2006; Copelovitch 2010). It has been argued that some countries – particularly allies of the United States – often received preferential treatment during times of economic contraction, receiving easier terms of restructuring and fewer penalties for failing to meet terms of agreement. The United States is also a major food exporter, and often provided agricultural imports at submarket prices. This might suggest an alternative explanation for my expectation that autocracies that spend more on food imports are more likely to default: These countries lack a powerful ally, and thus cannot get access either to cheap food imports or to concessional terms on their conditional loans. To account for the possibility that geopolitical proximity to major powers could affect default decisions, I introduce a measure that captures whether a country was a *US ally* or *USSR ally*,[16] drawn from data on UN voting patterns provided by Voeten and Merdzanovic (2009).[17] In addition, I introduce a direct measure of whether a country currently had any *IMF program* in place, as coded by Dreher (2006).

Finally, in order to test my hypotheses regarding pressures that hungry urban consumers put on autocrats fearful of revolt, and of rural farming blocs on elected incumbents in democratic regimes, I include a measure of *urbanization*, which measures the percentage of the total population in a country which lives in an urban area.[18] In addition, to capture the greater fiscal burden of cheap food policies for food importers, I include also a measure of the value of food imports into a given country, scaled by GDP. In order to construct this measure of food imports, I make use of data reporting "food imports as a proportion of merchandise imports," which come from the United Nations Statistics Division's Comtrade database. These are then combined with data on "Total Merchandise Imports" for each country, taken from the WTO, to generate a (current US) dollar amount of food imports into each country in a given year. However, as food imports should be scaled by country size, I take this measure of total food imports and divide it by the GDP of each country, producing a measure of *food imports over GDP*.

---

[14] Taken from the Penn World Tables. [15] Data from the WDI.
[16] This becomes a measure of alliance with Russia following the collapse of the Soviet Union.
[17] As a number of defaulting countries were also former colonies, I additionally collected data on whether a country was an ally of Britain, France, or Spain, under the assumption that perhaps these great powers might intervene to assist countries under their former influence. However, none of these controls proved significant, and their inclusion did not change any of my results, so I have suppressed these here.
[18] Taken from the WDI.

My baseline empirical model is of the following form:

$$default_{it} = \beta_1 urban_{it-1} + \beta_2 food_{it-1} + \gamma X_{it-1} + \mu_i + \theta_t + \epsilon_{it} \quad (3.1)$$

where β_1 and β_2 are my two main effects of interest to be estimated, X_{it-1} is a vector of the macroeconomic controls as well as the other correlates of urbanization introduced above, γ is a vector of coefficients to be estimated on each of these macroeconomic factors, μ_i and θ_t are country and year fixed effects, and ϵ_{it} is the error term, with standard errors clustered at the country level to account for within-country correlations including serial autocorrelation in the data.[19] Given my hypotheses, I expect both more food imports and higher levels of urbanization to make autocracies more likely to default (I expect $\beta_1 > 0$ and $\beta_2 > 0$ in autocracies). However, under the assumption of rural biases in many democracies, I expect less urbanized democratic regimes to be more likely to default, and expect food imports to play no systematic role in the reform decisions these governments face (I expect $\beta_1 < 0$ and $\beta_2 = 0$ in democracies). Given the binary nature of my outcome of interest, I follow standard practice in the literature in estimating this equation as a probit model, and demonstrate in the technical appendix that the primary results are not substantively changed when instead estimated using OLS, fixed-effects or conditional logit, or random-effects probit.

Before moving to the regression results, there is an additional methodological issue that requires some attention. I found that there existed nontrivial amounts of missing data scattered throughout several of the macroeconomic factors identified as important correlates of sovereign default. The standard approach of dealing with such missing data is to simply remove any observations for which even a single covariate is missing, often referred to as "listwise deletion." While this approach is reasonable in cases with fairly limited missingness in the data, in my case estimation of a model with a full set of covariates reduces the sample by approximately 80 percent. On the one hand, this reduction in usable data can be concerning due to the implied statistical inefficiency of throwing away useful information. However, recent work on the implications of listwise deletion, particularly for research in political economy, has suggested a more serious concern with this approach: Lall (2016) argues – following the insights of Hollyer, Rosendorff, and Vreeland (2011) and others – that country data are often not missing at random, but may in fact be correlated with important political or economic dynamics. Lall especially cautions researchers considering the effects of democratic regime type, along with economic development, on various outcomes, as he notes that countries that report data more diligently may also be more likely to be democracies and to have greater economic capacity. If true, estimation on the sample of observations with no missingness is likely to result in biased inferences. In the current exercise, the role of

---

[19] To reduce concerns over simultaneity bias, as is standard I lag all right-hand side covariates by one period.

political regime type is of central importance, and the capacity of countries to service their existing debt is almost certainly in part a function of their level of economic development. As such, rather than using listwise deletion to deal with observations with missing data below, I instead follow recommended practice and employ multiple imputation techniques to supplement and analyze my data (King, Honaker, Joseph and Scheve 2001).[20]

3.3 RESULTS

Table 3.3 reports results from my baseline specifications for sovereign default in autocracies and democracies. Generally speaking, both democratic and autocratic countries with higher debt levels are more likely to be in default, as are countries facing some parallel form of economic crisis.[21] As reported in Column 1, in support of my theoretical expectations, more urbanized autocracies are significantly more likely to default on their international debt, as are autocracies that import more of their food. Note, however, that in the democratic subsample reported in Column 3, the exact opposite relationship holds between urbanization and democratic default: it is more rural democracies that are found to be more likely to renege on their financial obligations. In addition, as expected, while food imports are a robustly positive predictor of autocratic default, there does not appear to be any systematic relationship between food imports and default in democratic countries.

Not only are these associations between urbanization and food trade status with default significant statistically, they are of a profound substantive magnitude. For point of reference, I first consider the predicted effect of an increase in the amount of debt held by a country, as one of the most straightforward expectations for factors likely to increase sovereign default rates. Holding all other factors at their average levels, moving from an autocracy with below average levels of debt-to-GDP (of 32.19 percent) to one with above average levels of debt-to-GDP (of 87.96 percent) increases the probability of default by about 4.3 percentage points.[22] As mentioned in Chapter 1, the (unconditional) average likelihood of default across the entire sample is approximately 13 percent, so the effect of rising debt burdens is to increase default rates by approximately one-third the baseline rate. Compare this, first, to the effect of

---

[20] Note that my baseline findings of the effects of urbanization and food imports on sovereign default do not depend on the use of multiple imputation – a full discussion of the imputation procedures taken, as well as presentation of results on nonimputed data, is presented in an online appendix to this chapter.
[21] Interestingly, it appears that democracies under IMF programs are somewhat more likely to default; however, this effect does not persist among autocracies. This asymmetry merits additional study in future work.
[22] This range is derived by subtracting or adding half a standard deviation from the mean *debt/GDP* ratio, such that this represents an increase of one standard deviation in debt levels. Marginal effects estimated using Clarify (Tomz, Wittenberg, and King 2003).

TABLE 3.3. *Food imports, urbanization, and debt default, 1960–2009*

VARIABLES	(1) Autoc.	(2) Autoc.	(3) Democ.	(4) Democ.
Urban Population (%)	0.116**	0.162**	−0.117**	−0.153***
	(0.051)	(0.069)	(0.052)	(0.057)
Food imports	25.391***	67.211***	2.036	27.619
	(9.801)	(23.334)	(12.090)	(43.392)
GDP per capita (log)	−0.047	−0.087	0.310	0.440
	(0.312)	(0.310)	(0.408)	(0.470)
Δ GDP	−0.040	−0.130	−0.138	−0.098
	(0.411)	(0.472)	(0.566)	(0.637)
Debt/GDP	0.011***	0.010***	0.022***	0.025***
	(0.003)	(0.003)	(0.005)	(0.006)
Crisis	1.824***	1.722***	0.849***	0.850***
	(0.285)	(0.297)	(0.271)	(0.294)
Current account (% GDP)	0.011	−0.021	0.052**	0.047
	(0.021)	(0.030)	(0.021)	(0.036)
Population (log)	0.065	−0.027	7.031***	9.943***
	(0.294)	(0.371)	(2.486)	(2.506)
Agricultural share of GDP	0.047*	0.056**	0.032	0.034
	(0.025)	(0.025)	(0.031)	(0.035)
US ally	0.460	−0.010	−1.049	−0.113
	(1.094)	(1.188)	(1.018)	(1.070)
Russian ally	2.874*	2.587*	1.186	1.448
	(1.658)	(1.545)	(0.923)	(1.124)
IMF agreement	−0.050	−0.017	0.554**	0.682**
	(0.222)	(0.225)	(0.267)	(0.320)
Imports (% GDP)		−0.052*		−0.045
		(0.029)		(0.035)
Exports (% GDP)		0.051**		0.029
		(0.026)		(0.037)
Foreign res./imports		−6.728**		−7.906
		(3.166)		(5.500)
Upcoming election		0.167		0.405**
		(0.178)		(0.160)
Oil rents		−0.000		0.000
		(0.001)		(0.001)
Govt. consumption		−4.108**		0.189
		(1.846)		(2.825)
Military size		0.036		1.569***
		(0.409)		(0.572)
Regime age		−0.015		−0.014
		(0.016)		(0.017)
Urban * Food imp.		−0.849		−0.377
		(0.550)		(0.749)
Observations	984	984	647	626
Countries	33	33	23	22

Robust standard errors clustered by country in parentheses
*** $p < 0.01$, ** $p < 0.05$, * $p < 0.1$
Table reports estimates of probit regressions of *default* on *urbanization* and *food imports over GDP*, as well as several controls, for nondemocracies in Columns 1 and 2 and democracies in Columns 3 and 4 from 1960 to 2009. The table reports multiple imputation estimates of the probit coefficients for each variable and robust standard errors, clustered at the country level, in parentheses. Country and year fixed effects were included in each regression, but are suppressed for presentation.

moving from an autocracy with below average levels of food imports (of 1.95 percent of GDP) to above average food import costs (of 5.05 percent), which is estimated to increase the probability of default by 10.9 percentage points.[23] Autocracies with high food import costs have nearly double the baseline rate of default compared to those with low levels of food imports, an effect that is almost triple the substantive size of rising debt-to-GDP levels. The effect of high rates of urbanization in autocracy are of similarly large magnitude: moving from a dictatorship with below average urban share of the population (of 36.1 percent) to above average urbanization (of 55.3 percent) increases the probability of default by 11.9 percentage points, again nearly doubling the baseline rate of default.[24]

Contrast this against the effect of urbanization on default in democracies: Moving from a below average level of urbanization (of 46.8 percent) to an above average urban population (of 66.1 percent) *decreases* the probability of default by nearly 45 percentage points![25] While this effect is massive, these point estimates should be interpreted cautiously. The normal *ceteris paribus* assumption in these estimations holds all else equal in a country except for the change in one factor of interest. Of course, an increase in the urban population share of 20 percent would likely also correspond to a number of other changes in the broader macroeconomy that might also feed into pressures against default. That said, given standard estimation approaches, it is clear that the mirror-image relationships between urbanization and default in autocracies and democracies are not only highly statistically significant, but are also of important substantive magnitude.

3.4 ALTERNATE ACCOUNTS

Beyond those macroeconomic effects discussed above as part of my baseline covariate specification, there are several additional important potential alternate accounts that could affect political decisions to default. As default generates short-term survival benefits in exchange for long-run economic consequences, factors which influence the time horizons of incumbent rulers are likely to systematically influence the attractiveness of sovereign default. Particularly in democratic systems, the temporal proximity of upcoming elections has often been argued to force elected rulers into more short-term considerations; this suggests that default should be more likely to occur in democracies when elections are looming. To capture this, I include a measure of whether there

---

[23] As above, this range is estimated by subtracting or adding half a standard deviation to the autocratic sample mean of *food imports/GDP* measure, to generate the marginal effect of a one-standard-deviation increase in food import costs.

[24] This range generates a one-standard-deviation increase in urban population shares in the autocratic subsample.

[25] This range generates a one-standard-deviation increase in urban population shares in the democratic subsample.

is an *upcoming election* in the following year, drawing on electoral data from the National Elections Across Democracy and Autocracy (NELDA) dataset.[26] While I expect electoral proximity to be significantly associated with higher rates of default in democracies, it is unclear theoretically whether we should expect the same relationship to hold in autocratic countries where the function of elections is likely to differ substantially.

A country's engagement with world markets, especially through exports and imports, can have a critical bearing on its level of foreign reserves, and so I include separately standard measures of *imports* and *exports*, both scaled by GDP. Including a control for the relative share of a country's economy captured by imports is also important given my interest in the role of food imports specifically in driving default in nondemocracies – I would not want to falsely attribute a relationship between food imports and sovereign default to food specifically if instead this were merely a story of higher imports in general reducing the availability of scarce foreign reserves. I also attempt to capture debt servicing capacity more directly by including a measure of *foreign reserves/months of imports*.[27]

If the costs of reneging on international obligations are likely to include reduced access to capital markets in the future, certain regimes may be less concerned about ability to borrow from foreign lenders, especially when they have access to alternate sources of financing. This may be especially relevant in countries that rely heavily on the sale of natural resources – particularly oil – to generate funding for the state, as such regimes are likely to be less reliant on debt markets for access to capital. In order to address concerns that some countries may be more likely to have additional sources of sovereign finance due to sales of natural resources like oil, I include a measure of *oil rents per capita*.[28] Governments may also vary in their need for debt financing due to higher or lower expenditures: While my theory of political survival posits that rulers will generally want to maximize their fiscal capacity in order to please as many important constituencies as they can, governments do vary in their overall spending targets, and it may be that credit access is less vital to those regimes with lower expenditures overall.[29] To account for this possibility, I also include a measure of *government consumption* as a fraction of GDP.[30]

While I have emphasized in Chapter 2 the importance of unrest as a threat to sitting dictators, my theory neglects another potential strategy that autocrats facing masses in the streets may choose: repression. When facing the prospect of revolution as consequence of economic reforms, some dictators may still be able to avoid default if they are better able to keep citizens in check.

---

[26] See https://nelda.co/.
[27] Data on trade and foreign reserves from the WDI.   [28] Taken from Dunning (2008).
[29] Note that these countries would also arguably be less likely to take on debt in the first place, which might reduce their need for default.
[30] Data from Penn World Tables.

3.4 Alternate Accounts

While repressive capacity is notoriously difficult to capture empirically,[31] Svolik (2012) emphasizes that, particularly when facing large-scale unrest, the role of the military as a means of executing wide-spread violence is key. In order to capture the relative capacity of leaders to employ violence against citizens, I therefore generate a measure of the *size of the military*, which is constructed as the (log) ratio of standing army soldiers to the total size of the population.[32] Finally, there is a tendency for countries to become more urbanized over time, which will be correlated with the age of a regime that stays in power. Perhaps the relationship between urbanization and default I have found arises only in older, more brittle regimes, and so to address this concern, I include a measure of *regime age*.[33] To address the possibility that there may be nonlinear effects between urbanization and food imports, I also include an interaction term between the two.[34]

Column 2 of Table 3.3 reports results from inclusion of these additional alternative accounts for the political decision to default to the autocratic subsample. In nondemocracies, greater levels of foreign reserves decrease default probability significantly, as is predicted by standard economic accounts. In addition, government consumption is negatively associated with default in nondemocracies; as might be expected, governments with greater expenditures (that presumably also favor continued access to capital markets for financing) are somewhat less likely to default on their international loans. Somewhat more surprisingly, it appears that autocracies that import more in general are less likely to default, a finding that contrasts quite strongly with the strong positive impact of food imports in particular. However, introduction of these additional controls does not affect the substantive magnitude or the statistical significance of my main factors of interest: more urban and more food-importing dictatorships are still significantly more likely to be in default.

My core results of interest in the democratic sample are likewise retained after adding these alternative controls in Column 4; urbanization remains strongly negatively associated with default in democracies. In addition, as expected by my model, impending elections are also found to be significantly positively associated with democratic default, as such periods are likely to be characterized by shortened time horizons for incumbents worried about the prospect of reelection. Intriguingly, democracies with larger standing armies are also found to be significantly more likely to default on their sovereign debt; this unexpected finding lies outside of my core predictions, and merits further study in future work.

---

[31] If citizens have internalized the threats of reprisal in the most repressive regimes, they may never trangress, and so we should not observe the need to actually employ violence against citizens in such cases.

[32] Data on military size taken from the Correlates of War. [33] From the *DD* database.

[34] This interaction term is never statistically significant; I include a discussion of interpretation of my results in an interactive framework in the online appendix to this chapter.

3.5 TEMPORAL/SYSTEMIC FACTORS

While I have so far demonstrated support for my theory linking food imports and urban population size to sovereign default, there exist a number of broader concerns relating to the evolution of the international financial system over time that have yet to be addressed. To begin, as emphasized by Copelovitch (2010) and others, the composition of sovereign borrowing has evolved over the past half century – while earlier sovereign debt tended to be distributed either by large commercial banks or directly between countries in "bilateral" loans, over time these forms of lending have been eclipsed by the sale of sovereign bonds to potentially tens of thousands of private bond traders. Earlier patterns of lending between a few large entities and states often encouraged a more constructive dialog between lenders and borrowers, but the coordination problems inherent in organizing the disparate interests of private bondholders has often been blamed for greater complexity in resolving modern debt crises, as evidenced by concerns over the effects of so-called vulture funds that swoop in on discounted sovereign bonds and then take countries to court, blocking negotiations on debt resolution and even pushing Argentina back into default in 2014.

To address concerns that changing composition of borrowing could affect the political dynamics I consider, I therefore introduce additional controls for each of the main forms of international sovereign borrowing, across both "public and publicly guaranteed" (PPG) as well as "private nonguaranteed" (PNG) lending, capturing borrowing by sovereigns from *PPG bonds, PPG commercial banks, PPG IBRD/IDA, PNG bonds,* and *PNG commercial banks*.[35] Beyond changes in the composition of international finance, an additional structural factor affecting flows of money across borders that has changed over time relates to restrictions on capital mobility. Following standard practice, I introduce a measure of *capital openness*, drawing on work by Chinn and Ito (2008).

Finally, given my particular interest in the relationship between urbanization and default over time, there remains a concern that my results could potentially be driven by more secular demographic trends that simply happen to overlap with evolving risks in the international financial system. For example, if countries tend to become more urban over time, and if risks in the financial system have also grown since the start of the period (especially following reliberalization of capital controls after the end of Bretton Woods), then we might expect to find a correlation between higher rates of urbanization as well as greater likelihood of default driven not by the logic I develop, but by simple trends over time.[36] While in earlier specifications I have included year fixed effects which should remove any common variation across countries

---

[35] Data from the International Debt Statistics (IDS).
[36] Note, however, that this type of concern would still not be able to account for the opposite association in democracies.

3.5 Temporal/Systemic Factors

within a given year, such an approach does not necessarily account directly for the possibility of secular trends; work by Carter and Signorino (2010) has suggested that a straightforward means of doing so is to include a cubic polynomial of time to the specification. I follow this suggestion as well, adding *time*, *time*,^{2} and *time*^{3} to the regression.[37] Alternately, if certain countries suffer from "serial default" – as suggested by Reinhart and Rogoff (2009) and others – an alternative form of dependence might exist between prior default instances and my outcome. To capture this potential form of temporal dependence, I construct a measure of the *time since last default* by country, as well as the quadratic and cubic polynomials of this factor.[38]

Table 3.4 reports results after including this additional set of systemic factors; I mirror the presentation of results in Table 3.3 by estimating with my "baseline" and "alternate" sets of covariates separately. In support of work emphasizing the geopolitical reach of US influence in the international financial system, I do find that autocratic allies of the United States are significantly less likely to default on their external debt; while this effect is significant in democracies as well when only including the baseline set of covariates, it loses significance after the fuller set of controls are added.[39] Beyond these findings, however, none of the other included controls appears to systematically drive default; most importantly, even after introducing this host of additional covariates, I still continue to find that food imports and urban population size are significantly associated with sovereign default in autocracies, while rurality remains a significant predictor of democratic default.[40] Following this set of robustness checks against spurious correlation arising due to omitted variables and systemic factors, there exists robust quantitative support for my primary theoretical claims.

---

[37] In this specification, I drop the use of year fixed effects. Carter and Signorino (2010) argues that the inclusion of linear, quadratic and cubic polynomials of time avoids potential implementation issues (such as quasi-complete separation) with other common methods, and generally outperforms such methods in Monte Carlo simulations, and so I follow their recommendation in respecifying my approach to account for potential temporal dynamics. I note, however, that this specification would not necessarily account for a more complicated set of interactions between the international financial system and particular elements of domestic politics; see Oatley (2011) and Chaudoin, Milner, and Pang (2015) for more detailed discussion.

[38] In the online appendix, I also demonstrate that my main findings are replicated if, given concerns of dependence across outcomes for periods of continual default (across multiple years), I drop subsequent years of default from my sample and instead regress a measure of the *first year of default* only.

[39] Note that this is different from the estimations in Table 3.1; this difference likely arises from the lack of year fixed effects in these estimations, which may absorb much of the cross-country alliance variation within a given year.

[40] Given the importance of times of economic crisis to my discussion on default pressures in Chapter 2, I report in the online appendix to this chapter results after subsetting on times of crisis. Interestingly, I do find that the effects of food imports on autocratic default are most pronounced during times of crisis; in contrast, the effects of urbanization on default appear both during times of crisis as well as during more "normal" times. I thank an anonymous reviewer for this suggestion.

TABLE 3.4. *Systemic effects and debt default, 1960–2009*

VARIABLES	(1) Autoc.	(2) Autoc.	(3) Autoc.	(4) Democ.	(5) Democ.	(6) Democ.
Urban Population (%)	0.105**	0.138**	0.107**	−0.099**	−0.148***	−0.137***
	(0.045)	(0.062)	(0.049)	(0.049)	(0.052)	(0.053)
Food imports	23.275***	61.022***	52.098**	−2.963	0.497	−0.284
	(7.368)	(20.500)	(22.498)	(11.304)	(37.238)	(37.037)
GDP per capita (log)	0.110	0.090	0.046	−0.094	0.193	0.173
	(0.347)	(0.363)	(0.447)	(0.366)	(0.393)	(0.451)
Δ GDP	−0.213	−0.186	−0.095	0.062	0.088	−0.168
	(0.360)	(0.386)	(0.416)	(0.597)	(0.604)	(0.695)
Debt/GDP	0.010***	0.009**	0.006	0.021***	0.024***	0.022***
	(0.004)	(0.004)	(0.004)	(0.005)	(0.006)	(0.007)
Crisis	1.511***	1.436***	1.052***	0.695***	0.696***	0.486*
	(0.236)	(0.251)	(0.233)	(0.240)	(0.243)	(0.249)
Current account (% GDP)	0.008	−0.025	−0.030	0.040**	0.029	0.013
	(0.023)	(0.032)	(0.029)	(0.017)	(0.027)	(0.027)
Population (log)	0.109	0.036	−0.004	5.834**	8.099***	7.019***
	(0.212)	(0.325)	(0.281)	(2.305)	(2.357)	(2.022)
Agricultural share of GDP	0.037	0.047*	0.030	0.013	0.003	−0.013
	(0.026)	(0.026)	(0.027)	(0.025)	(0.028)	(0.032)
US ally	−1.925***	−2.382***	−1.840***	−1.776*	−1.313	−0.999
	(0.685)	(0.632)	(0.666)	(1.001)	(1.033)	(0.925)
Russian ally	0.683	0.490	0.502	0.823	0.743	0.579
	(0.842)	(0.770)	(0.750)	(0.634)	(0.625)	(0.622)
IMF agreement	0.062	0.099	0.065	0.440*	0.596**	0.531*
	(0.177)	(0.172)	(0.193)	(0.252)	(0.299)	(0.298)
PPG bonds	−29.582	−30.135	−18.490	−8.384	−12.107	−10.430
	(39.953)	(39.285)	(33.948)	(16.127)	(16.036)	(16.849)
PPG commercial	−6.050	−9.110	−6.688	−20.521	−17.964	−19.152
	(7.437)	(9.926)	(8.695)	(17.949)	(20.044)	(20.185)
PPG IBRD	−15.030	−33.326	−26.151	21.992	20.107	−1.336
	(28.314)	(31.637)	(34.516)	(39.428)	(42.036)	(36.048)

	(1)	(2)	(3)	(4)	(5)	(6)
PPG IDA	139.205 (256.840)	223.864 (340.523)	237.026 (389.830)	−258.115 (258.321)	−180.931 (296.317)	−130.474 (279.850)
PNG bonds	−1.606 (85.139)	−15.784 (84.163)	14.865 (67.352)	−38.526 (54.459)	−19.037 (55.273)	−9.967 (69.257)
PNG commercial	0.563 (8.831)	−0.592 (10.465)	−4.458 (11.836)	−9.352 (13.381)	−13.109 (13.587)	−9.569 (13.653)
Chinn-Ito index	−0.303 (0.544)	−0.387 (0.546)	−0.377 (0.593)	0.044 (0.509)	−0.031 (0.599)	0.072 (0.618)
Urban * Food imp.		−0.801 (0.531)	−0.767 (0.530)		−0.010 (0.706)	0.134 (0.729)
Imports (% GDP)		−0.050* (0.027)	−0.033 (0.025)		−0.036 (0.028)	−0.057** (0.027)
Exports (% GDP)		0.058** (0.023)	0.037 (0.023)		0.016 (0.029)	0.029 (0.029)
Foreign res./imports		−5.681* (3.189)	−2.540 (2.615)		−3.824 (5.172)	−4.780 (5.638)
Upcoming election		0.141 (0.185)	0.092 (0.207)		0.443*** (0.114)	0.476*** (0.115)
Oil rents		−0.001 (0.001)	−0.001 (0.001)		0.000 (0.001)	0.000 (0.001)
Govt. consumption		−2.706 (1.831)	−2.239 (1.883)		−1.064 (2.349)	−1.062 (2.328)
Military size		0.053 (0.391)	−0.001 (0.318)		1.082** (0.488)	1.018** (0.411)
Regime age		−0.014 (0.014)	−0.014 (0.011)		−0.018 (0.017)	−0.018 (0.017)
Observations	984	984	984	694	670	670
Countries	33	33	33	23	22	22

Robust standard errors clustered by country in parentheses
*** p < 0.01, ** p < 0.05, * p < 0.1

Table reports estimates of probit regressions of *default* on *urbanization* and *food imports*, as well as several controls, for nondemocracies in Columns 1–3, and democracies in Columns 4–6, from 1960 to 2009. The table reports multiple imputation estimates of the probit coefficients and robust standard errors, clustered at the country level, in parentheses. Country fixed effects, as well as a cubic temporal polynomial, were included in each regression but are suppressed for presentation; cubic polynomials for time since default were included in columns 3 and 6.

Yet one may worry that the tests I have run so far on democratic default in particular are not a fair representation of the theoretical predictions borne by the formal model in the previous chapter – while it is true that my model finds that countries with larger and more electorally critical rural populations should be more likely to default on their sovereign debt, it also suggests that the fiscal burden of domestic agricultural subsidization should be felt primarily in countries that are net food exporters. As nearly all countries export at least some tiny amount of food products, it would not be possible to generate a sample of countries for which food exports were literally equal to zero. Instead, I have identified countries that are *net food exporters* as those countries for which the value of food exports exceeds the value of food imports in a given year. Recall that, absent my theory, much of the literature on default would suggest that food exporters would be less likely, all else equal, to be forced to default on their sovereign debt, as agricultural exports often provided a source of much needed foreign reserves. In contrast, one might worry especially about the opposite group, those that import food, as being particularly vulnerable to debt troubles, as critical food imports would compete with debt repayment for scarce foreign currency.

I therefore repeat in Table 3.5 the regression from Column 6 of Table 3.4, dividing the sample first into only those democracies that were net food exporters (Column 1) and then focusing instead on countries that were net food importers (Column 2). Once I divide my sample of countries into net food exporters and importers, I find that while the positive effect of rural population shares remains a strong and significant predictor of default in food exporting democracies, the effect vanishes when we turn to the food importing subsample, exactly as my theory would predict if what is truly driving these default decisions by democratic leaders is the fiscal burden imposed by large agricultural subsidy policies.[41]

3.6 SUBSIDY COSTS

While the hypotheses generated by my formal model in Chapter 2 are important for interpreting the mirror-image effects of urbanization and food trade status across autocracies and democracies, the ultimate driver of the fiscal consequences of food policy in my model are food price policies. Ideally, I would be able to analyze such subsidies as they exist in my full sample of countries; unfortunately, to the best of my knowledge, such wide-ranging data do not exist. However, a recent research program hosted by the World Bank

---

[41] It is important to note that the results do not suggest that the coefficients on urbanization are significantly different from one another across the two subsamples: instead, the size of the standard error in food importing countries is so large as to suggest no systematic relationship between rurality and default.

3.6 Subsidy Costs

TABLE 3.5. *Food export status and democratic default, 1960–2009*

VARIABLES	(1) Food exporter	(2) Non food exp.
Urban Population (%)	−0.216**	−0.017
	(0.098)	(0.291)
Food imports	11.873	−76.707
	(23.849)	(80.093)
GDP per capita (log)	1.416**	−2.880
	(0.689)	(3.160)
Δ GDP	0.406	−2.392*
	(0.705)	(1.399)
Debt/GDP	0.037**	0.024
	(0.016)	(0.018)
Crisis	0.464	0.250
	(0.422)	(0.579)
Imports (% GDP)	−0.057	−0.232*
	(0.057)	(0.121)
Exports (% GDP)	0.026	−0.014
	(0.060)	(0.124)
Current account (% GDP)	0.048	−0.038
	(0.043)	(0.149)
Foreign res./imports	−4.616	−10.158
	(8.623)	(12.701)
Population (log)	9.288***	55.612***
	(2.749)	(19.085)
Agricultural share of GDP	−0.028	−0.096
	(0.048)	(0.166)
Upcoming election	0.462**	0.774
	(0.193)	(0.575)
Oil rents	−0.002	0.001
	(0.002)	(0.003)
Govt. consumption	1.332	−2.022
	(4.018)	(8.202)
Military size	0.837	6.581**
	(0.683)	(2.617)
Regime age	−0.041	−0.183
	(0.031)	(0.174)
US ally	−2.571*	2.018
	(1.326)	(1.367)
Russian ally	−0.128	0.048
	(1.217)	(1.343)
IMF agreement	0.970**	−0.321
	(0.444)	(0.989)
PPG bonds	−18.543	25.751
	(19.338)	(61.834)

TABLE 3.5. *Continued*

VARIABLES	(1) Food exporter	(2) Non food exp.
PPG commercial	−44.958	−0.497
	(31.006)	(59.862)
PPG IBRD	−35.329	−22.976
	(61.579)	(206.288)
PPG IDA	−424.757	1,590.606
	(543.884)	(1,089.742)
PNG bonds	−43.788	151.266
	(109.458)	(232.650)
PNG commercial	−9.937	−1.918
	(19.334)	(71.664)
Chinn–Ito index	0.302	−2.692*
	(0.997)	(1.468)
Observations	403	252
Countries	17	13

Robust standard errors clustered by country in parentheses
*** $p < 0.01$, ** $p < 0.05$, * $p < 0.1$
Table reports estimates of probit regressions of *default* on *urbanization* and *food imports*, as well as several controls, for net food exporting democracies in Column 1, and net food importing democracies in Column 2, from 1960 to 2009. The table reports multiple imputation estimates of the probit coefficients and robust standard errors, clustered at the country level, in parentheses. Country fixed effects, as well as a cubic temporal polynomial and cubic polynomial in time since last default, were included in each regression, but are suppressed for presentation.

on Distortions to Agricultural Incentives (DAI) in many developing countries provides relevant measures for a subset of my full sample.

Of particular relevance for my interests in relative biases towards urban or rural citizens, the DAI project has attempted to quantify the relative weight of policies benefitting rural agricultural producers, as opposed to urban citizens, across a number of countries. After totalling benefits to each group in a given country-year, these data are used to construct the "relative rate of assistance to agriculture" (RRA), as a measure of relative bias towards rural farmers; a value of zero on this measure implies no bias towards either urban or rural groups, whereas more positive values imply greater revealed bias towards farmers, and more negative values imply greater bias towards consumers. I report the raw distribution of this measure below in Figure 3.3. The vertical lines represent mean values for RRA for each regime type, with the average value below zero (in favor of urban consumers) in nondemocratic countries as opposed to a positive mean value (in favor of rural producers) in democracies.[42] As can be

[42] Kolmorogov–Smirnov tests of equality of distribution across regime type rejects the null hypothesis of equal distributions at the 0.001% level.

3.6 Subsidy Costs

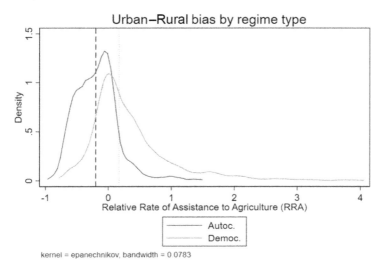

FIGURE 3.3. Relative Rate of Assistance (RRA) to agriculture, by regime type.

seen, these data provide strong support for one of the core suppositions of my theory: Democratic regimes are (on average) much more likely to place greater emphasis on pro-farmer polices, whereas autocratic regimes are significantly more likely to display antiagricultural biases in their food price policy (Hendrix and Haggard 2014).

Yet, many of the factors that play into this RRA score, as collected by the World Bank, may not necessarily imply a direct fiscal burden to the state, as the project additionally considers benefits such as favorable exchange rate polices. More directly relevant to my core argument is another measure constructed by the DAI: the "gross subsidy equivalent to farmers" (GSE) of such agricultural pricing policies, which calculates a (US dollar) equivalent cost of all food pricing policies in place. As with the RRA measure, a value of zero for the GSE implies no bias in subsidy policy, whereas a negative value implies price reducing subsidies while positive values are associated with pro-farmer price increases on food. As with the RRA measure, autocracies and democracies differ significantly in their average behavior of implied subsidies, with mean autocratic values falling below zero, whereas mean democratic values are significantly positive.[43] As I expect the fiscal consequences of food policy, as a function of urban population shares, to be most pronounced for those

---

[43] Similar to the RRA distribution, a Kolmorogov–Smirnov test of equality of distribution across regime type rejects the null hypothesis of equal distributions for the GSE measure at the 0.001% level.

countries that engage in heavy subsidization of either urban consumers or rural producers, I use this measure of GSE to create a dummy measure of *high urban subsidy* for autocracies and *high rural subsidy* for democracies, which takes a value of one for those countries in the lowest or highest third of their respective distributions. While including this measure of subsidy costs significantly reduces the number of countries in my sample (to 17 autocracies and only 13 democracies), given the centrality of this measure to my core theory, I demonstrate in Table 3.6 that the effects of urbanization on default in autocracies is indeed only statistically significant for those countries engaged in heavy subsidies for consumers; similarly, while there exists a weakly significant negative association between urbanization and default in democracies without high rural subsidies,[44] this relationship is significantly magnified among those democratic regimes that provide heavy pro-farmer price supports.[45]

3.7 DISCUSSION

After subjecting my main results on the positive association between food imports, urbanization, and debt default across autocracies and democracies to a number of robustness checks, including controlling for omitted variables, systemic factors, and an explicit measure of subsidy costs, I find robust support for my primary theoretical expectations that urban pressures drive default in nondemocracies, whereas rural farm support affects this choice in democratic systems. In an online appendix, I demonstrate that these core results remain across a wealth of additional empirical tests meant to address a number of additional concerns, including use of different estimating models, reestimation using differently specified independent and dependent variables, and analysis on nonimputed data. In the following chapter, I substantiate these aggregate associations with more detailed country-level evidence that providing food cheaply for restive urban dwellers was a major concern for ruling autocratic leaders, and that the fiscal costs that arose from such cheap food policies became a major source of contention once these countries eventually faced fiscal crisis. In addition, I show in much greater historical detail in Chapter 5 that rural-biased democracies do indeed face severe fiscal costs from agricultural subsidy programs, and that they are particularly unwilling to remove these subsidies when facing electoral challenges, leading even to default on their sovereign debt.

---

[44] As might be expected if part of this effect could proxy for economic development.
[45] Inclusion of measures of *regime age* or *government consumption* led to failure to complete multiple imputation estimates in these specifications, and so I have dropped these two controls here.

3.7 Discussion

TABLE 3.6. *High subsidies and debt default, 1960–2009*

VARIABLES	(1) Autoc.	(2) Democ.
Urban Population (%)	0.192	−0.406*
	(0.137)	(0.221)
High urban subsidy	−2.466**	
	(1.199)	
High urban subsidy * Urban	0.056**	
	(0.022)	
High rural subsidy		30.498***
		(9.973)
High rural subsidy * Urban		−1.378***
		(0.431)
GDP per capita (log)	1.528*	5.098**
	(0.787)	(2.190)
Δ GDP	−0.887	−0.471
	(0.672)	(1.317)
Debt/GDP	0.013**	0.077***
	(0.005)	(0.026)
Crisis	1.806***	1.609*
	(0.556)	(0.877)
Imports (% GDP)	−0.056	−0.295***
	(0.055)	(0.094)
Exports (% GDP)	0.142**	0.182*
	(0.056)	(0.110)
Current account (% GDP)	−0.068	−0.013
	(0.064)	(0.107)
Foreign res./imports	−8.101	−22.925
	(7.932)	(19.581)
Population (log)	4.080	24.446**
	(3.843)	(11.147)
Agricultural share of GDP	0.146***	0.175**
	(0.051)	(0.083)
Upcoming election	0.382*	1.042**
	(0.218)	(0.411)
Oil rents	0.002	−0.001
	(0.003)	(0.007)
Military size	−0.770	3.388
	(0.671)	(2.489)
US ally	4.497	1.717
	(2.927)	(3.030)
Russian ally	5.616	3.600
	(3.662)	(3.078)
IMF agreement	−0.342	0.398
	(0.433)	(0.801)
Observations	396	253
Countries	17	13

Robust standard errors clustered by country in parentheses
*** $p < 0.01$, ** $p < 0.05$, * $p < 0.1$
Table reports estimates of probit regressions of *default* on *urbanization* and *high subsidies*, as well as several controls, for nondemocracies in Column 1 and democracies in Column 2 from 1960 to 2009. The table reports multiple imputation estimates of the probit coefficients for each variable and robust standard errors, clustered at the country level, in parentheses. Country and year fixed effects were included in each regression, but are suppressed for presentation.

4

Default Pressures in Closed versus Electoral Autocracy
Zambia and Malaysia

> [IMF conditionality] is becoming more difficult and politically more unacceptable ... There is no point in accepting a program that, following mass demonstrations, has to be scrapped.
>
> Governor of the Bank of Zambia, as quoted in Clark and Allison (1989, 57–58)

> Hungry workers and angry farmers present a tempting target for opposition politicians looking for political support. Agrarian reform has social and economic effects, but the primary objectives are ultimately political. It attempts to win the support of target groups, create or restore political stability [and] legitimize the government.
>
> Bruce Drury (1988, 292) "The Limits of Conservative Reform: Agricultural Policy in Malaysia"

4.1 INTRODUCTION

In the preceding two chapters, I have argued theoretically and tested empirically the claim that, on average, nondemocratic regimes with large urban populations – and heavily reliant on food imports – will be unwilling to reform cheap food policies when faced with fiscal crisis due to the fear of unrest that would ensue. Yet, despite a wealth of empirical tests to suggest that the relationship between urbanization, food imports, and autocratic default is remarkably robust, it is difficult to prove that this is a result of the particular mechanisms I have highlighted in the theory. In order to demonstrate that the fear of urban unrest due to increased costs of food does indeed affect default decisions by elites in closed autocracies, in this chapter I provide a detailed historical account of sovereign default in Zambia, which was selected as a "best fit" case for illustrating the mechanisms I have emphasized. As a heavily urbanized country that existed under one-party rule for much of the 1970s and 1980s, the

4.1 Introduction

Zambian case proves a fertile testing ground for my claims about the political difficulty in undoing urban-biased subsidies during times of fiscal crisis. Yet, the discussion in Chapter 2 also highlights that, when electoral autocracies depend on mobilization of large blocs of rural voters in order to generate electoral supermajorities, the standard bias towards consumers in cities may be attenuated. The chapter also includes a case study of Malaysia, in which heavy reliance on rural Malay farmers led to much more pro-agricultural government intervention from the 1960s through the 1980s, despite the fact that the country is characterized as a nondemocratic one for this historical period.

In analyzing accounts of historical political dynamics, there often exists concern in identifying the "true" preferences of relevant actors. This can prove particularly difficult in cases involving back and forth between domestic governments and international agencies, when strategic incentives may exist for actors on both ends to conceal their actual views (Putnam 1988). To address these concerns, in all of the qualitative case material that I investigate in the following three chapters, I complement expert opinion from the secondary literature with my own original research drawing on close reading of hundreds of declassified documents from the IMF's archives. These primary sources are of particular use for identifying core views of relevant political and institutional actors during periods of fiscal crisis, as most of these documents were originally classified from public view and thus participants tended to be both more blunt and more honest in their discussions. As becomes apparent when reading, for example, the actual minutes of meetings of the executive directors at the Fund, the public statements put forward by the IMF sometimes papered over more significant internal division over the proper course of action in a given country; importantly, letters to the Fund from Ministers of Finance (and even occasional appearances by heads of state themselves) help identify in the words of the relevant actors themselves the areas that were of primary concern during the times of fiscal crisis around which my theory revolves.

This use of IMF documents is of additional relevance in consideration of the fact that, not only was the IMF the dominant international financial agency pushing for economic reforms at the time, but the country reports that it produced were frequently sought out by a multitude of other private actors as well. Given accounts that have emphasized the importance of considering in tandem not only the influence of IMF donor states, but also the corporate interests of IMF agents themselves (Copelovitch 2010), these declassified documents provide a unique window into the internal operations of the most important international financial agency in the world, and identify in great qualitative detail the conflicting priorities of the international financial markets as opposed to the domestic political concerns of particular country leaders. Additionally, recent efforts by the IMF to make scanned versions of these documents available at an online archival repository allow me throughout the book to employ suggested best practices in qualitative research by implementing "active citation" strategies, including in-text hyperlinks to precise documents, allowing for greater transparency and replicability of my historical research (Moravcsik 2010).

In order to investigate whether the role of food policy and urban–rural pressure were significant determinants of the decision to default by autocrats, I read through every available document in the IMF Archives for Zambia and Malaysia for the years prior to and following particular instances of fiscal crisis, and supplemented these primary sources with the secondary literature on the subject.[1] As can be seen Section 4.2.3 in the Zambian case, the combination of internal IMF documents and previous historical accounts helps identify that concerns over the fiscal ramifications of cheap food policies were of central importance at the time, and to demonstrate the extreme reluctance of autocratic rulers to remove these policies for fear of the political backlash that would ensue.

4.2 ZAMBIA

4.2.1 Case Selection

Zambia is an excellent case for investigating the role of urban bias in autocratic policymaking. As noted by Bates and Collier (1993, 388), for example, "By 1980, 43 percent of Zambia's population lived in the cities, a figure nearly double that of the rest of Sub-Saharan Africa ... Zambia is thus urban and industrial to a degree that is unusual in Africa." Given the role pressure from large urban populations exerts over autocratic survival in my theory, Zambia fits the bill well. In response, food policy had become a major political issue for the autocratic United National Independence Party (UNIP) regime, which ruled from the time of independence until the 1990s. In addition, the Zambian economy is largely focused around a few key commodities, with its agricultural market heavily centered on consumption of maize, making it easier to identify the ramifications of policies for particular commodities on Zambian macroeconomic stability.

4.2.2 Early History

Immediately following granting of independence in 1964, initial elections in Zambia appeared to take place in an environment of multiparty competition under the "First Republic," with competition primarily centering around the United National Independence Party (UNIP), which drew support from Northern regions and the Copperbelt against the African National Congress (ANC), which based its support in the South. After securing control of government in the elections of 1966, Kenneth Kaunda's UNIP in 1967 held elections for

---

[1] Specifically, for Zambia, I read over all documents available in the IMF Archive for the years 1976–1987, while for Malaysia I read all documents available for the years 1970–1986.

important positions in the Central Committee. However, internal (and regional) divisions within the party soon spilled out into open conflict; when a slate of UNIP candidates from the Western Province broke away to form their own independent party, this was initially banned following some political violence. In response, these breakaway actors chose to ally themselves instead with the primary opposition ANC party; in consequence, by 1968, the ANC had gained control over three of Zambia's eight provinces. This threat to UNIP dominance continued over the next few years, as another splinter faction of UNIP, dissatisfied with Kaunda's direction, subsequently formed an actual opposition party in the United Progressive Party (UPP).

This proved particularly threatening to continued UNIP rule, as the UPP's political base was drawn from the Copperbelt at the literal and figurative heart of Zambian politics. As discussed by Bates and Collier (1993, 398–399), "had UPP taken Northern Province and the Copperbelt in the elections of 1973, then UNIP would have lost five of the nine provinces and become a minority party. In December of 1971, the UNIP government therefore detained over 100 UPP organizers; in February of 1972, the government made Zambia a single-party state, with UNIP the sole legal party." Beyond declaring UNIP the only legal political party, Kaunda added additional changes to the constitution of the "Second Republic" which disallowed future possibility of any alternative party formation, thus cementing his control over both party and government (Rakner 2003, 52).

4.2.3 Urban Bias under Kaunda

At the time of independence, the urban labor movement proved a crucially important mobilizing force in Zambian politics. This mobilizational capacity functioned as a central component of UNIP's initial electoral success. Following the dissolution of the multiparty system, Kaunda feared the potential of a social counterweight that could arise from union capacity for strike and protest mobilization. In an attempt to weaken the capacity for unions to form an effective source of political opposition to his one-party state, Kaunda implemented the 1971 Industrial Relations Act, which made union affiliation with the Zambia Congress of Trade Unions (ZCTU) mandatory, as well as enforcement of the policy of "one industry one union." Given that ZCTU leadership was closely affiliated with UNIP at the time, the consequence was to place all labor unions under an umbrella organization with favorable relations with the government (Rakner 2003, 50).

Beyond securing its dominance over the political sphere, UNIP under Kaunda also nationalized large swaths of the economy – starting with two major copper companies – as part of the "Mulungushi" reforms beginning in April 1968. This nationalization was meant to establish domestic sovereign control over the economy after a colonial history of foreign dominance; while initially exceptionally popular with domestic audiences, the result of this acquisition of private production by the government was, predictably, a cessation in continued foreign investment in the country (Rakner 2003, 45). While copper prices remained high on international markets, this collapse of foreign funding was not perceived to be immediately threatening to the government's plans for development, as it was able to secure foreign exchange through copper exports. In addition, as domestic agricultural production collapsed under antirural discriminatory policies, Clark and Allison (1989, 5) note while "Zambia's agricultural sector was ill-equipped to provide the cheap food needed by the country's large urban population, this problem could be contained – for a while – by using a large part of Zambia's copper revenues to fund food subsidies for urban people."

Heavy government intervention in the economy was perceived as threatening as well to many domestic business elites. As the government developed an increasingly large panoply of state-owned enterprises to directly produce and market consumer goods, local business owners without direct access to government-subsidized input prices feared the consequences of noncompetitive economic policies made by the government on their bottom line. In addition, despite initial cooperation between UNIP and organized labor, government attempts to limit public wage bills by imposing wage restraint quickly met with opposition from labor groups (Rakner 2003). Indeed, as expected given the heavy rates of urbanization that Zambia experienced in this period, Bates and Collier (1993, 397) note that "While economically important, these groups [organized labor and the business community] were politically marginal; they lay outside the Party's core constituency which, as we shall see, consisted of urban consumers and state-owned industries."

Like so many underdeveloped countries blessed with mineral wealth, at the time of independence Zambia's economy was almost entirely based around its vast copper deposits. Copper exports accounted for over 90 percent of all foreign reserves earnings, and the growing "Copperbelt" region was seen as both the literal and figurative center of Zambian development.[2] As high international prices for copper generated strong incentives for expansion of the mineral sector, wages for copper miners skyrocketed, leading to a situation of economic dualism so common to resource-rich states: rising returns to labor created a large and growing urban agglomeration around the Copperbelt, as rural subsistence farmers heard tales of get-rich-quick schemes working for mining companies that promised wages that seemed almost too good to be true.

Sadly, of course, the massive rural–urban migration that followed this push meant that labor for mining activities quickly became vastly oversupplied; while the growth of downstream industries meant that there were still some other urban jobs to be had, even these became quickly filled, leading to the presence of a large accumulation in urban areas in Zambia of working-age men who lacked

[2] The Copperbelt is located almost perfectly in the middle of Zambia.

4.2 Zambia

sufficiently remunerative employment.[3] This situation was depicted openly by the Zambian government in 1972, which noted that

> Zambia's wealth is heavily concentrated in the urban sector ... It will be seen that the nation represents an extreme example of economic dualism, with a rich import/export-oriented mining sector and a poor subsistence sector almost wholly outside the money economy. This dualism has been broken to some extent by the rapid growth of the urban areas as a result of migration of rural people. It is estimated that between 40 and 60 per cent of Zambia's adult male population are now, at least temporarily, resident in the urban sector.[4]

Work on collective action has commonly found that age and gender map closely onto potential for political mobilization: Young men are generally the most likely social subgroup to take part in protest or rebellion, especially in urban areas. With over half of the adult male population concentrated in urban centers, but with far fewer jobs available to actually employ these men, the potential political consequences of this urban dissatisfaction were not lost on the Zambian regime. In order to forestall unrest among these urban populations, UNIP quickly began making use of the then-abundant economic rents from valuable copper exports to engage in a number of urban-biased policies, especially the subsidization of cheap food.[5] Secondary accounts are virtually unanimous in emphasizing the centrality of urban consumers to the government's political survival concerns; for example, Hawkins (1991, 842–843) argues that "[d]espite inherent economic problems [in the government's agricultural policies], the model created a constituency for the government among the very elements of society that could potentially be the most threatening to the government. The most important part of this constituency was the urban population." This is echoed as well by Bates and Collier (1993, 406), who state (in almost perfect summary of my theoretical account of politics in urban-biased autocracies) that "the structure of political competition within the Second Republic created political incentives that induced a preference on the part of politicians in favor of interventionalist policies that protected the interest of urban consumers."

Accounts of Zambian food policy make clear that this urban bias took a number of particular forms. First, having inherited a system of agricultural marketing agencies from the colonial period, the government exercised monopsonist marketing power for rural agricultural goods through the National Agricultural Marketing Board (NAMBOARD), especially for maize. That this marketing board was not used to the benefit of maize farmers is summarized

---

[3] Callaghy (1990, 287) notes that by 1986, Zambia was 48 percent urbanized – "the highest rate in black-ruled Africa."
[4] Lombard and Tweedie (1974, 1).
[5] See Callaghy (1990) for a more detailed discussion of the political dynamics in Zambia at the time of Independence.

well in the following quotation from a Zambian government report on agricultural policy:

> Undoubtedly the most important crop handled by NAMBOARD is maize. In 1970–71, 4.2 million bags of maize were consumed in the money economy. As it is Zambia's staple food, the marketing of maize is controlled by the Government, and NAMBOARD has to ensure that Zambia is adequately supplied from internal production and through importation when necessary. The control of maize is implemented by law through the Minister of Rural Development, and any part of Zambia can be declared a controlled area at any time. In a controlled area a farmer must sell all his surplus maize to NAMBOARD or to a designated agent.[6]

This control of domestic agricultural production was secured principally through monopsonist power on line-of-rail access by government agencies. At the time, essentially the only means for transporting rural goods to urban markets for resale involved putting these goods on trains that ran to the cities; farmers usually sold their goods to middlemen along the line-of-rail, who were then responsible for actually transmitting and selling the goods at their final point of destination. However, the Zambian government claimed sole right to these transactions along the line-of-rail, which effectively left rural producers with no outside option to secure better prices for their produce. In addition, as is made clear in the summary, the government possessed the power to declare any region in the country a "controlled area"; in these controlled zones, farmers were mandated by law to sell their surplus maize to government agents. In such a price-setting environment, the government could squeeze excess rents from rural producers, and did so in order to maintain a source of cheap food for urban consumers. The following quote (again, from a Zambian government publication) helps demonstrate that these transfers were viewed explicitly in terms of urban–rural biases:

> The Government also maintains a cheap food policy and has introduced statutory retail prices for some essential foodstuffs, for example maize meal, milk and meat. Such a policy is expensive in subsidies to statutory boards, as the prices have lagged far behind the general level of inflation, and of course the urban consumer is the main beneficiary. Indeed, a large proportion of the subsidies allocated to the Ministry of **Rural** Development have in fact subsidized the **urban** consumer.[7]

An additional policy tool used by NAMBOARD to repress domestic food prices involved the subsidization of fertilizer. At first glance, this policy may seem evidence of a more pro-rural attitude. However, a greater understanding of the mechanism by which domestic agricultural prices were set helps to clarify that, again, this policy represented largely an overriding concern with urban food prices. Marketing prices were technically set in a "cost-plus" method, which was theoretically designed to guarantee farmers some fixed return to their investment beyond any costs incurred. In theory, of course, if government

---

[6] Lombard and Tweedie (1974, 17).   [7] Lombard and Tweedie (1974, 72, boldface in original).

held additional returns to farmers fixed, any decrease in their costs through subsidization would represent an improvement in the profitability of food production. In practice, however, the Zambian authorities frequently squeezed domestic farmers by accompanying suppression on the "cost" margin via subsidized fertilizer with simultaneous reductions on the "plus" margin that they were guaranteed by government marketing agencies. Note, as expected in a system where rural agents lacked much political influence, that these anti-rural biases occurred despite the fact that a majority of the population at the time still depended on agriculture for their livelihood (Saasa 1996, 9).

Beyond its powers to control marketing and pricing for agricultural goods, NAMBOARD also enjoyed monopsonist importation rights for most key food commodities, including maize, vegetables, fruit, and milk. The government therefore provided cheap food to urban dwellers both from rural domestic production (which was secured at reduced prices via abuse of marketing power) as well as from imports of food which were resold at a rate below the current world price; this matches nearly perfectly the formal approach I adopt in Chapter 2 to describe urban-biased cheap food policies. While such a policy may have seemed feasible when rural agricultural production was largely sufficient to cover urban consumption, over time these subsidized food imports, particularly on maize, constituted an increasingly large part of Zambian fiscal imbalance. IMF concern over the financial burden of these policies is made clear as early as 1976; given its centrality to my theory, I quote at length a summary by the IMF of Zambian agricultural pricing policy:

> In the past the authorities have attempted to protect the consumer by maintaining selected retail prices and producer prices for agricultural products at an artificially low level. This policy has necessitated the *direct payment of consumption subsidies for maize*, the staple food, as well as the subsidization of fertilizer. In addition, subsidies and other forms of payments have been made to cover the financial losses of parastatal enterprises relating not only to management inefficiencies but also to low retail prices of products such as maize, bread and cooking oil.
>
> With the *increase in import prices*, and the need to increase producer prices in 1974 and 1975, subsidies increased by K 10 million in 1974 and by K 35 million in 1975...The failure to increase gradually consumer prices, as reflected by the increase in subsidy payments, *has aggravated the overall budget position* and made it more difficult to eliminate subsidies.[8]

Despite shocks to its terms of trade arising from the twin oil crises of the 1970s and the collapse in copper prices from the ensuing international recession, UNIP chose to shield domestic consumers from these international dislocations primarily through resorting to massive expansion in foreign borrowing (Rakner 2003, 54). Compounded by falling prices for copper, the rising fiscal burden of cheap food policies increasingly became a target of concern. By 1979, despite a better-than-average fiscal performance in the previous

[8] IMF (1976c, 6), emphasis added.

year, Zambian authorities were already "concerned about the emergence of an excess in Treasury lending associated with problems encountered by the National Agricultural Marketing Board (NAMBOARD). These problems arose from the inflexibility of the pricing structure."[9] Given this recognition that food subsidies were becoming a severe drain on the government budget, why didn't the authorities simply do away with such policies? Certainly it was not for lack of recommendation: IMF reports from 1976, 1977, 1979, 1981, 1983, 1984, and 1985 all cite food subsidies as a large and increasing source of budgetary imbalance.[10] This accords with Sano (1988, 565)'s account of Zambian negotiations with the IMF, who states that "[i]n particular, the IMF urged the abolition of agricultural subsidies. The latter had occupied a prominent place in all Zambian-IMF negotiations since 1978. According to the IMF's view, these subsidies were not only instrumental in raising the fluctuating level of budget deficits and thus in fueling inflation, but they also gave rise to grave distortions of the Zambian food market and particularly that of maize. During 1980, when the subsidies were at their highest level prior to the IMF-Zambian accord, the total subsidies for agriculture accounted for almost 19 percent of total recurrent government spending."

In addition, several IMF reviews of the Zambian economy repeatedly stressed the need for diversification away from copper, and argued that agriculture offered the greatest promise for immediate gains. Yet, the core of these recommended policies required improving terms of trade for rural farmers that would come at the expense of urban consumers; as noted by an executive director in the minutes of the Executive Board meeting on October 29, 1979, "it had to be recognized that it was not easy to make a major adjustment in pricing policy, which affected Zambia's principal consumer goods ... The price adjustment imposed a considerable burden on the urban population in particular."[11] The resulting inability to reform domestic economic policies, however, led to an explosion of sovereign debt, such that, "by 1984 Zambia was the most indebted country in the world relative to its GDP."[12] While budgetary imbalances also arose from factors outside of food pricing policy, Saasa (1996, 8)'s discussion of the reform process makes clear the centrality of the maize subsidy in particular to the overall budget position, noting that the "budgetary implications of the pre-reforms heavy maize subsidies were significant. In particular, between 1980 and 1990, maize subsidies ranged between 21 percent and 145 percent of the total budget deficit."

4.2.4 Response to Fiscal Crisis

Zambian food policy to protect urban consumers was initially funded by foreign reserve earnings from copper exports; when these dried up, the government

---

[9] IMF (1979c, 3).
[10] See IMF (1976c, 23), IMF (1977b, 9), IMF (1979c, 3), IMF (1981d, 4), IMF (1983d, throughout), IMF (1984h, 7), IMF (1985j, 20).
[11] IMF (1979c, 8). [12] Bates and Collier (1993, 389).

4.2 Zambia

turned to borrowing to continue this politically-important policy. While this may have seemed more feasible in the environment of easier access to private lending during the 1970s and early 1980s, Mexico's default on its international debt marked the end of such "easy" money. Thus, 1983 marked an inflection point when, with external options for financing drying up, Zambia was forced to confront its economic imbalances directly in order to retain access to lending of last resort from the IMF (Rakner 2003, 57). The government attempted reforms to a host of state-owned enterprises and marketing agencies, raising the price of a number of consumer goods while also exerting downward pressure on wages in an attempt to control deficits. Importantly, however, despite wide-ranging efforts by the government to shore up its budgetary balances, there remained one area in which government intervention continued to persist: the price of maize. While the government did permit some lessening of subsidies in food markets, in direct evidence of the political centrality of this policy, Bates and Collier (1993, 421) note that "[t]hroughout the economic reforms, maize remained the one commodity subject to price control." Secondary accounts of the danger that reforms posed to Kaunda are in concert: Hawkins (1991, 845) captures the consensus view that while "[t]hese new [reforms under IMF programs] were designed to improve performance in certain sectors ... they had the unavoidable result of harming the model's political base: the urban working class."[13]

In the face of rising fiscal problems associated with food subsidies, Zambia repeatedly promised reduction or removal of distortionary agricultural price policies. Internal discussions of several conditional loans packages make clear that the Zambian government worked to continually provide the appearance of reforming cheap food policies, often declaring that prices in the economy had been decontrolled. Yet despite being continually identified by the IMF as a significant source of fiscal trouble since the mid-1970s, nearly ten years later the director of the IMF still highlighted the main fiscal objectives for Zambia in 1986 as "improved expenditure control, as well as restraint on the growth of personal emoluments, containment of budgetary subsidies (particularly on maize and fertilizer), and control of current transfers to parastatals."[14] By the beginning of 1986, Zambia was deep in the throes of fiscal crisis, a crisis due in no small part to its policy of subsidizing imported food for urban consumers.[15]

Beyond its use of food subsidies as a means of benefitting urban consumers, the Zambian regime had also maintained an over-valued exchange rate to keep down the costs of imported goods, including food (as well as industrial inputs for state-owned enterprises).[16] In an international environment of rapidly receding finance, the IMF hardened its demands for concrete reforms as part

---

[13] See also, e.g., Rakner (2003, 58). [14] IMF (1985j, 39).
[15] Loxley (1990) claims that subsidies on maize meal alone consumed nearly 15% of government revenue in certain years, an enormous share of total government resources.
[16] Bates and Collier (1993, 407).

of its package in 1985. While still unwilling to decontrol maize prices, the Zambian government did accede to conditions associated with the exchange rate, introducing in October 1985 a foreign exchange auction intended to allow the value of the kwacha to be set by free market demand, not governmental fiat. Upon introduction of the auction, the kwacha did indeed depreciate significantly, falling in value by 35 percent in the first nine months of the program and by nearly 85 percent by the end of 1986.[17] Devaluation of the currency was intended, of course, to discourage additional imports and to make Zambian exports more competitive on world markets, which (it was hoped) would lead to a lessening of the balance of payments problems faced by the government.

However, despite significant depreciation, Zambian exports failed to experience pronounced gains, due in part to continued weakness in international demand compounded with the inability of Zambian enterprises to immediately enjoy competitive gains following decades of reliance on the state. Even more problematic, the devaluation had two additional deleterious consequences for the likelihood of successful maintenance of reforms in Zambia. First, for a country largely reliant on foreign-currency-denominated borrowing, one consequence of the devaluation of the kwacha was to further expand the pain associated with debt service payments (Clark and Allison 1989, 12). This had the effect, therefore, of further requiring that government emphasize its external obligations at the expense of programs for domestic beneficiaries, which ought to prove unsavory for most incumbents.

Of more direct relevance to my own theoretical account, for a country heavily reliant on imports of food to feed its urban population, the devaluation of the currency also led to an increase in food costs for domestic consumers. Clark and Allison (1989, 28–30) recount that, for "the urban poor the IMF-inspired auction meant increasing unemployment and soaring prices for imported goods, many of which – such as soap and kerosene – are seen as essentials. Domestic goods also started to rise in price as inflation got out of control ... This had a sharp effect on the food consumption of poor families." Initial response to this erosion of urban purchasing power was an attempt by several unions to stage a series of strikes in late 1985 and early 1986; however, by leaning on its labor market influence, the government was initially able to withstand this pressure against austerity through extended labor repression (Rakner 2003, 59). Fearful of additional unrest, the government did attempt to reintervene in foreign exchange markets in July of 1986; however, the IMF was quick to identify this government interference as unwarranted under the terms of the structural adjustment assistance, leading the government to move away from these interventions.

By late 1986, IMF patience with the lack of real reform of Zambian subsidization policies had worn thin; failure to conform with implementation

[17] Clark and Allison (1989, 18; 30).

4.2 Zambia

of policy measures led the existing arrangement between the IMF and Zambia to become inoperative. Desperately hoping to regain IMF approval (especially given that loans from other official sources required normalized relations with the Fund), the Zambian representative to the IMF explained to the board of directors that "the slippages should not be interpreted as a lack of commitment to adjustment on their part. Implementation of the adjustment had been unsatisfactory because it had *touched on sensitive policy areas*. Nevertheless, the authorities had been engaged in concerted efforts to muster the political consensus that was needed to ensure successful implementation of the program, and that consensus had been largely secured."[18] Facing a dire budgetary shortage, the Zambian authorities pieced together a change to the maize pricing policy that they believed could simultaneously reduce its fiscal footprint while still avoiding potentially destabilizing unrest.

In response to a growing awareness that the financial burdens of cheap food policies were unsustainable, in December 1986 the Zambian government removed the official subsidy on higher-quality maize meal. The subsidy on lower-grade maize was maintained, on the theory that this would still protect the purchasing power of the poorest consumers (who would not mind the lower-quality grain) while passing on costs of adjustment to the more well-off who could presumably bear the higher prices for food (and who preferred the better maize meal). However, the response of private millers largely undermined the government's intentions – once the price ceiling for high-quality maize was removed, the millers shifted production almost entirely to this finer grain, thereby leading to a serious shortage of the (still-subsidized) coarse maize meal and a rapid run-up in prices.

Callaghy (1990, 296) recounts the effect of removing the maize subsidy: "Serious rioting broke out in the Copperbelt in which fifteen people died. The outbursts in Lusaka itself were less serious, but still frightening. Badly shaken by the riots, President Kaunda immediately reversed the maize price increase and nationalized all the large private maize mills." Facing the largest outpouring of mass unrest since Independence, the Zambian regime found itself caught between two horns of a particularly difficult dilemma – on the one side, demands for austerity in order to remain current on its debt payments, and on the other, angry urban citizens willing to take to the streets to protest rapidly rising food prices. The linkage between food prices, unrest, and political survival at this point are quite explicit in secondary accounts, such as in Rakner (2003, 59)'s discussion of how "[r]ioting shook the Copperbelt and Lusaka and left 15 people dead. These events profoundly shook the UNIP government and its immediate response was to restore the subsidies, nationalize the milling companies and blame the IMF ... Increasingly, political survival needs dictated economic policies."

---

[18] IMF (1986e, 3).

Statements by the Zambian representative to the IMF in January 1987 make explicitly clear the role that unrest played in affecting government reversal in food price policy, arguing that "the civil disturbances that had occurred in late 1986, including some loss of life, had created *new political realities that could not be ignored.*" In specifying what those new realities entailed, the representative read a letter sent to the IMF from the Zambian Minister of Finance, which noted that with "regard to the government budget, the major expenditure slippage will be in respect of the maize meal subsidy. I am confident that we will find appropriate ways of substantially offsetting or financing the additional subsidy."[19] In other words, the maize subsidy was here to stay. This is echoed by Bates and Collier (1993, 422), who argue that after the riots, "economic reforms were no longer debated in terms of growth rates or allocational efficiency; they were instead debated in terms of their impact on political stability – i.e., on the capacity of incumbents to retain power."

The blatant statement that the maize subsidy would not be reduced further, and that means for financing it would have to be found, constitutes an incredible about-face in the language of these negotiations from the previous fifteen years. Indeed, in every internal account I could find up to this point, the Zambian authorities expressed their regret at the distortions caused by food subsidies, and always implied that subsidy reduction was an important policy priority for the near future. In simply stating that the subsidy would no longer be on the table for adjustment, the authorities presented an entirely different political orientation, one motivated explicitly in reaction to the large-scale violent response to its previous attempt to increase the price of maize. In reply, the director of the IMF expressed that "it was most regrettable that without the benefit of offsetting savings as yet, the maize subsidy – which accounted for a significant part of the fiscal deficit – had to be reinstated fully."[20] Sano (1988, 563)'s account of reform discussions makes clear the centrality of maize subsidies to the difficulty of successful reform, noting that the "crux of the argument between Zambia and the IMF concerned the rising level of the Zambian budget deficit as a result of the failure of the government to reduce its maize consumer subsidies. These had been reintroduced following the riots in the copperbelt and Lusaka in December 1986 after an initial doubling of high grade mealie-meal (maize flour) prices."

Caught in such a dilemma, a self-interested politician concerned with remaining in power might rationally refuse to implement economic adjustment, especially if citizen unrest was viewed as damaging to regime stability. With single-party elections scheduled for 1988, Kaunda may have been particularly sensitive to the potential for urban unrest to threaten his rule.[21] In fact, Callaghy (1990, 296, emphasis added) argues that "Zambian officials believed

---

[19] IMF (1987, 5). [20] IMF (1987, 6).
[21] These were not multiparty elections, and thus the case is still coded as a closed autocracy.

4.2 Zambia

that the elections were crucial to the legitimacy, *and thus the stability*, of the single-party state [and that] a severe embarrassment in the elections might foster divisive and centrifugal political and social tendencies." The Zambian government at the time viewed food price riots explicitly in terms of their potentially destabilizing impact, and facing such pressure, Kaunda chose to call off reforms intended to improve budgetary balances and continue debt servicing. After doing so, access to international financial resources was essentially stopped, and "[f]inally, on May Day 1987, President Kaunda announced that Zambia was suspending its IMF reform effort, abolishing the auction, freezing prices, reintroducing price controls, resurrecting the import licensing system of allocating foreign exchange, and limiting debt service to well under 10 percent of foreign exchange earnings" (Callaghy 1990, 298). In other words, when faced with the threat of regime instability driven by urban riots against rising food prices due to economic adjustment, the Zambian government chose instead to renege on its international borrowing agreements, and defaulted on its sovereign debt.[22]

4.2.5 Postelectoral Reforms in Zambia

The case of sovereign default in Zambia helps make clear, through use of both primary and secondary sources, that concerns over urban food prices were central to the survival calculations of incumbent autocrats. Yet these cheap food policies were expensive, and when faced with inevitable fiscal crisis, were explicitly targeted by international financial institutions as important sources of disequilibrium that were necessary for the rebalancing of government budgets. Despite this external pressure for reform, the UNIP party apparatus in Zambia faced an equally powerful domestic pressure against austerity: the threat of mass unrest against rapidly rising food prices. In this case, in the end the fear of short-term survival threats outweighed the long-run economic costs of default.

Yet the ouster of Kaunda following reimposition of competitive elections in 1991 coincided with a period of relative success in removing urban-biased food subsidies. What explains this about-face in government's willingness to reform cheap food policy? Why might elected incumbents have less to fear from urban consumers? When survival in office is predicated upon winning votes, not suppressing unrest, do the political incentives for sovereign default change? Having demonstrated robust quantitative and historical support for my theory of default in closed autocracies like Zambia, before turning explicitly to consideration of the democratic side of the coin in Chapter 5, I consider in the remainder of this chapter the ways in which the introduction of multiparty elections, even in autocracies, may affect the relative balance of political influence between urban and rural citizens.

---

[22] Clark and Allison (1989, 19) argues that the political effects of the foreign exchange auction and food subsidies were the two main causes of Zambia's break with the IMF.

4.3 MALAYSIA

4.3.1 Case Selection

While the case of Zambia emphasized the importance of appeasing urban consumers in order to forestall unrest in autocratic regimes, not every dictator has targeted benefits exclusively to urban areas. Observers of the Malaysian regime have often noted its emphasis on providing for the many poor and rural farmers that inhabit the countryside; at the same time, experts have continued to identify Malaysian politics as nondemocratic under the long rule of the dominant UMNO party. This explicit emphasis on provision of public programs for rural areas – primarily in the agricultural sector – may seem somewhat jarring when juxtaposed against autocracies such as the Zambian case considered in the first half of this chapter, where far-flung farmers were either ignored or actively discriminated against in a quest to maintain lower costs of living for urban citizens. What explains this difference in the Malaysian case? Does this interest in supporting rural areas contradict my more general theory of autocratic survival?

I argue that the presence of multiparty elections in Malaysia, in a country where a large fraction of the population lives in rural areas, has generated incentives for the incumbent regime to provide at least some minimal level of transfers to farming communities. In particular, this has often taken the form of government supported minimum-price levels for basic food commodities. While such policies have protected the material interests of rural agents, they have also often resulted in higher food prices in the cities. This strategy of rural provision has proven to be an incredibly successful means of securing stability for UMNO; in particular, by generating the expectation of perpetual electoral conquest, this has meant that elections in Malaysia serve to bind the interests of common Malays to continued party rule, while also demonstrating to potential defectors that opposition is likely to be fruitless. Thus, while multiparty elections in Malaysia are not expected to actually lead to turnover in power, they do serve an important stabilizing function for the government. Critically, given the conceptual focus of this book, this electoral linkage turns on the mobilization of vast numbers of rural voters, which produces systematic incentives for the ruling government to actually pay attention to the material needs of farmers, in sharp contrast to the closed autocracies discussed in the beginning of this chapter.

4.3.2 Early History

The discovery of high quality tin within the territories of what would become Malaysia made it an attractive target for colonial expansion. As British control of the area was consolidated, expansion of economic production in Malaysia was generally accompanied by migration from other areas, especially ethnic

4.3 Malaysia

Chinese workers who flocked to several major mining centers including Kuala Lampur, the future political capital, which was initially established around a series of tin mines (Yaakob, Masron, and Masami 2010, 88). Over time, this practice led to an overlapping alignment of ethnicity, geography, and economic activity in Malaysia, with much of the benefit of development accruing to ethnic Chinese and Indians in growing urban centers, while ethnic Malays (still a majority of the overall population) languished in poor rural areas and generally engaged in subsistence agriculture (Yusof and Bhattasali 2008).

By the middle of the twentieth century, as the rumblings of independence movements began to spread across colonial regions, this alignment of geography, ethnicity and economy had created a set of palpable political tensions, with the majority Malay population increasingly expressing discontentment at having been denied the fruits of economic advancement that were instead enjoyed by "outsiders" (Narayanan 1996, 870). Early work done in constructing the Malaysian constitution recognized "the need for safeguarding the *special position of the Malays* in a manner consistent with the legitimate interest of other communities,"[23] which led to the enshrinement of Article 153 of the Constitution, which explicitly identified the need for government to "safeguard the special position of the Malays," generally interpreted as particular political and economic support for the largely agricultural-based traditional members of the dominant ethnic majority.

While initial elections in Malaysia witnessed a seemingly successful cross-ethnic coalition between the major Malay (UMNO), Chinese (MCA), and Indian (MIC) political parties in the Alliance front, not all was settled in terms of a continued sense of disparity, particularly among ethnic Malays and other indigenous peoples, commonly referred to as the "Bumiputera" (or "sons of the the soil"). In 1963, the Federation of Malaya expanded to include North Borneo, Sarawak and Singapore, leading to the advent of new opposition parties – especially the the ethnically Chinese People's Action Party (PAP), based in Singapore – which campaigned explicitly in the 1964 elections for a "Malaysian Malaysia," or a call for equal treatment of all Malaysian citizens regardless of ethnicity. Government concern over the possibility of a repeated showing for the PAP in future elections that might siphon off Chinese supporters of Alliance, along with rising tensions between Singaporean and Malaysian citizens, led to the expulsion of Singapore from Malaysia in the following year.

Yet, if anything, this strategy of expulsion in order to retain Chinese loyalty appears to have backfired. By the time of the third parliamentary elections in 1969, two new opposition parties had formed – the Parti Gerakan Rakyat Malaysia (Gerakan) and the Democratic Action Party (DAP) – drawing support largely from urban Chinese voters; both campaigned explicitly against the special privileges afforded by Article 153. These calls against discrimination

---

[23] Reid Report (1957, 7).

were to prove electorally appealing – the DAP and Gerakan collectively won nearly 20 percent of the vote share, which in addition to a strong showing by the PMIP (which earned another 21 percent of votes cast) led to the governing Alliance Party capturing a mere 44 percent of votes, which while enough to ensure a bare majority of legislative seats (at 51 percent), resulted in the first time ever that the Alliance Party did not control the supermajority of seats required, among other things, to pass constitutional amendments.

Savoring what appeared to be a true competitive opening in a previously Alliance-dominated electoral environment, several of the opposition parties took to the streets in the wake of the elections to celebrate their new political influence. This included a victory rally held in Kuala Lumpur on May 12, at which DAP and Gerakan supporters allegedly engaged in the use of racial epithets against Malay bystanders. In response to this, the primary Malay party of the Alliance bloc, UMNO, organized its own counter-protests to be held in the capital; as Kuala Lampur was primarily a Chinese city, however, this required the transportation of thousands of ethnic Malays from rural areas to the city (Horowitz 2001). While the counter-rally initially appeared peaceful, by early evening of May 13, anti-Chinese violence had broken out across the city, including rioting, looting and destruction of property. As Chinese and Indian citizens began to organize for violent reprisals against Malays, the army finally mobilized and imposed a national curfew while also occupying major strategic centers. Following the declaration of a state of emergency, Parliament was disbanded, and governance of Malaysia was passed to the newly established National Operations Council, headed by the sitting leader of UMNO.

4.3.3 Elections and Political Geography in Malaysia

The breakdown of elections and ensuing civil violence that occurred in what has since become known as the "May 13 Incident" represented a crucial pivot for Malaysian politics. Given the costliness of designing and implementing political institutions, it is rare to observe radical change in the institutional structure of a country. Indeed, especially given the self-reinforcing nature of most institutional arrangements, it is only during times of serious crisis that we may expect existing equilibria to become "punctuated," thereby allowing for the possibility of new alignments (Baumgartner and Jones 2010). With military intervention and cessation of elections in Malaysia, the incumbent UMNO regime surely faced a difficult choice in deciding how to restructure Malaysia's political system. In similar cases of interethnic violence, one common approach has been for a regime party to annul all formal opposition, identifying electoral competition with social strife and thereby securing for the regime sole access to elections. Yet this was not the path pursued in the Malaysian case. Instead, Parliament was reconvened in 1971, and parliamentary elections – with multiple opposition parties — were resumed in 1974. It is recognized that the subsequent electoral environment did not constitute a fully democratic one, and so the case is generally agreed to be an electoral autocracy (Pepinsky 2007).

In expressing a willingness to use force to interrupt electoral outcomes that were perceived as threatening to its primacy, UMNO revealed that its dedication to elections went only so far as those elections produced the "right" results. Indeed, it is precisely for this reason that Malaysia is used as the textbook case to illustrate the importance of the "consolidation rule" for identifying democracies in Przeworski, Cheibub, Limongi and Alvarez (2000, 21–22), which argues that "1969 served notice to the Alliance leadership that it might have to one day face the prospect of an electoral defeat ... The rules of the game of Malaysian democracy were therefore set for modification after 1969 because the prospect of a zero-sum electoral result would be unacceptable if Malay political supremacy was not to be assured." Yet, this poses something of a puzzle: Why bother returning to multiparty elections at all? In a country where a majority of the army was ethnically Malay, why not simply rely on ethnic connections to ensure support for the government, as has been done in several other dictatorial regimes?

As discussed in Chapter 2, when autocrats rely on turnout of large super-majorities of voters in order to project an "aura of invincibility" (Magaloni 2006), this creates systematic pressures to provide support to the large blocs of voters that live in rural areas in the developing world. Secondary accounts of the UMNO government's survival strategy in this period are in concert on the central role that rural peasants played in providing a base of support for the regime. For example, Drury (1988, 295) argues that "UMNO's base of support has been in the countryside, and thus the party has directed many programmes towards rural areas in order to maintain the power base. Rural development was and is desirable because land, jobs, and prosperity for the rural Malay masses should ensure votes and continued power for UMNO." The advantages of large population shares in rural areas was further compounded by institutional design in the Malaysian electoral system, which provided systematic overrepresentation to rural areas. Pepinsky (2007, 144) notes that "the electoral system strongly favors rural – and hence Malay – voters. The government's willingness to gerrymander electoral constituencies to its political advantage has increased over time, ensuring that the effective weight of Malay votes far exceeds that of non-Malay votes."[24]

This more complex set of supporters has critical implications for the sorts of agricultural policies we expect dictators to pursue. In particular, note that the strategy of providing cheap food for urban consumers by exploiting the monopsonist power of rural marketing boards is likely to result in significant opposition from farmers; if these farmers are expected to form an important part of the electoral coalition, we should expect less systematic discrimination against rural producers. In fact, to the extent that autocrats seek to tie farmers

[24] See also, e.g., Drury (1988, 291).

to the regime through government transfers, this suggests that electoral autocracies may even be characterized by the sorts of farm support policies I describe in subsequent chapters as an important component of the agricultural system that arises in many democratic states seeking to court rural voters. Yet, when elections are not seen as a viable means of replacing the executive, we should still suspect that citizens who are unhappy with the regime may consider revolt when their interests are ignored completely. Given this still-present threat of potential rebellion, and following the obvious collective action advantages for mass mobilization of urban areas discussed at length in Chapter 2, it is unlikely that autocrats will be able to dedicate all their attention to the numerically-advantaged rural areas, as doing so would likely leave the regime still at risk of facing urban unrest.

4.3.4 The New Economic Policy (NEP)

While the eruption of violence surrounding elections in the May 13 incident provided the UMNO regime with an opportunity to restructure politics, the decision to return to multiparty elections likely resulted from awareness that political survival could be best secured by generating electoral supermajorities centered on rural Malay votes. In order to function, however, this required a series of government benefits for loyal voters, especially concentrated among rural farmers. While it can often be difficult to identify precisely a given regime's economic goals, in the Malaysian case the resumption of Parliament coincided with an explicit detailing of the government's targets for economic development in the form of the New Economic Policy (NEP), published in 1971.

This reorientation of the economy was clearly viewed through the lens of recent unrest; as argued by Aziz (2012, 30), "the 1969 riot was a major catalyst for the creation of the New Economic Policy." Thus, the May 13 incident helped to clarify that political security would continue to be threatened by social instability, unless the government addressed a series of underlying imbalances between rural Malay farmers and urban Chinese manufacturers.[25] In a summary of economic developments in 1972, the IMF captured well the political tensions motivating the government's new policies:

Although considerable economic growth was achieved during the First Malaysia Plan, poverty, unemployment and economic and social imbalances continued to prevail. Economic imbalances in Malaysia are reflected in the uneven distribution of income, employment, and ownership of wealth, which tend to coincide with the racial origin and place of livelihood of the population. Thus, the bulk of Malaysians of Malay origin live in rural areas and are largely engaged in paddy cultivation and other small-scale agricultural activities, where income levels are generally lower ... The "New Economic Policy" calls for the Government to take a more active role in attempting to correct these imbalances through placing more emphasis on the social aspects

---

[25] See discussion in IMF (1983e, 5).

4.3 Malaysia

of economic development. The "New Economic Policy" aims at achieving a better distribution of income and employment among the various ethnic groups and regions through eradicating poverty irrespective of race and restructuring society to reduce and eventually eliminate the identification of race with economic function.[26]

The guiding philosophy for government intervention in the economy, as outlined in the NEP, was explicitly framed in terms of the need to eliminate poverty (largely concentrated among rural Malays), and to eventually eliminate the association of identity with economic productivity. Yet how, precisely, was this reorientation to be brought about? Coincident with publication of the NEP in 1971, the government also developed a new Second Malaysia Plan (SMP), which was to serve as the basis for economic planning for the next five years. As described by the IMF, "the Second Malaysia Plan is an expression of the 'New Economic Policy' and aims at developing the economically depressed rural areas and increasing the share of Malays and other indigenous people in the ownership and control of the means of production in the modern sector; such people now manage and own less than 10 percent of the commercial and industrial enterprises in Malaysia."[27]

It is important to note the striking difference in emphasis here – with a direct focus on rural development – as compared to the urban-biased regimes discussed in the Zambian case. The SMP was explicitly targeted toward alleviation of rural poverty; as noted, of course, the vast majority of rural producers in Malaysia at the time were engaged in agriculture, largely either as smallholders producing rice for domestic consumption or rubber for international export. Equally important, of course, was the political effect of such reforms, which Drury (1988, 287) describes as including the maintenance of "a stable political base for the ruling group [which required] an agricultural reform package that was intended to reduce poverty, increase productivity, and reduce inequities in the distribution of wealth."

What did these rural poverty alleviation programs look like explicitly? Of direct relevance to my formal theory, one of the major interventions of the SMP established a "Guaranteed Minimum Price Scheme, [under which] rice farmers are guaranteed a minimum price for paddy at the farm level."[28] Beyond providing a guaranteed minimum support price for rice, the Malaysian government also provided a host of other development-related rural expenditures, including increased irrigation investment, cheap access to credit, and subsidized fertilizer. In addition, government agricultural agencies increasingly supported smallholder paddy farmers in developing techniques to improve "double-cropping" opportunities, in which a single plot could produce multiple harvests throughout the year. As a result of these interventions, Malaysia became

---

[26] IMF (1972, 25). [27] IMF (1972, 25).
[28] See IMF (1972, 14). Note that, prior to implementation of the New Economic Policy, the Malaysian government did not provide direct cash subsidies to rice farmers; see, for example, discussion of this point in IMF (1971b, 30).

largely-self sufficient in rice, with domestic production meeting approximately 90 percent of domestic demand in most years. However, while this self-sufficiency in rice was certainly an advantage in years when international rice prices rose, this was not the primary purpose of such rural policies; indeed, Malaysian authorities were explicit in statements to the IMF that "while rice self-sufficiency is desirable for strategic reasons, the primary objective of promoting rice production is to provide farmers with an increased source of income."[29] For a regime reliant on rural support in elections, then, a main focus of the SMP was to improve rural incomes by intervening in agricultural production.

While the government did support the wellbeing of existing paddy farmers, one of its major development projects involved the settling of new agricultural property – largely accomplished under the Federal Land Development Agency (FELDA) – for production of rubber and palm oil; somewhat conspicuously missing from this farm expansion was additional land for rice paddy. In fact, while "irrigation and drainage facilities are being expanded in certain designated rice bowl areas ... farmers outside these areas are being discouraged from growing paddy."[30] For a government interested in increasing rural welfare, why did it discourage additional rice farmers? Wouldn't production of excess paddy only serve to further reinforce the food needs of the state?

In fact, as explained by Malaysian representatives to the IMF at the time, "official policy is to achieve not more than 90 percent self-sufficiency and to avoid *accumulating wasteful surpluses* which would be *difficult to dispose of in the world market* since Malaysia is a relatively high cost producer of paddy."[31] This statement reveals several key insights into the Malaysian government's priorities at the time. First, note that this recognizes that Malaysian domestically grown paddy was more expensive than rice that could be purchased on international markets; a report from a few years later agreed by stating that "Malaysia's costs of rice production is high; the National Paddy and Rice Authority (LPN) provided a subsidy of M$165.4 per metric ton of paddy purchased from farmers while maintaining the retail price of rice at M$1,070 per metric ton, a level that is about 50 percent higher than that in Thailand."[32] With rice prices half again as expensive as in neighboring countries, it is difficult to believe that the Malaysian government was solely concerned with maintaining cheap food for urban consumers – if so, why didn't the government simply cease to support domestic farmers, and save a great deal of money by importing much cheaper rice? Thus, Malaysian agricultural policy seems consistent only with a government concerned with maintaining the support of rural farmers.

Yet, importantly, the government was also able to exercise restraint in its provision of support to rice growers, as indicated by its discouragement of additional farmers turning to grow (now heavily subsidized) rice, as would

[29] IMF (1979b, 6).   [30] IMF (1972, 14).   [31] IMF (1972, 14), emphasis added.   [32] IMF (1985i, 20).

4.3 Malaysia

likely occur under a more open economy. My formal theory in Chapter 2 highlights that fiscal costs of crop support prices should be most pronounced for countries that generate surplus production of agricultural goods. In light of this insight, the government's stated motivation for this restriction of the expansion of paddy farming is revealing. As a result of its high costs of production, excess rice surpluses would be difficult to resell on international markets; lacking market power on the international market, this would require the Malaysian government to sell more expensive Malaysian rice at a loss in order to offload excess production in exports. The subtext, then, is that the regime did not rely on additional rice production precisely because of the fiscal burden that would result therefrom.

What differentiates the Malaysian case from, for example, the Turkish case discussed in subsequent chapters, where electoral competition led to a bidding war among various candidates to be seen as the greatest supporter of rural interests? Here, again, we must consider carefully the difference between autocratic and democratic multiparty elections. For elections to be considered democratic, there must exist some positive probability that opposition parties can break into power. So long as this threat of gaining control of government is possible, opposition efforts to peel off previous supporters of the incumbent by promising even greater government largess can be considered credible by voters; this pressure by opposition parties requires that incumbents also increase the benefits they would promise to important constituencies, so as to not lose critical components of their electoral base.

In this sort of environment, if a viable opposition to UMNO existed, they could have captured an increasing share of rural votes by promising to further expand paddy support policies to a broader swath of the rural population, thereby forcing the government to respond in kind. Instead, elections in Malaysia did not serve to give opposition candidates a realistic chance of assuming control, and so any bids provided by opposition candidates would likely have been rejected by most voters as unrealistic (Magaloni 2006). Lacking this threat of a true opposition, the Malaysian government was able to use elections to deliver benefits to critical constituencies, but was also able to do so in a manner that did not require (at least initially) a serious strain on the budget. What was the political impact of this support? As noted by Pepinsky (2009, 65), "development grants to the rural and agricultural sectors ensured political stability, with the effect that rural Malays constituted the main supporters of UMNO."

4.3.5 Urban Counterpressure

While rural farmers therefore served as the primary electoral base of continued party rule, this did not mean that urban interests could be ignored completely. Indeed, in the immediate aftermath of the May 13 incident, the Malaysian government frequently expressed serious concern about the potential for additional unrest in the capital as driven by urban unemployment.[33] While extensive unemployment is likely to be a political risk for all kinds of regimes, the particular characteristics of unemployment in Malaysia, as summarized in an IMF report, suggested three dynamics likely to make unrest particularly threatening, noting that "several significant characteristics are discernible with respect to unemployment in Malaysia. Firstly it is concentrated among persons of younger age groups ... Secondly, more than 91 percent of the unemployed as revealed by the 1967/68 labor force survey had a primary and/or higher educational background. Thirdly, the young and educated unemployed are more heavily concentrated in urban areas."[34] A primer on triggers for collective action would be hard pressed to find a potentially more active group of citizens: young, educated, and urban. Having witnessed recent civil unrest on the streets of the capital, UMNO leaders could not ignore the threat of urban protest completely.

In order to defuse this potentially volatile employment situation, the government pursued a number of policies. While the NEP did emphasize the role of some state development investment in manufacturing, it was recognized that

> the rate of growth of manufacturing activities in Malaysia and elsewhere was not enough to absorb the large influx of younger people, thereby turning underemployment among smallholders in rural sectors to more apparent unemployment in urban centers. Be that as it may, the Malaysian authorities give a very high priority to an employment policy aimed at both stimulating aggregate employment opportunities and correcting regional imbalances in the employment pattern. Deliberate efforts are being made to accelerate job opportunities in the agricultural sector through land development schemes.[35]

In particular, UMNO sought to promote labor-intensive types of production, especially in agriculture, as a means of absorbing excess labor supply; a staff report to the IMF in 1973 went so far as to argue that Malaysian "employment policy is based mainly on land settlement schemes."[36] By relocating workers to rural farms under FELDA, this served the dual purpose of dispersing the urban jobless to more remote parts of the country, while also tying their employment status to government support, thereby limiting the potential for greater urban unrest.

Yet this policy of rural relocation could not absorb the entirety of the urban proletariat. If not constrained to maintain rural electoral support, the regime might have chosen to intervene in food markets in order to keep the remaining urban dwellers content, as was done in the Zambian case. But, if driving down food prices would also create dissatisfaction among the large rural group of farmers who produced food for domestic consumption, such a policy could threaten the basis of continued political stability secured through rural

---

[33] IMF (1970a, 5). [34] IMF (1972, 22). [35] IMF (1973b, 26).
[36] See IMF (1973a, 2). For more for discussions with IMF of promotion of labor-intense agriculture, see, for example, IMF (1970b,c, 1971a).

4.3 Malaysia

electoral supermajorities. As highlighted in Drury (1988, 292)'s summary of political conditions in Malaysia, "[h]ungry workers and angry farmers present a tempting target for opposition politicians looking for political support." What else could the government do?

Outside of food, housing in urban areas is another source of largely inelastic demand for city dwellers – regardless of the price of housing, individuals still need shelter from the elements and a place to sleep (not to mention the arguably "moral economic" value of having a home for one's family). Given a largely inelastic demand for urban housing, this suggests another policy avenue that autocrats wary of unrest might pursue, if limited in their ability to manipulate food prices: Provide subsidized government housing instead. By 1976, as the Third Malaysia Plan was being developed, this combined emphasis on rural relocation and urban subsidized housing was identified explicitly by Malaysian representatives to the IMF, noting that the "[Third Malaysia] Plan will focus on programs to reduce both rural and urban poverty and to move people to areas which provide better employment opportunities. In agriculture, the Plan would aim at developing at least one million acres of new land. In urban areas emphasis will be placed on providing housing, health, and other facilities."[37] Beyond direct government support for housing production, urban housing costs were also kept low by subsidizing the cost of inputs, including direct government control over pricing of cement, bricks, tiles, and steel rods.[38]

Of course, while cheap housing might have allowed urban consumers to divert more of their income to other priorities, this did not in and of itself guarantee that food would always remain affordable. When domestic food production largely sufficed to cover domestic demand, the Malaysian authorities were able to sustain an environment of price stability that helped limit unrest in urban areas by keeping the price of food largely constant. However, in years when the price of imported food rose, as occurred in 1973–1974 as a result of worldwide shortages, UMNO officials behaved as we might expect dictators worried about urban protests to do: they subsidized the price of rice for urban consumption. As noted in a summary of economic developments in 1974, "to reduce the impact on domestic prices of rising world market prices of rice, the Government decided to subsidize imported rice on a temporary basis. The 1973 budget provided M$13.8 million for rice subsidies, while the 1974 budget has allocated M$65 million for this purpose."[39]

In a political system in which the potential for urban violence had already been demonstrated, UMNO clearly could not ignore the specter of food riots as a source of instability; despite its largely rural base of electoral support, the Malaysian regime still needed to protect the cost of living in urban centers. Did

---

[37] See IMF (1974b, 3). The account continued by identifying that "agriculture will account for 28.2 percent of new employment and manufacturing for 24.2 percent. The land development program continues to be the most important means for expanding agricultural employment."
[38] See, for example, IMF (1981c,b).   [39] IMF (1974a, 19).

these food subsidies affect the budget? In discussion of the economic conditions in Malaysia among the executive directors at the IMF, it was argued explicitly that "the main reason for the expansionary budget in 1974 ... was the granting of considerable subsidies in order to cope with the sharp increase in the cost of living in 1974, when the rate of inflation had reached a peak of 24 percent at one point. There were other factors, but the cost of the subsidies had had a significant effect on the budget deficit, which already in 1974 had reached 7 percent of GNO."[40]

That rising food import costs would lead to greater subsidies in the short term, and that these subsidies might put pressure on the government's budget, should not be surprising at this point. What is more interesting, however, was the Malaysian response to this situation. A government report identified that Malaysia remained reliant on food imports for a number of its food requirements outside of rice, "including meat, dairy products, fruit and vegetables; the prices of these commodities rose sharply in 1973. Consequently, Government policy is now directed toward accelerating food production."[41] While shifting to new types of agricultural production takes some time, existing production incentives particularly in rice meant that, even given an international environment of higher rice prices in 1975, "the volume of rice imports has declined substantially because of the increase in domestic production."[42] By the following year, it was argued that Malaysia's "success in combating inflation was due to a wise and flexible demand and exchange rate policy combined with timely provision for supply of essential goods as, for instance, rice."[43]

In many ways, this policy response seems almost painfully obvious: If imported food is too expensive, why not simply encourage domestic farmers to produce the food required instead? And, in fact, a number of dictators have expressed a desire to increase domestic agricultural production for precisely this reason. The problem, of course, is that it is reliant upon the cooperation of rural farmers in order to be successful. In an urban-biased regime, in which food production is already discriminated against by monopsonist government marketing boards, demands to grow additional agricultural products is unlikely to be viewed favorably by impoverished rural agents.[44] On the other hand, in a regime like Malaysia's, where farm products often received direct government support, the appeal of food diversification would have been considered much more credibly by farmers whose loyalty was tied to UMNO's rule through agricultural benefits. That is, unlike in regimes that ignored or actively repressed rural well-being, in Malaysia a policy that directed additional resources to rural areas was actively aligned with the coalition of support for UMNO.

This dual-pronged approach – combining price supports for rural food production with subsidized housing for city dwellers – was to become enshrined

[40] IMF (1976b, 16). [41] IMF (1974a, 12). [42] IMF (1975, 40). [43] IMF (1976a, 6).
[44] See, e.g., discussion in Bates (1982) on ways in which anti-agricultural biases have exacerbated food needs for many African dictatorships.

4.3 Malaysia

TABLE 4.1. *Malaysia: Compliance with lending guidelines, selected sectors*

	Minimum requirements	Actual performance	Share at end December 1981
Commercial banks' lending			
Bumiputra	17.0	29.8	18.6
Small-scale enterprises	20.0	28.9	16.0
Agricultural food production	6.0	9.5	6.0
Finance companies' lending			
Bumiputra	17.0	34.7	22.1
Housing	20.0	27.2	17.3
Small-scale enterprises	28.0	47.4	30.3

Source: IMF (1981b, 28).

in the primary development goals of the regime for the next decade and a half; in multiple reports, Malaysian representatives to the IMF emphasized the high priority assigned to these two goals.[45] Perhaps nowhere was the importance to the regime of these goals made more explicit than in its use of "directed credit requirement" policies, by which the government mandated that both domestic commercial banks and financial companies allocate a sufficient share of their financing towards regime priorities, and also required that these groups be provided with "preferential" (that is, submarket) rates of interest. Table 4.1, which is drawn from an IMF summary of economic developments in Malaysia in 1981, identifies explicitly which groups had been targeted as these regime priorities: Bumiputras, small-scale enterprises, agricultural food producers, and housing developers.

While the beneficiaries of transfers to ethnic Malays (most of whom lived in rural areas), agricultural food producers, and housing developers are clear, the document also subsequently clarified that "small-scale enterprises are defined as registered businesses and enterprises engaged in agriculture with net assets of up to M$250,000; practicing professionals, individual persons who are not registered to carry on business activities (other than farmers and persons engaged in agriculture), and non productive businesses were excluded from the scheme."[46] Thus, even among this residual group, it is clear that rural farmers were still anticipated to be a primary beneficiary of concessional lending rates, especially those that were food growers. Other than these rural interests, there was one additional source of targeted lending: agents that built urban housing. Identified by the regime explicitly as "priority" sectors, these groups fit perfectly with an account of an authoritarian government seeking to simultaneously secure rural electoral support, while also keeping down urban costs especially via

---

[45] See, for example, IMF (1976b, 17). [46] IMF (1981b, 28).

the provision of cheap housing.[47] Note, however, that these targeted credit policies – which effectively amount to a subsidy on borrowing costs for rural farmers and urban housing builders – were achieved at essentially no cost to the government's budget. That is, these reduced borrowing rates offered by domestic financial institutions were not compensated by the government, but were instead largely the product of moral suasion and financial policy.

4.3.6 Growth of Urban Malay Base

While early emphasis of the NEP was directed towards agricultural policy, beginning in the mid-1970s the UMNO government began pursuing a secondary strategy to increase the economic wellbeing of ethnic Malays: The use of industrial requirements that mandated Bumiputera ownership. As described earlier in the chapter, at the time of independence, domestic ownership of capital in Malaysia was almost entirely concentrated in the small urban Chinese population of merchants and businesspersons. As part of the NEP, the government also set out guidelines for equity ownership to be achieved by the program's end; Rasiah and Shari (2001, 60) note that, in "corporate equity terms, Bumiputera, non-Bumiputera, and foreign participation was set at 30%, 40% and 30% respectively for 1990. It was 2.4%, 32.3% and 63.3% respectively in 1970." Of course, such demands for expanded ownership were not well-received among local Chinese investors; in response, "[p]resumably to overcome the continued resistance of local capital (mostly Chinese) to the restructuring exercise, the Industrial Coordination Act (ICA) was passed in 1975 requiring all new and existing industrial establishments ... to apply for new manufacturing licenses. The issuing of these licenses permitted the government to impose new conditions. The business community interpreted the ICA as having the primary aim of increasing the corporate share of the Malays" (Narayanan 1996, 870). Crucially, this industrial policy mandated at least 30 percent ownership by ethnic Malays in any new industrial enterprise; over time this lead to the development of a domestic Malay capitalist class.

Yet, as the direct association of "Bumiputera" with "rural agriculturalist" began to break down, this had consequences for the dominant base of support for UMNO. Over time, while ethnic Malays still remained the dominant share of agriculturalists, there developed an urban set of Malay workers employed in professional and managerial positions (Aziz 2012, 35). This also included the rise of a new set of Malay entrepreneurs, many of whom were direct beneficiaries of ICA reforms mandating greater ethnic diversification of asset ownership. For a party based largely on ethnic loyalties of the dominant ethnicity, the consequence "was the changing nature of UMNO. By the 1980s

---

[47] Over time, the government also increasingly targeted cheap credit toward manufacturing interests as well as the economy gradually developed; see, for example, IMF (1979a, 34).

4.3 Malaysia

UMNO had changed from a party dominated by rural interests ... to one in which a more critical and competitive group of professionals and businessmen played the dominant role" (Funston 1988, 365). This shifting of greater party attention from rural to urban (particularly manufacturing) interests was to play a crucial role in the impending fiscal trouble – and capacity for reform – that Malaysia was to face in the 1980s.

4.3.7 Fiscal Crisis and Reform

Upon return to multiparty elections following the May 13 incident, UMNO ensured political dominance by creating a series of rural development programs aimed at improving the welfare of Malay farmers, while also ensuring that urban cost of living was moderated by stable food prices and subsidized housing. Yet, while development expenditures were certainly consistent sources of fiscal outlay, the regime was careful in limiting the degree to which either rural farm supports, or urban price subsidies, could become a significant drain on the budget. This general environment of economic stability was continually lauded in internal IMF discussion throughout the 1970s; this assessment of essentially sound economic management, even facing the hints of a downturn in the international economy, was captured in a staff report from 1979 that noted simply "the country has no critical short-run macroeconomic problems."[48] With government policies generally in line with existing revenue sources, Malaysia lacked much need for external borrowing, and ended the 1970s with very little external sovereign debt. Indeed, an IMF summary of economic conditions in early 1980 noted that "the external public debt of the Federal Government has remained relatively small. In 1979, the ratio of the Federal Government's disbursed external public debt to GNP was about 11 percent."[49]

However, this stellar fiscal performance for the Malaysian regime was not to last long. For an economy that relied on exports of primary commodities for a substantial share of its growth, the rapid deceleration of the international economy at the beginning of the 1980s – in part a response to the second OPEC crisis of 1979 along with deflationary pressure generated by more hawkish monetary policy at the US Federal Reserve – proved much more threatening than these originally sanguine estimations suggested. Weakness in international markets beginning in 1980 led to a serious decline in several major Malaysian enterprises, as well as concomitant declines in government revenue. However, rather than retrench from its expanding role in the economy, UMNO responded instead by accelerating the government's push into a number of additional projects. In part, this expansion was believed to be sound due to extremely low external indebtedness at the beginning of the decade; as noted by Sheng (1996, 6–7), given "its strong financial position and to counteract the impact

[48] IMF (1979b, 15). [49] IMF (1980, 57).

of the severe international recession of 1980–82, the Government embarked in 1980 on a counter-cyclical policy to build up infrastructure and an industrial base, relying primarily on external borrowing."

At the center of this government expansion was a critical reorientation of Malaysian development policy, which had heavily focused on agricultural support programs in the 1970s, to a new emphasis on heavy industry. This policy was largely the brainchild of then-Minister for Trade and Industry Mahathir bin Mohamad, who argued that growth of heavy industries in Malaysia would generate further upstream and downstream industrial linkages, spurring additional development and growth. However, this explosion of government-backed industrial products maintained the ethnic ownership requirements introduced under the ICA; Rasiah and Shari (2001, 65) argue that this policy was therefore also intended as a political project to further expand manufacturing ownership by the Bumiputera supporters of the regime. When the former head of UMNO, Hussein Onn, relinquished control of the party in 1981 due to failing health, Mahathir was appointed unopposed as the successor for Prime Minister, moving an increased concern over Malay manufacturing to the very pinnacle of the political system.

Yet, while initial estimates of the international economic downturn hoped for quick turnaround, by early 1983 conditions looked increasingly dire for an export-led economy like Malaysia's. With external demand for many of its products collapsing, the Malaysian government engaged in an incredible expansion of government fiscal intervention; as a result, "the overall budget deficit increased to about 16 percent of GNP as government expenditure increased to over 44 percent of GNP."[50] While some of this deficit was covered in 1982 by "borrowing" from the rainy day funds of the state-run oil company, Petronas, by the subsequent year this domestic source of funds had been largely exhausted and, "in these circumstances, the Government plans to reduce domestic borrowing...and rely somewhat more on borrowing from foreign markets to cover the fiscal gap. Such borrowing is projected to increase Federal Government external debt to 27 percent at the end of 1983."[51] While this explosion of government borrowing was initially perceived of as resulting from temporary counter-cyclical policies, by 1983 the IMF had already begun to argue that "the fundamental fiscal imbalance derives from the excessively rapid growth in budgetary expenditure since 1979. Consequently, the fiscal imbalance should not be viewed as either temporary or cyclical. In these circumstances, the staff would urge a comprehensive review of project and other nonstatutory expenditure priorities, with a view to achieving a substantial reduction in such expenditures and the fiscal deficit over the medium term."[52]

When called upon to reduce its expenditures, the Malaysian government did manage to successfully limit spending in 1982 by M$1.4 billion. In so

---

[50] IMF (1983e, 7).   [51] IMF (1983e, 21).
[52] See IMF (1983e, 26). Note that the prior section in this document also highlights that fiscal adjustment via increasing revenue was likely to prove infeasible.

doing, however, the government explicitly identified the priority projects that would not be touched by spending cuts, describing that "the determination of expenditure cuts was made so as to minimize disruptions to the economy without sacrificing the economic and social objectives of the New Economic Policy."[53] Of course, the targets of NEP projects were precisely the rural voters that had been targeted all along, in addition to various urban housing interests and a number of newly developed manufacturing projects. Fearing that extensive government deficits would not be sustainable in the medium run, the IMF continued to pressure the Malaysian regime for more cuts in expenditure.[54]

In summarizing its budget from 1983, at first it appeared as though the Malaysian government had pushed through an amazing reform of its development expenditure, highlighting that transfer payments were expected to have declined by 60 percent and arguing that the "share of transfer payments in development expenditure was reduced from 24 percent in 1982 to less than 10 percent in 1983."[55] However, subsequent analysis revealed that much of this "reduction" in government expenditure had been accomplished by budgetary sleight of hand: when official government development expenditure was reduced, the development expenditures of a host of major "off-budget agencies" (OBA) exploded. While nominally private development agencies, these OBAs were implicitly backed by the government, as operating losses of these agencies were met by government borrowing. This budgetary trickery was initially identified by a seeming impossibility: Despite supposedly reducing official government external financing needs, Malaysia still saw *growth* of net long-term inflow of capital;[56] had government need for external financing fallen, it would be difficult to explain why there was a net increase in foreign debt. The culprit, however, was quickly identified, with the IMF estimating that "borrowings by off-budget public agencies almost doubled to US$0.5 billion, following a substantial increase in 1982."[57] Once identified, the Malaysian government promised to open inquiries into means of including these OBAs into official fiscal calculations, but without much firm reform in this manner, Malaysian sovereign debt continued to skyrocket in 1984 and 1985.

Part of the government's unwillingness to enact reforms in 1983 and 1984 stemmed from a series of domestic sources of political instability (Narayanan 1996, 874). This included a major bank failure (the "Bumiputera Malaysian Finance" scandal) at a Malay-dominant bank where highly placed ethnic Malays at the bank were eventually determined to have taken large bribes from real estate developers in Hong Kong in exchange for investment in property development on the island. Among some circles in the public, this raised doubts about the state-led push to expand Malay ownership of capital. More central

---

53 IMF (1983c, 36).
54 See extended discussion on this point by several IMF executive directors in IMF (1983b).
55 IMF (1983c, 38). 56 IMF (1984g, 71). 57 IMF (1984g, 71).

to the political realm, 1983 also witnessed a constitutional crisis between the dominant party UMNO and the nominal head of state, the "Yang Di Pertuan Agong" or "elected King" of Malaysia. While the monarch was established in 1957 as part of Malaysian independence and its role was largely seen as ceremonial, the constitution of Malaysia did technically grant the king the power to refuse the Prime Minister's request to dissolve Parliament. In an environment of political realignment in which the sitting Yang Di Pertuan Agong was preparing to end his term, UMNO put forth a constitutional amendment that would have essentially established the political primacy of Parliament (and, by extension, UMNO) over the monarch by limiting the capacity to veto Parliamentary changes. As noted by Pathmanathan (1985, 213), "it was widely speculated that one of the government's motives for bringing about the constitutional amendment was … the feeling that with the end of the term of office of the current Yang Di Pertuan Agong, the new candidate could prove to be somewhat strong willed vis-a-vis the [Mahathir] administration … He was reported to have said in a speech that the people 'have given us the power to be their protectors and it is up to the people if they want to take it back.'" Despite a brief period of political drama, however, UMNO dominance of Parliament led to a supermajority vote in early 1984 affirming the subordination of the Yang Di Pertuan Agong to Parliament, thereby eliminating one potential source of political opposition to Mahathir.

Beyond financial scandals and constitutional challenges,[58] arguably the most important political event in this period was the (internal) UMNO party elections in 1984. As summarized by Pathmanathan (1985, 215), "the UMNO party elections were more significant than the general elections of 1980. The importance of the struggle for political office within UMNO cannot be underestimated, since UMNO determines the direction and strength of the government as both the leading party and the dominant element within the Barisan coalition." Yet, internecine struggles for dominance in UMNO had begun brewing with the appointment of Mahathir as head in 1981, and these schisms threatened to break out into more open conflict as a result of competition for party positions at UMNO's general conference.

At the heart of this evolution of internal elections as a seriously competitive arena was the rise of new money in the hands of ethnic Malay backers, which generated a serious possibility of upsetting previous arrangements for executive survival; as argued by Milne (1986, 1373), "[t]he more extensive use of money in UMNO elections has raised the danger that the procedure for selecting the country's rulers, which has generally worked well in the past, may be destroyed by a new process that would make the deployment of massive wealth the

[58] This period also saw internal divisions within other "Alliance" coalition members, including the MCA and Gerakan, as well as direct government conflict with the Islamist PAS party; see Pathmanathan (1985, 223–225) for more detailed discussion.

4.3 Malaysia

chief criterion for high office." That this was tied to shifting rural–urban bases of support for the regime is made explicit in the following account, which I reproduce at length:

> Another consequence of the affluence of a limited, but growing, number of Bumiputeras has been the greater importance of money in UMNO elections, which are more decisive in selecting the country's political elites than the general elections. Until the mid-1970s, votes at the UMNO General Assembly had usually been cast as a bloc, according to the wishes of the Menteri Besar (chief minister) of each state ... However, by the 1980s the demand for votes had risen ... At the same time, the supply of money available for buying votes was greater than ever before, swollen by Bumiputera affluence. At the 1984 UMNO elections the total money spent on votes was allegedly well in excess of M$20 million, the highest ever. It was said, also, that for the first time more Malay money was spent than Chinese money. As a result, influence over UMNO elections is shifting from rural areas, where Malay school teachers were often the leaders, to urban areas, the base of Malay capitalists.[59]

Thus, precisely in the period in which costly government interventions were driving a large expansion in Malaysian external debt, the geographic base of support for the dominant regime was also undergoing a shift from a predominantly rural focus, to one that increasingly took the interests of urban capitalists into account. To be clear, this is not to say that the government had forsaken the importance of rural voting blocs entirely – indeed, for generating electoral supermajorities in general elections, rural voters still formed a crucial component of the regime's survival strategy. However, evolving internal party dynamics also suggested the increasing importance of access to funds to conduct successful elections to high-ranking UMNO positions, which increasingly came to rely on funding from wealthy Malay entrepreneurs.[60] As noted by Pathmanathan (1985, 217), the "struggle for party position and the personality clashes during the course of the campaign brought to the front emerging trends perceived as dangerous to UMNO. The implementation of the New Economic Policy had resulted, since 1969, in the growth of a new Malay entrepreneurial and commercial elite which was beginning to flex its economic muscle in search of political patronage and power ... During the course of the campaign, an UMNO veteran was quoted as saying that 'Money is what political patronage once meant. Now the bumiputra-oriented New Economic Policy has created so many millionaires, each of them is a source of patronage, each of them a source of power.'"

During this period of relative sclerosis in Malaysian policymaking, the budgetary consequences of consistently high deficits became increasingly alarming

---

[59] Milne (1986, 1371–1372).
[60] This dual focus of executives on "votes" and "campaign contributions" falls outside the core logic of my theory but fits well with accounts, for example, of trade policymaking developed by Grossman and Helpman (1994).

to IMF officials. This sentiment was well summarized by an executive director in a meeting of the executive board of the IMF:

> We are increasingly struck by the very rapid buildup of Malaysia's foreign debt, from 34 percent of GNP in 1981 to nearly 65 percent last year and 76 percent expected this year. At the same time, the debt service ratio has risen from a low 8 percent in 1981 to more than 15 percent in 1985 and to more than 19 percent expected in 1986. In sum, Malaysia has rapidly moved into the ranks of the heavily indebted developing countries ... it is hard to avoid the conclusion that the past good image of Malaysia in international financial markets may now be in jeopardy, not just because of the present higher level of debt, but in the light of the medium-term outlook as well.[61]

Thus, by early 1986, Malaysia was clearly in the throes of a fiscal crisis, with deep concern among international financial institutions of the medium-term viability of its current course. This crisis of the Malaysian economy was further exacerbated by the failure of several domestic financial firms in late 1985, and the collapse of expected revenues in 1986 with a fall in international oil prices, a significant source of export revenue. Surely, if ever there was a time in which the pressures on a government to default should have materialized, the overlapping series of political and economic crises facing the broader Malaysian macroeconomy of the mid-1980s should have fit the bill.[62]

Yet, after finally securing elections for his dominant proteges, Mahathir introduced a program of reform for the Malaysian economy in his "Look East" doctrine, modeled in part on emulation of the successful state-driven development in the Japanese and Korean examples. This involved imposition of a series of economic changes. One of the most important was the need to do away with what Mahathir called a "subsidy mentality" among rural agriculturalists, who were argued to have become dependent upon the state for handouts rather than relying on their own hard work for production (Pathmanathan 1985, 226). This reorientation of official support for rural areas was to be accomplished under the New Agricultural Policy (NAP), which involved gradual reduction in government subsidies for food producers. However, while this removal of rural subsidies was sure to meet with some opposition from farmers, this was to coincide with increasing efforts at development of "rural manufacturing" projects, intended to construct manufacturing centers in rural areas. As noted by Milne (1986, 1380), the effect was "intended to offer new opportunities for Bumiputeras. The New Agricultural Policy should benefit some of the poorer peasants (who are in general Bumiputeras), while the heavy industry proposals should provide jobs for some of those who leave the land."

---

[61] IMF (1986c, 26).

[62] It is worth noting that the government of Malaysia did not ever turn to the IMF for official lender of last resort facilities during this period; as with subsequent financial crises, this was argued to be due to political unwillingness to abide by IMF demands for reforms (Athukorala 2013, 4).

4.3 Malaysia

A second major thrust of the new direction for Malaysian development was centered around privatization of government-owned enterprises. In the Zambian case, as well as in a number of cases discussed later in the chapter, reform of these SOEs proved extremely politically difficult, as they were generally used to transfer benefits to important political constituencies, often at great budgetary cost. And yet, in contrast to this expectation, the Malaysian government did actually succeed in fully privatizing or disbanding a host of the OBAs that had contributed to its fiscal imbalance. How was it able to do this? While even the IMF was unsure of the exact identify of these "nonfinancial public enterprises" at first, by 1986 the Malaysian government had compiled a comprehensive list of these agencies and began the process of reducing government fiscal exposure by severing their link to government finance, the vast majority of which were engaged in either heavy industrialization, or transportation infrastructure.[63] While such programs were still likely to remain of importance to an economy increasingly shifting towards greater balance between agriculture and manufacturing, the rise of a Malay capitalist class provided an important opportunity for privatization to deliver benefits to a crucial constituency that was becoming central to Mahathir's continued political rule.

Secondary accounts of the "success" of privatization in this period largely agree that this process of "reform" was actually a means of transferring additional resources to important members of UMNO's coalition. For example, Narayanan (1996, 878) argues that "privatization was a carefully managed exercise that subjugated other goals, like relieving the financial burden of the government and improving efficiency, to serve NEP interests ... in keeping with the NEP spirit, all public share issues under privatization reserved a portion for bumiputera institutions, while another third of the shares in the primary issue were given to bumiputera institutions and individuals. In this manner, privatization probably increased rather than curtailed Malay corporate wealth accumulation."[64] That these reforms served regime-supporting ends is further supported by the observation that the "task was made that much easier because a large proportion of UMNO's younger voting members belong to the new professional and entrepreneurial classes that have benefited directly from the pro-business stance of fiscal policy" (Narayanan 1996, 879). Indeed, many of the resulting winners from such privatizations were to become important domestic capitalists that subsequently formed a critical core of the UMNO coalition discussed by Pepinsky (2009) in his account of the political dynamics surrounding reform during the East Asian Financial Crisis. As such, when faced with mounting pressures for privatization in order to reestablish economic

---

[63] For example, of the 26 nonfinancial public enterprises identified in IMF (1986d, 140), only two are arguably from outside the manufacturing sector: the Federal Land Consolidation and Rehabilitation Authority (FELCA), and the Sabah Forest Industries.
[64] See also, e.g., Rasiah and Shari (2001, 73) or Milne (1986, 1375).

efficiency, much of the privatization was accomplished without substantial political backlash.

Importantly, however, while cuts to developmental expenditure were taken in order to restore the fiscal standing of the Malaysian government, it was clear that certain types of programs were likely to retain a protected status. For example, in an earlier discussion of recent austerity programs, the Malaysian representative to the IMF noted that "austerity measures instituted by the Government would be continued in the remaining year of the Fourth National Plan up to 1985, but the authorities were committed to implementing in full the priority programs aimed at attacking poverty, particularly those designed to assist small landholders, paddy farmers, fishermen, essential workers, and the urban poor."[65] Thus, while it was more able to reform expensive industrial development agencies, UMNO explicitly identified that development projects for rural agriculturalists and the urban poor, while temporarily reduced in some cases, would remain a high priority. Perhaps nowhere is this intertwining of development strategy and political purpose made more clear than in the response by the Malaysian representative to the IMF to a series of concerns regarding the sustainability of government reforms:

> Responding to those who had questioned whether the fiscal deficit projected for the medium term would be sustainable, Mr. Jafaar [the Malaysian representative] observed, the intention was to reduce the deficit to 5 percent of GNP or even less by 1989. Painful cuts had already been made in projects aimed at alleviating poverty in rural areas, where three fourths of Malaysia's population lived ... However, the authorities in Kuala Lumpur recognized that external constraints made it imperative that the new economic policy objective be temporarily compromised somewhat in the interest of stability. The Fifth Malaysia Development Plan would reflect that recognition. Of course, cuts in development expenditure of the magnitude made over the past three years could not be taken indefinitely, as they would bring about hardship and minimize the impact of the development momentum thus far achieved. For both *political and social reasons*, the authorities would not permit those developments to occur; hence, for the future, development projects would be looked at closely with attention to quality and efficiency that was consistent with stability.[66]

Put plainly, moving forward, development expenditures targeted at the rural base of UMNO's stability would remain a high priority. In point of fact, the Malaysian authorities appear to have been largely successful in sticking to this promise. While still maintaining the use of rural support programs to ensure loyalty of rural farmers to the regime, Malaysian sovereign debt (after peaking in 1987 at nearly 75 percent of GDP) declined steadily over the next decade, falling to under 30 percent on the eve of the East Asian Financial crisis (Reinhart and Rogoff 2010).

Despite facing a crisis of potentially epic scale in the mid-1980s, the Malaysian regime was largely successful in reforming its fiscal policy, by

---

[65] IMF (1984f, 27).   [66] IMF (1985h, 31–32).

privatizing industrial development agencies while still maintaining those rural development programs that helped stabilize its hold on power by ensuring a continued supermajority of rural electoral support. Crucially, with competing rural and urban political pressures, at no point did agricultural policy in Malaysia become so unilaterally biased in one direction as to impose permanent fiscal deficits; in addition, as UMNO's base of support expanded to include urban entrepreneurs and Malay "middle class" voters, the regime managed to successfully reorient its economy in a manner that more evenly divided government attention between rural agriculturalists and urban manufacturers. Lacking overwhelming geographic pressure, despite a rapid buildup of external debt in the early 1980s, Malaysia managed to implement a series of reform measures and thereby avoid the costly long-term damage of default.

4.4 DISCUSSION

This chapter began with an account of Zambia, a closed autocracy that faced a large and restive urban population. As expected by my theoretical predictions, concern by political leaders over the destabilizing effects of urban unrest led to large and costly government interventions into food prices; however, when combined especially with large food import needs, these cheap food policies became consistent targets for reform by international financial institutions seeking to right the fiscal ship of state. After facing large-scale violence by urban citizens in an attempt to do away with crucial food subsidies, the Zambian regime chose ultimately to instead renege on its international financial obligations than face continued threat to its short-term survival.

Yet, as the second half of this chapter makes clear in its discussion of the Malaysian case, not all dictators can ignore rural agriculturalists and expect to stay in power. This is most likely to occur in electoral autocracies where the generation of voting supermajorities requires the support of the rural farm vote, and this attentiveness to rural interests limits the capacity of autocrats to impose anti-farmer food policies in order to keep food cheap in the cities. The Malaysian case helps make clear that, in a regime that successfully balanced the competing needs of urban consumers and rural producers – including explicit attention to limiting exports of costly Malaysian rice – the fiscal consequences of rule did not reach unsustainable levels. In addition, the Malaysian case helps make clear that, as the geographic base of support began to move from a largely rural to a more urban one, the state managed to succeed in economic reforms due to implementation of policies that were still consistent with its central bases of political support. Having demonstrated historical qualitative support for my primary predictions surrounding political survival and sovereign default in non-democratic systems, in the following chapter I turn subsequently to consideration of how these incentives are affected by the presence of true electoral competition in democracies.

5

Default Pressures in Consolidated versus Contentious Democracy

Costa Rica and Jamaica

> Democracy today is a democracy of groups. It is the group, and not the individual, which now possesses sufficient potential to be the subject of politics. The man who is not integrated into a group – irrespective of class – remains outside of the democratic game.
>
> Oscar Arias Sanchez, future president of Costa Rica, (1971)
> *Pressure Groups in Costa Rica*

> [T]hose with the greatest material needs and deprivations within the party become most involved in rank and file party activism. Their only resource is bringing in the vote, and violence. Interparty hostility and violence emerged in the early period of party politics and escalated to alarming proportions in the 1980 elections ... This violence is often orchestrated by the political elites in their quest for power.
>
> Carlene Edie (1989, 14) "From Manley to Seaga: The Persistence of Clientelist Politics in Jamaica"

5.1 THEORETICAL PREDICTIONS FOR DEMOCRATIC DEFAULT

In contrast to the two historical cases discussed in the previous chapter, a defining characteristic of democratic regimes is that incumbent survival is dictated, first and foremost, by winning elections. In consolidated democracies where political violence carries little influence, elected politicians should be particularly sensitive to electorally important voting groups. As suggested by the formal model developed in Chapter 2, there are two characteristics of groups that should make them more likely to garner attention from politicians: a "median voter" advantage, as well as a "bloc mobilization" advantage. Concerning the former, there exists a simple mathematical relationship between group size and the number of votes that can be won by catering to a given

5.1 Theoretical Predictions for Democratic Default

group. This suggests, all else equal, that groups with larger populations should be more likely to be favored with policies they prefer, even if such policies may be fiscally costly. Of course, in some cases, even large groups may not always mobilize together successfully, which may dilute the simple advantages of size; conversely, those groups that can successfully channel the votes of a large fraction of their members should be viewed as especially crucial for politicians looking to swing the outcome of an election. Where there exist groups that link electoral turnout to specific government interventions, these should be especially likely to receive political favors in democracies.

I have argued in Chapter 2 that, in many developing democracies, rural agents are likely to be electorally crucial for both of these reasons. First, a defining characteristic of most developing countries is that a large fraction of the population lives in rural areas; in the sample of countries analyzed in Chapter 3, for example, the average level of urbanization in the non-OECD countries in 1960 was 40.3 percent. When the majority of the population lives in rural areas, simple median voter models would point to the clear electoral advantages of targeting farmers as a crucial source of votes. Beyond this mathematical effect of group size, however, I also argue that the nature of agricultural production means that this sector is more likely to be characterized by direct interaction between farmers and government programs, which heightens the visibility of the linkage between government policies and electoral support.

More specifically, as agricultural surplus in rural areas must be transferred to urban centers in order to be sold to consumers, and as limited infrastructure in the rural parts of developing countries makes transportation by farmers themselves quite costly, a common feature of rural communities in these countries is the presence of a government marketing board. These agencies are tasked with procuring surplus food production from farmers – often at a significant markup – as well as sometimes providing subsidized agricultural inputs (especially credit and fertilizer); the centrality of these actions to the direct financial sustainability of rural producers means the salience of such agencies is likely to be high. Given a relatively limited set of specific government policies with clear consequences for the economic wellbeing of such communities, this greatly heightens the likelihood that farmers will mobilize together to vote en masse for agricultural support policies.

Due to the combination of both "median voter" as well as "bloc mobilization" advantages, we should observe that rural voters receive government benefits in exchange for their support during elections. The most direct form that this support generally takes is through guaranteed price supports for food products: Governments act to insure farmers against negative price shocks in agricultural markets by essentially guaranteeing the existence of demand for their surplus at a favorable price. Beyond these price supports, governments also frequently intervene to improve farmer profits by driving down input costs. The nature of agricultural production – with long temporal lags between planting season (when inputs must be purchased all at once) and harvest season (when surplus production is sold in bulk for profit) – makes access to credit a crucial component of the costs faced by farmers. As such, governments seeking rural favoritism often provide agricultural loans at sub-market interest rates, effectively subsidizing the input costs of production. In extreme cases, when farmers have faced failed crops or collapsing demand for their products, elected politicians have also often campaigned on promises of debt forgiveness for rural agents, a policy that has proven extremely popular at the polls recently in India, for example.[1] Finally, governments will also often provide other agricultural inputs – such as fertilizers or seed – at reduced prices, thereby further protecting the profitability of farmers.

Of course, all of these subsidization schemes generate deficits for state agricultural agencies. Buying food at supra-market prices can be costly, especially if the government must offload excess production on world markets where a lower commodity price prevails. Additionally, if some governments seek to shield domestic consumers from artificially high food prices, this can lead to budgetary troubles even without exports of surplus, as the government guarantees that it loses money by reselling food products it has purchased at a higher price for a lower value. Subsidized inputs, particularly in the form of interest-rate subsidies on agricultural loans, can evolve into particularly heavy fiscal burdens when these funds result from governmental borrowing abroad in foreign currency, which can become substantially more costly following rising international rates or depreciation pressure on a domestic currency. Finally, when governments go so far as to allow rural debt forgiveness, this can of course constitute a large fiscal hit for the state in cases where a great numbers of farmers avail themselves of the opportunity to rid themselves of debt. Given the negative fiscal consequences of these government interventions into agricultural markets, such policies are likely to be targeted for reform when governments face fiscal crisis. Yet it is precisely because rural producers are so electorally critical that it can become politically difficult to reform these programs; especially in the lead-up to elections, when incumbents are particularly nervous about alienating electorally critical groups of voters, these pressures against reform may drive the state to renege on its international debt obligations, rather than face the threat of electoral suicide. Thus, I expect that – in consolidated democracies where rural producers are electorally critical – difficulty in reforming costly agricultural support policies will be associated with greater likelihood of sovereign default.

---

[1] See story on "India farm loan waivers raise fear about credit discipline," www.ft.com/content/921d7a8a-65fc-11e7-8526-7b38dcaef614?segmentId=6132a895-e068-7ddc-4cec-a1abfa5c8378.

5.2 COSTA RICA

5.2.1 Case Selection

In many regards, Costa Rica is an ideal test case for these core hypotheses. To begin with, it is a country that has been characterized by stable democratic rule since the civil war of 1948. Not only has the country witnessed peaceful transition of power between opposing parties multiple times in the postwar era, it is one of the best cases in the developing world of a democratic regime where the use of violence in politics is almost completely shunned. For example, Wilson (1998, 45) emphasizes that "Costa Rica's post-civil war political stability is largely a function of the elite-level compromise concerning the manner in which competition for political power should take place ... This compromise was reflected in a series of new electoral laws that have facilitated the smooth transfer of political power among competing political parties and effectively prevented the use of violence for political ends since the conclusion of the civil war." Likewise, Ameringer (1982, 1)'s summary of the nature of Costa Rican politics begins with the observation that the Costa Rican people "do not like unpleasantness and shun extremes and fanaticism. Disputes are resolved *a la tica* – that is, the *tico* way: with civility and without rancor." The "pure type" of democracy that I consider theoretically is one in which the systematic use of violence by citizens is not afforded political weight in determining electoral survival; there are few countries that would better fit this condition than modern Costa Rica.

In addition, Costa Rica is a country in which the rural farmer has played an important role throughout its history. Ameringer (1982, 2–3) notes, for example, that the "schoolteacher and civilian statesman represent Costa Rican democracy, but the picture is not complete without the yeoman farmer. Alberto Cañas (1978) describes the small proprietor as the backbone of Costa Rican democracy." Nelson (1992, 237) likewise discusses the Costa Rican case as one in which electoral arrangements "overrepresent rural areas," further cementing the political centrality of agriculturalists. Nor was this perception of a central role of farmers in Costa Rican society limited to academic analysts. For example, in justifying government intervention to help cushion agriculturalists against falling commodity prices in the late 1950s, then Minister of Agriculture Jorge Borbon argued that "[w]e are essentially a country of farmers ... If the majority of Costa Ricans, who are farmers, are left to their fate, we cannot expect much from the opportunities of the industrialists" (Wilson 1998, 92).

My justification for focusing on rural-biased policies is premised on the assumption that rural producers will be an electorally-salient group. Explicit recognition by government officials that a large fraction of the population was engaged in farming establishes a baseline "median voter" potential advantage for rural agents. In addition, the role of agricultural production agencies in serving as conduits for mobilized rural votes is also clearly present in Costa Rica. While difficult to validate empirically, a study of political activity by

Costa Ricans in the late 1970s found, in contrast to earlier expectations of rural citizens as politically inert, that there was greater community project activism among peasants than urbanites, as well as "significantly higher group membership rate among peasants" (Booth and Seligson 1979, 42). Depictions of agricultural production in Costa Rica help make clear that such groups tended to center around agricultural activities, such as marketing boards and credit agencies, that directly linked government benefits to local rural activity (Edelman 1990).

Of course, by the 1970s, Costa Rican society was not only composed of farmers, following a series of industrialization programs that saw the growth of urbanization. While there is evidence to suggest greater likelihood of partaking in community projects by rural groups, do we really know that this was viewed as a political asset by politicians at the time? Absent direct access to the internal musings of political candidates, it can often be difficult to firmly determine those factors politicians consider as representing significant political influence. Here the Costa Rican case presents a fortuitous opportunity in that one of its most prominent presidents – Óscar Arias Sánchez – was trained as a political scientist before joining politics more directly. As part of his academic career, Arias also penned a book analyzing political conditions as he saw them in Costa Rica in the 1970s. The title of the book, *Pressure Groups in Costa Rica*, makes clear the primary subject of the work: as indicated in the epigraph to this chapter, the central premise of the book was that "we have passed from the 'democracy of individuals' to the 'democracy of groups.' In this day, it is the group that is our true political subject."[2] Arias argued that the modern Costa Rican political system tended to prioritize the preferences of agents that were capable of organizing themselves into "pressure groups," as opposed to a more atomistic style of democracy that catered to individuals directly.

This general conceptualization matches nearly perfectly with the predictions from my theoretical model that democratic systems should tend to focus on groups capable of mobilizing voters in large blocs. That the size of a group would be a benefit in this regard is articulated directly by Arias, who argued that "the two most important elements in determining the power of these groups are the number of their members and their financial capacity. In a pluralist democratic regime like our own, in which every four years you hold elections to consult the people (*pueblo*) whether their opinion is in accordance or not with the governing party, the number of members that constitute a group is a determining factor."[3] Yet which groups did Arias view as having successfully organized themselves into effective conduits of political influence? Here again Arias's account of those conditions that make group mobilization more likely echo those factors emphasized theoretically in Chapter 2: "the group integrated by its similarities acquires more unity and strength, by which it is better prepared for action. In the agricultural camp Costa Rica has

---

[2] Arias Sánchez (1971, 79), author translation.   [3] Arias Sánchez (1971, 74), author translation.

5.2 Costa Rica

several producer organizations (the Cooperative of Atlantic Cocoa Producers, Cooperative of Tobacco Producers, Guanacaste Rice Cooperative, etc.)."[4] It is worth emphasizing here that, in identifying specific instances of pressure groups in Costa Rica, the very first sector mentioned is agriculture. This accords with Nelson (1990, 355)'s account of Costa Rican politics at the time, arguing that "[w]here large farmers do swing considerable political weight, they are often tied into the very political/economic system that orthodox structural reforms seek to dismantle." Thus, Costa Rica is an excellent fit for the theoretical conditions I outline in Chapter 2 as likely to lead to costly agricultural subsidies that may be politically difficult to reform during times of fiscal crisis. Selected as a "best case" fit, if the historical record does not indicate that rural electoral pressure was a factor increasing the likelihood of default in Costa Rica when facing budgetary troubles, this would serve to falsify my account. Conversely, as I will demonstrate, there is substantial qualitative support for my primary mechanism linking agricultural political influence to difficulties reforming farm support programs, which ultimately proved fatal to a series of attempts to restore fiscal balance in the Costa Rican economy, triggering default.

5.2.2 Potential Challenges with Costa Rican Case

While there are many aspects of the Costa Rican system that make the country an excellent fit for the theoretical conditions I outline as important in consolidated democracies, it is important to discuss two major factors that could make the case more difficult to test my core hypotheses about the importance of domestic political considerations in driving sovereign default conditions: *term limits* and *geopolitics*.

Term limits
As emphasized repeatedly in Chapter 2, my main hypotheses start from the assumption that politicians are office-motivated, and that they will go to great lengths to ensure their survival as incumbents. In this regard, those familiar with the Costa Rican case might point to an institutional characteristic of Costa Rican politics that may complicate this assumption: Presidents in Costa Rica are constitutionally barred from serving more than one term. That is, all presidents are "lame ducks" from the moment they enter office, as they cannot compete for the highest office again once their term expires. All else equal, this suggests that presidents in Costa Rica may actually be less concerned with the electoral consequences of the policy decisions they take; indeed, one might even expect that this could completely insulate the presidency from popular resistance to necessary economic reforms. This issue is exacerbated by the fact that legislative deputies are also disallowed from seeking immediate re-election, although deputies may return to the legislature following a break

---

[4] Arias Sánchez (1971, 68), author translation.

from serving in office. As emphasized by Wilson (1998, 1999), despite the fact that Costa Rica operates a closed-list PR system (an institutional form traditionally associated with strong party discipline and control), this has led to a relatively weak capacity of political parties to enforce legislative discipline within their own ranks. All of these factors might be expected to mitigate the importance of electoral survival considerations, a core component of my theory.

However, further consideration of the operation of elections in Costa Rica makes clear that electoral calculus is still an important factor in policymaking decisions by incumbents. Despite lacking the capacity to immediately run for office again as a deputy, many "career" politicians in Costa Rica extend their time in government by managing to be nominated for governmental non-elected positions, such as heads of ministries or important state-owned enterprises, which allows these individuals to continue to maintain contact with the machinery of government and the resources that such access provides. The end result of this system is to continue to motivate deputies to consider the effects of government policy on upcoming electoral outcomes; critically, however, this is not done to ensure their own re-election (which is institutionally disallowed), but rather to connect themselves to future elected executives. As clarified by Wilson (1999, 764), "deputies interested in perpetuating their political careers must necessarily link their careers to the fortunes not of the incumbent president – who is a lame-duck president himself – but of a future presidential contender. It is these contenders, not the sitting president, who are in a position to offer an incumbent deputy a political appointment [which can] can extend the length of a deputy's political career beyond the 4-year legislative term." Thus, while term limits may reduce concerns somewhat of sitting presidents for the future electoral consequences of their actions, to the extent that the next candidate for office will still need to successfully win a new election, and as continued government access for politically minded deputies is contingent upon securing the support of these new candidates, there will still arise opposition to policy reforms that might be deemed important to electorally-crucial groups. Given the nature of Costa Rican politics, this suggests that such pressures should indeed be greatest in the lead-up to new elections, whereas insulation of a newly-installed president immediately following an electoral campaign may be associated with a weakening of direct consideration of electoral consequences of economic reform.[5]

Geopolitics

Beyond challenges to my theoretical assumption of office-motivated incumbents as a function of term limits, a second potential threat to my focus on

---

[5] Note that, as emphasized in my model's attention to political "time horizons," we might expect this postelectoral reform capacity to hold more generally across countries; here I emphasize that particular institutional arrangements in Costa Rica suggest these factors should be especially pronounced.

the domestic political consequences of policy reform comes from the special geopolitical situation Costa Rica enjoyed during the period I consider. More specifically, as emphasized by a host of secondary work, despite its small size Costa Rica enjoyed the strong support of the government of the United States during the late 1970s and into the 1980s. In large part, this arose as a result of the eruption of civil conflict in the region, particularly the Sandinista movement in Nicaragua as well as civil war in El Salvador. The importance of maintaining a friendly democratic regime in Central America meant, firstly, that the US placed a high value on Costa Rica responding to its crisis conditions as a "success" story. Relatedly, partly in response to allowing the US to use Costa Rican territory to supply rebels during the Contra War against Nicaragua, the US successfully steered large amounts of foreign funds to the Costa Rican government, especially through the provision of massive funding from USAID projects meant to help cushion the reform of different sectors of the ailing Costa Rican economy (Hansen-Kuhn 1993, 8).

My theory emphasizes that sovereign default is particularly likely to occur in cases where domestic governments face difficulty in reforming costly programs, often in response to demands from international financial institutions in the face of dwindling access to foreign funds. Yet, if Costa Rica enjoyed special importance in the eyes of the United States during this period, and if this influence translated into softer conditions from the IMF and World Bank, or if continued access to special funding from agencies like USAID limited the fiscal constraints placed on the Costa Rican government, this could serve to weaken the conditions under which I expect incumbent politicians to consider reneging on international financial obligations rather than face domestic electoral blowback. In this regard, the geopolitical importance of the Costa Rican regime constitutes a "hard test" for a theory like my own that emphasizes the importance of domestic political considerations. As will be revealed in Section 5.2.4, the special place of Costa Rica was clearly a factor that worked in its favor in terms of limiting overall conditionality and granting it preferential access to easy money from international agencies. Yet, despite these geopolitical advantages, I still continue to find historical support for concern by elected politicians over the consequences of reform policies on their likelihood of winning subsequent elections; in particular, the role of agricultural support programs stands out in this case despite more successful reform of other kinds of government policies.

5.2.3 Rise of the PLN (1953–1982)

While prewar political movements in Costa Rica were often organized around individual political personalities, the restoration of electoral competition in the postwar period gave rise to the first major consolidated programmatic party in the the Party of National Liberation (*Partido Liberación Nacional*, or PLN). Founded as a social democratic party, the PLN established a dominant political brand characterized by expansion of the welfare state to benefit key electoral constituencies. While early PLN programs were focused almost exclusively on rural agricultural development,[6] over the course of the 1950s and early 1960s, the party also expanded government employment in the highly organized public sector. Wilson (1998, 83) argues that "the PLN, in part, viewed its programs to increase government employment and create new entitlement programs...as fostering the formation of new social sectors that might become loyal to the PLN and dependent upon its programs." While the party did narrowly lose the presidency in 1958 and 1966, Wilson (1998, 81) still notes that the "PLN quickly became the dominant political force in postwar Costa Rican politics," describing the period as one of "PLN's electoral dominance." This dominance was fostered both by the strength of the PLN's electoral support from large voting blocs like farmers and public sector workers, but was also aided by the relative disunity of opposition parties – even in cases where the PLN lost elections, power was ceded to a coalition of opposition groups that eventually coalesced into Costa Rica's second main political party, the PUSC, which tended to represent both Catholic conservative values voters, as well as right-wing opposition to the welfare state policies promoted extensively by the PLN.

During much of the 1950s, Costa Rica's economy was largely dominated by two major export industries: coffee and bananas. Agricultural exports generated the lion's share of foreign reserves for the country, and fully two-thirds of the Costa Rican population was employed in agriculture (Wilson 1998, 83). Given this sectoral dominance, it is unsurprising that the PLN initially focused heavily on provision of government funding for farmers in exchange for electoral support; for example, Wilson (1998, 91) notes that (despite expressing interest in a proindustrialization program), "the [PLN] government did not venture beyond facilitating infrastructure and agricultural diversification" during its initial term in office. This heavy focus on rural producers by government was made particularly apparent when, in response to deteriorating terms of trade for Costa Rican agricultural products at the end of the 1950s, the government proposed an economic promotion plan whose "principal intent was to bail out the traditional agroexporters with state-owned bank credits and funds that were borrowed from international commercial banks and funneled through the state banks. Industrialists, who had celebrated the passage of the economic promotion plan, were very disappointed with its implementation and complained loudly that the agricultural sector should not receive the lion's share of the available funds" (Wilson 1998, 91). The government's justification for this focus on agriculturalists, however, was captured in the quote from the Agriculture Minister above: "We are essentially a country of farmers." This relative lack of attention to industry can be observed in the fact that, from 1950 to 1962, the overall share of the economy accounted for

---

[6] See discussion of 1950s PLN agricultural programs in Wilson (1998).

5.2 Costa Rica

by manufacturing remained virtually unchanged, growing from 13.4 percent of GDP to 14 percent (Wilson 1998, 94).

Over the period of PLN dominance, support for rural producers expanded tremendously. In an account of peasant life in Costa Rica at the time, Edelman (1999, 68–69) details this extensively, noting that

> state institutions came to permeate virtually every aspect of rural life and of agricultural and agroindustrial production. By the late 1970s, a medium-sized (or even small) maize farmer might, for example, obtain subsidized credit from the National Banking System for renting land, planting, cultivating, and harvesting the crop, and perhaps for machinery or other capital investments. The bank would require him to purchase crop insurance from the National Insurance Institute. He could obtain inexpensive fertilizer from the nationalized fertilizer company, and technical assistance from the Ministry of Agriculture and Livestock or from one of the several other agencies that provide extension services. He would then likely sell most of the crop to the CNP at an artificially high price and, should he need maize for feeding poultry or for his family, then or later, he could purchase it at artificially low prices in a CNP retail outlet or a private grocery store (where maximum prices for staple foods were also set by a government board). If he were a member of an agrarian reform or other cooperative, he would have access to the extension and credit programs of the reform agency or the institutions serving the cooperative sector.

Thus, in a period in which the farm vote was a critical electoral component, we observe substantial investment by the state into programs meant to improve agricultural profitability, including direct purchase of farm goods at inflated prices, exactly as expected in my formal model of democratic policymaking.

However, the sensitivity to international market gyrations of a development model largely reliant upon two dominant export crops became increasingly clear over this period. While young Costa Rican industries would have been hard pressed to compete with imported industrial goods from the developed world, the creation of a regional trading agreement in the Central American Common Market (CACM) provided precisely the sort of infant industry protection that was believed to be necessary to ensure the survival of nascent businesses. Several additional programs were created to encourage the development of Costa Rican industrial products designed for export to the expanded consumer base of the CACM, which enjoyed substantial import protection against goods from outside the region. Combined with generally favorable international market conditions for its agricultural products, this led to a period of halcyon growth throughout the 1960s for the Costa Rican economy, with per capita GDP expanding from rough parity with most of its neighbors to significantly better standards of living over time.

The first major shock to the system arose in 1973, largely due to conditions outside of the direct control of the government. For a country reliant on export-led growth, rapidly rising oil prices (with most oil imported from abroad) combined with falling coffee prices led to a significant deterioration in the terms of trade. However, rather than respond to this major shock to government revenue by reducing government expenditures on politically popular social programs, the Figueres administration "avoided the contraction by increasing the foreign debt and substantially expanding domestic credit ... Costa Rica's public external debt increased from $296 million in 1973 to $379 million in 1974 and $511 million in 1975" (González Vega 1984, 25). It is worth noting that this expansion in external borrowing was made possible, in part, by relatively low outstanding Costa Rican debt at the beginning of the period; in the context of my theoretical account, this captures well a situation in which a government facing economic trouble did not face a binding fiscal constraint, and thus was able to avoid pressures for reform of costly support policies.

This gamble by the government appeared to have paid off by the mid-1970s, which saw both the resumption of lower oil prices as well as a significant rise in international coffee prices. González Vega (1984, 26–27) argues that, during this period, "what was actually a transitory increase in income [due to the coffee boom] was viewed as a new higher level of permanent income, and aggregate spending was adjusted accordingly ... Moreover, given the attractive terms prevailing in the international capital markets, Costa Rica's foreign borrowing increased rapidly. The country's public external debt grew to $646 million in 1976 and to $834 million in 1977. By early 1978 the Oduber government was still borrowing abroad, at shorter terms and more restrictive conditions, merely to pile up international monetary reserves."

In the lead-up to the presidential election of 1978, the main opposition candidate – Rodrigo Carazo Odio, himself a former member of the PLN who left the party in 1970 after failing to win the party's nomination – campaigned in part on a message of the need to rein in the fiscal excesses of (as well as concerns over corruption within) the incumbent PLN regime; clearly, a tripling of external borrowing over a five year period was not a signal of confidence in the Costa Rican economy. Pulling together a diverse coalition of opposition groups, Carazo managed to upset the PLN by capturing a narrow majority of the presidential vote. However, despite losing control of the presidency, the PLN retained its dominance in the legislature, limiting Carazo's capacity for policy reform from the outset. Even absent this opposition force in the Assembly, Carazo's ability to implement changes to the economy were likely to have been hindered by a series of international crises that occurred almost immediately upon taking power. First among these was the second oil crisis in 1978, which (as in 1973) coincided with a collapse in coffee prices and dramatically worsened Costa Rica's terms of trade. Beyond this, the eruption of civil violence in Nicaragua and El Salvador also brought the export markets in the CACM crashing down, further limiting Costa Rica's capacity for export production.

With collapsing state revenues – and in contrast to earlier PLN governments – the more right-leaning Carazo initially proposed a series of austerity measures meant to try and right the listing fiscal ship of state by slashing state services. Such a move could surely have resulted in loss of support from

5.2 Costa Rica

key constituencies; as noted in Section 5.2.2, for a president operating at the beginning of his term and without any prospect for re-election, we might expect that this would be precisely the case in which reforms should have enjoyed greatest success. However, as noted by Wilson (1998, 105),

> although President Carazo had not caused the economic crisis, his response and his lack of control over the Legislative Assembly, the Autonomous Institutions, the bureaucracy, and his own cabinet made it difficult to either implement an effective austerity program or quickly adjust the economy. As the economy spiraled out of control, Unidad deputies looked to further their own political careers by aligning themselves with the likely next presidential candidate rather than designing solutions to the crisis. The government's first response was to increase government expenditure on public works programs, expand public employment, and increase taxes. Although the public works programs went ahead, the Legislative Assembly blocked the tax increases. As a result, the public-sector deficit grew to 12 percent of GDP.

Thus, ignoring the likely opposition to reforms in popular programs by PLN deputies who constituted a majority in the Assembly, Carazo faced defections of support even from his own coalition, who in order to protect their own political futures approved an expansion of government spending while simultaneously rejecting an increase in government revenue.

As the economic crisis continued to play out, the Costa Rican government was forced to turn to the major international financial institutions, particularly the IMF and World Bank, in order to acquire emergency lending; by this point, having dramatically expanded its external debt over the past several years, it was clear that the Costa Rican regime was facing fiscal crisis. As generally occurs in such cases, the IMF imposed a series of reform conditions as part of its release of emergency loans. This culminated, in 1980, in the government securing a $300 million bailout loan from the IMF, to be dispersed over three years, for which the government agreed to a wide-ranging series of economic reforms meant to limit government expenditure, control monetary supply (including a devaluation of the currency), and increase government revenue. By the middle of the following year, however, consultation of internal IMF documents makes clear that the government had already reneged on a host of these reforms. Chief among these was a much larger than expected deficit at the central government level; the summary notes that "the central government deficit amounted to ₡3 billion compared with a projection of ₡1.6 billion."[7] In identifying specific areas of failed reforms, the document highlighted failed increase in revenue necessary to cover salary increases and lower than expected revenues from export taxes due to falling volumes of coffee and banana exports. Additionally, the IMF highlighted in particular that several public enterprises that had been slated for fiscal improvement actually observed significant expansion in their deficits, noting that "within the public sector, deviations occurred mainly in the operations of the State Production

---

[7] IMF (1981a, 4).

Council (CNP), the National Oil Refinery (RECOPE), and the Costa Rican Development Corporation (CODESA)."[8]

Despite promises in letters from the Minister of Finance to the IMF that 1981 would see greater dedication to economic reforms to government finances, almost immediately upon securing the initial tranche of IMF funds, vocal opposition to the austerity measures erupted from the Chambers of Industry and Commerce, leading to the revocation of the degrees by Carazo. Following initial cessation of negotiations by the IMF in protest against the government's reneging on promises of reform, in 1981, "President Carazo became so frustrated with the IMF demands that he expelled the IMF's Costa Rican mission, stating that given the choice 'between eating and paying the external debt, we cannot accept anything other than the first option.'"[9] That an incumbent politician – even a lame duck with no direct prospects of re-election himself – would be unwilling to follow through on reforms to the economy in the face of popular opposition in the lead up to a new round of elections, serves as support at a generic level for my propositions about democratic default. While expanding deficits at the state agricultural agency (CNP) were explicitly highlighted as a source of project failure, so too were a host of other support programs, suggesting that opposition to economic reform was successful both within and outside the agricultural sector. Yet, closer consideration of the negotiations between the newly elected Monge government and the IMF help make clear the role played by opposition by agricultural interests, and the particular difficulty of reforming farm support policies, in the face of expected electoral fallout.

5.2.4 The Monge Presidency

During the presidential campaign in 1982, the PLN's candidate – Luis Alberto Monge – capitalized on broad public dissatisfaction with the incumbent government's handling of economic crisis gripping the country. While in truth many of the factors that drove Costa Rica into fiscal trouble were outside the direct control of Carazo, Monge was largely successful in painting the situation as a result of mismanagement by the Unidad administration (Wilson 1998, 113). Beyond complaining about Carazo's inability to resolve the crisis, Monge also campaigned on a traditional PLN platform of social welfare support without necessarily providing specifics on precisely which policies would be promoted. This strategy proved to be electorally successful; Wilson (1998, 115–116) notes that "large numbers of traditionally non-PLN supporters voted for the PLN in 1982 in hopes that the party could end the economic crisis and restore their pre-1980 standard of living. Thus, in February 1982, the PLN won an overwhelming electoral victory, with the largest share of the popular vote since the civil war." Amazingly, just prior to taking office, surveys of the Costa Rican

---

[8] IMF (1981a, 4–6). [9] Wilson (1998, 105).

5.2 Costa Rica

public found that nearly 95 percent of respondents were either somewhat or very optimistic that the new president would pull the country out of crisis; as Wilson (1998, 116) notes, "this extraordinary level of public support gave the incoming government considerable freedom to enact unpopular policies in attempts to resolve the economic crisis."

Upon gaining office – despite campaigning on a platform of social welfare programs – Monge moved quickly to enact a series of austerity measures demanded by the IMF meant to restore Costa Rica to fiscal health. Interestingly, despite some initial concerns from observers of the Costa Rican system that these reforms would fall heaviest on the poorest segments of society, the government managed to limit the consequences of reform for particular groups by both rotating reforms across a wide swath of social actors, while also using compensatory spending to cushion the effects of the removal of state-sponsored programs.[10] In part, this compensation was facilitated by an enormous expansion of international financial support, particularly from the US Agency for International Development (USAID). As argued by Seligson and Muller (1987, 316),

> [a] major external factor that helped explain Monge's ability to stabilize the economy was the role of the United States. As Monge took office, concern was growing in the United States with the leftist character of the Sandinista regime in Nicaragua, Costa Rica's northern neighbor. The civil war in El Salvador only added to these concerns. The Reagan administration sought to strengthen the hand of its friends in Central America and approved a massive foreign aid program directed largely at El Salvador, Honduras, and Costa Rica. The U.S. Agency for International Development alone increased its assistance from $2.7 million in 1981 to $165 million in 1983.

The importance of this international influence clearly highlights the potential relevance of geopolitical considerations in affecting the decisions domestic governments make when faced with the need for reform. In fact, given the extraordinary commitment of external resources to limiting the consequences of austerity in Costa Rica, one might expect that the Costa Rican case would be one in which dismantling of previous social welfare programs could be completed without a hitch, thus preventing the need for government to face the difficult dilemma of choosing to avoid default against survival in office. Careful attention to the reform dynamics in this period, as made possible by primary archival research, paints a more complex political picture.

Discussions at the IMF in early 1983 make clear that there was a general sense of enthusiasm about the reforms successfully executed in the first year of the Monge administration. Indeed, reforms to pricing in the public sector more generally were credited with a strong improvement in government finances, with the annual deficit falling from approximately 14 percent in 1981 to around 3 percent in 1983. Yet, despite enjoying some successes in implementing reforms

---

[10] For extensive discussion of the strategies used by the Monge government to limit the electoral backlash of reforms, see Wilson (1998, 1999).

at the beginning of his term, "after eighteen months of austerity measures and consequent increased levels of popular protests, especially by the unionized public employees, President Monge sided publicly with the protesters and argued that the austerity measures were the result of IMF conditionality and were undermining the social fabric of the country (La Nacion, December 20, 1983). Monge refused to sign a new IMF standby agreement, ended some austerity measures, and increased social spending" (Wilson 1998, 117). This outpouring of dissatisfaction by public sector employees was met with a large wage expansion, among other expenditures, which subsequently derailed the original terms of the IMF loan.

Yet, Costa Rica still required significant assistance from the IFIs, and so returned to the negotiating table quickly. Explicit focus on the terms of continued reform, as demanded by the IMF and World Bank, are of particular use in identifying those programs that were considered politically sacred, even at a time when other state expenditures were successfully being slashed. Over this period, while lauded initially for executing some improvements in government finances, the IMF nonetheless continued to emphasize that, given the massive size of oustanding Costa Rican debt, the state would need to run a primary surplus for years before debt levels would reach more normal and manageable levels.[11] Beginning in 1983, and continuing for the next several years, discussion by the IFIs largely centered around the need for improvement in three major areas: wage restraint for public employees, budget deficits from autonomous institutions, and losses at the Central Bank. I discuss each in turn.

Public Sector Wages
While organized labor in Costa Rica had generally remained weak in the private sector due to anti-Communist activity during and following the civil war, unionization rates in the public sector were extremely high. As important conduits of blocs of voters come time for elections, the public sector unions were accorded significant political attention by the PLN. As my theory would expect, this translated into costly support policies from the government, the most straightforward of which was increased wages for public sector employees; for example, in an IMF report that noted that the public sector in Costa Rica provided employed approximately 20 percent of the workforce, it was also emphasized that "large nominal wage increases, in excess of the amounts that could be justified by the increase in the cost of living index, were awarded under pressure of the strong public sector labor unions."[12] While extremely politically popular, with large numbers of employees on the government's payroll, any effort to expand wages also translated directly into additional budgetary outlays for the state; unsurprisingly, González Vega (1984, 15)'s summary of fiscal issues faced by the Costa Rican government noted that "the rapid expansion of public sector employment has caused a growing fiscal

[11] See, e.g., IMF (1984c). [12] IMF (1984b, 20).

deficit, which is at the root of the more recent financial crisis. In turn, the importance of wages in public expenditures has made it politically difficult to cut government spending. The concentration of workers in large public institutions has facilitated their unionization. Public-sector unions are the strongest in the country and have managed to maintain higher wages than those for similar occupations in the private sector, while at the same time preventing any reduction in the absolute size of government." Given large outlays required to finance state employment, it is unsurprising that the IMF repeatedly identified public wage restraint as a crucial component in any effort to rein in government expenditure. While outside the realm of agricultural policy, I note that the dynamics relating electoral blocs to costly government policies fits quite closely to an expanded interpretation of my theory.

Autonomous Institution Deficits

In pressing for additional fiscal reforms, the IMF explicitly highlighted the budgetary issues that had arisen previously from the host of autonomous institutions that existed in Costa Rica; however, with most such institutions representing a tiny fraction of government budgetary support, attention was primarily focused on four major state enterprises: the state oil agency (RECOPE), electricity agency (ICE), agricultural marketing agency (CNP), and general development agency (CODESA).[13] Each of the three former institutions had been involved in some degree of price subsidization that generated deficits that required budgetary support by the central government, while CODESA encompassed an umbrella of state-supported development projects that were largely recognized as noncompetitive and which therefore required government intervention to keep afloat. For the first three agencies, IMF prescriptions were straightforward: Stop subsidizing the consumption of oil and electricity, and cease the practice of inflating producer prices for food farmers, as well as subsidized basic grain consumption for consumers. Regarding CODESA, the IMF recommended a dismantling of the agency via privatization of its subsidiary programs. I note here that, consistent with my expectations, the fiscal costs arising from agricultural support policies comprised one of the main targets of reform demands.

Central Bank Losses

While reforms to state finances were meant to stanch the need for the state to take on additional sovereign borrowing, Costa Rica still faced extremely severe pressure in the form of strenuous repayments on its heavy existing debt burden, much of which had been lent by private banks and not through multilateral agencies. Over the course of 1983, the Costa Rican authorities were able to reach consensus with their private lenders to restructure virtually the entirety of their outstanding debt into more favorable terms with delayed repayment.

[13] IMF (1985e, 17).

This restructuring proved important for several reasons. To begin with, during the course of negotiations with the private banks, it became clear that the financial health of the Costa Rican Central Bank was in worse shape than it had appeared in prior statements, largely due to the fact that when state enterprises ran deficits, these were financed via loans secured by the Central Bank from international creditors, and then passed on the agencies themselves. While such agencies were nominally considered "autonomous institutions," their de facto financial backing by the Central Bank made clear that these debts should be counted on the government's balance sheet, rather than hidden via accounting fiat.[14] As a term of the restructuring of private sector debt, the Costa Rican authorities agreed to move state enterprise loans onto the balance sheet for the Central Bank, so as to facilitate accounting for the financial health of the government.[15] However, once these agency deficits were explicitly accounted for, this had the effect of massively degrading the balance sheet of the Central Bank since it involved assuming ownership of a series of poorly performing loans generally owed to foreign financiers. As these costs became clearer to negotiators at the international financial institutions, reining in losses at the Central Bank became a consistent target of further reforms.

Besides the deficits acquired from state-owned enterprises (which were supposed to be eliminated following reforms at the autonomous institutions), Central Bank losses also arose from a practice of subsidizing interest rates for particularly important groups. Having nationalized the banking system at the end of the civil war, the Costa Rican government enjoyed an extra lever of control over development priorities in the broader economy, which was achieved by mandating favorable interest rates for particular sectors. Most pronounced among these practices was extreme favoritism toward agricultural producers, who were granted loans at exceptionally subsidized rates. For example, in 1982, while official interest rates for the general economy hovered around 25 percent, interest rates for small farmers and agricultural cooperatives averaged about 6 percent, while lending rates to the state-run agricultural production board (CNP) were set by law at a mere 2 percent![16] Vogel (1984, 134) concurs, noting that, regarding official interest rate policy, "agriculture tends to be favored relative to other sectors." Nor were these favorable lending policies for farmers of trivial fiscal consequence: on average, it is estimated that the interest rate subsidy for agriculture amounted to nearly 4 percent of GDP (Vogel 1984, 135).

The financial consequences of these loans to domestic farmers were particularly troubling given that most were financed by central government borrowing from abroad; the Central Bank faced risks that these costs could increase not only when international interest rates continued to rise (forcing greater implied subsidies to maintain lower domestic rates), but also exposed the government to the possibility of assuming completely nonperforming loans

---

[14] IMF (1985f, 6). [15] IMF (1985f, 17). [16] IMF (1984b, 42–43).

5.2 Costa Rica

in the cases where poor agricultural production led to widespread default by private agricultural producers. Given that Central Bank losses had to be covered by central government funding, the IMF increasingly focused on shoring up the balance sheet at the Central Bank in order to limit additional needs for external borrowing, including explicit emphasis on the need to end preferential interest rate programs for agricultural producers.

5.2.5 Institutional Cross-Conditionality and the 1986 Elections

In strong evidence of the catalytic role of the IMF, terms of private bank debt renegotiations were made explicitly conditional on Costa Rica remaining in good standing with its IMF programs. Here there entered an additional institutional wrinkle: At the same time that Costa Rica was interacting with the IMF over terms of its Stand-By Arrangement (SBA), it was simultaneously also negotiating terms of an agreement for a Structural Adjustment Loan (SAL) with the World Bank. While it has often been suggested that the IMF and World Bank worked hand-in-hand when dealing with countries in crisis over this period, consultation of the minutes of Executive Board meetings makes clear that, in this particular case, the linkage between IMF and World Bank programs was made an explicit condition of good standing. It appears that the two institutions decided to split up the issue areas over which reform was to be made an explicit condition, with the IMF terms largely focused around "short-term financial management and exchange rate policies," while the World Bank focused more specifically on reforming the public sector, financial sector, and trade reform.[17] Given the cross-conditionality of IMF and WB programs that began in 1983, this had the effect of making both public and private restructuring of Costa Rican debt (which was largely necessary to allow the state to avoid default on heavy repayments) explicitly tied to terms of both institutions' demands.

By 1985, attention to several external indicators should have pointed to a favorable resolution of the Costa Rican debt problem. As noted earlier, in the early and mid-1980s, Costa Rica enjoyed the financial support of the United States and had managed to successfully restructure its outstanding debt into much more favorable terms; in addition, by 1985, oil prices had fallen significantly and coffee prices had recovered, with a concomitant improvement in Costa Rica's terms of trade. Finally, in March of 1985, Costa Rica finalized the terms of a 13-month SBA with the IMF, paving the way for another round of restructuring talks with private financiers. This confluence of external factors should have been perfect conditions for successful implementation of economic reforms. However, despite all these favorable external forces, 1985 posed a particular challenge to the sitting government's attempts at further reform: it heralded the advent of the next round of national elections, to take place in 1986.

[17] IMF (1984a, 5).

In discussing the recently completed SBA, several IMF officials emphasized the importance of continued structural reforms under the World Bank's SAL. The importance of adherence to these reforms was also emphasized in May at a Paris Club meeting on official debt restructuring, which notes that terms of restructuring were contingent upon continued agreement with the IMF.[18] This critical nature of cross-conditionality was only further strengthened in discussions with private lenders, which also demanded that Costa Rica remain in good standing as a precondition for commercial bank lending to be rescheduled in 1985 and 1986.[19] Unfortunately, by September of 1985, it had become clear that Costa Rica was poised to fall out of standing with the IMF. In initial discussion by the IMF's executive directors, based upon a circulated summary of conditions in the country, it appeared as though Costa Rica was only in violation of a single reform condition that related to the permissible level of "arrears" the country could maintain while still counting as in good standing. In response to this, several executive directors noted that, in the past, it was common for countries to lapse on a particular term in their obligations, but to still retain the IMF's seal of approval so long as the spirit of reforms was being maintained. Several noted that a single condition was not necessarily cause for serious concern, and as the report emphasized that Costa Rica was essentially in compliance with all the other terms of the SBA, pressed for more details on why the country was set to lose good standing.[20]

In subsequent discussion with IMF internal staff, however, it became clear that the violation of the "arrears" term in the Costa Rican case was due to the country's inability to successfully restructure outstanding commercial debt, which had led to a much-higher level of outstanding loans than had been anticipated under the assumption of private creditor cooperation. Upon closer examination, it turned out that the failure to reschedule private debt had arisen due to Costa Rica's lack of compliance with the structural reforms identified as necessary for repairing fiscal imbalances that were included in the World Bank's SAL – as noted earlier, the commercial banks placed a heavy emphasis on the importance of the continued maintenance of these adjustments.[21] Thus, while Costa Rica was nominally only in violation of a single term of its obligations to the IMF, the research staff emphasized that the failure on the arrears term was actually symptomatic of much broader noncompliance with necessary adjustments, and thus should not have been viewed as merely temporary or minor.[22] While the minutes for this particular executive directors' meeting did not highlight the specific conditions under violation, it is possible to determine the details of this policy transgression by consulting the performance evaluation of the SAL generated by the World Bank itself.

One of the primary areas of structural reform targeted by the World Bank's SAL was the improvement of fiscal losses arising from parastatal organizations.

---

[18] IMF (1985k). [19] IMF (1985c, 67). [20] See extended discussion in IMF (1985a).
[21] IMF (1985b, 6). [22] IMF (1985b, 3,11).

5.2 Costa Rica

As was noted at the end of Section 5.2.4, these reforms were primarily targeted around the four largest autonomous institutions in Costa Rica: RECOPE, ICE, CNP, and CODESA. Each of these generated targeted benefits for particular constituencies, and thus may have been difficult to reform. To what degree did the Costa Rican government succeed in repairing the deficits of these agencies? As made clear by detailed budgetary summaries, by the mid-1980s, reforms to RECOPE and ICE had moved them into surplus; price reforms to oil and electricity are credited as actually contributing to government revenues in 1983.[23] Regarding CODESA, intended government divestment of a host of nonprofitable projects was further facilitated by the US "Caribbean Basin Initiative," funded by USAID, in which foreign grants were used to purchase these nonperforming agencies from the state. Clearly, this again demonstrates the importance of US geopolitical interest in Costa Rica in limiting the difficulty of implementing economic reforms: In the case of the state development agency, not only did sales of uncompetitive programs improve the fiscal performance of the nonfinancial enterprises by removing loss-making programs from the budget, but the sale of such projects funded by foreign grants constituted an additional source of government revenue (Wilson 1994, 161). Thus, by 1985, the Costa Rican government had already managed to effectively limit its budgetary exposure to oil and energy consumers, and was in the process of transferring government control over development projects from the state-run CODESA to the newly created "Costa Rican Coalition for Development Initiatives" (CINDE), responsible to USAID (Hansen-Kuhn 1993, 9).

However, unlike the other three main state-owned enterprises identified as targets for reform, the national agricultural marketing agency (CNP) was the only one which demonstrated significant fiscal decline over the period. Internal discussion at the IMF identified these cost overruns at the CNP explicitly as attempts to expand domestic agricultural production using supramarket price guarantees, precisely the sort of farm support policies I expect to result from rural electoral influence.[24] That such losses would arise precisely in the lead up to a fresh round of presidential elections only helps further tie the linkage between crucial rural votes and costly farm support programs – that this happened over a period when the three other primary autonomous institutions were largely successfully reformed highlights the particular difficulty of agricultural reform in democratic contexts where rural votes are electorally central (Hazell 1992, 574).

Yet, perhaps the World Bank was willing to overlook the failures of the government to constrain losses at the CNP? Perhaps these losses were deemed insignificant, or not worth delaying broader reform efforts? Following disbursement of an initial tranche of funds in September, by December 1985 the Bank had chosen to withhold the next tranche due to failed reforms by the Costa Rican government. In discussing the conditions that led to failure to

---

[23] IMF (1985d, 58–60). [24] See discussion in IMF (1986a) and IMF (1988).

disburse additional tranches of support money, the Bank highlighted that "three major conditions of second tranche release had not been met. The major tariff issues remained unresolved because they required approval by the Assembly, which had not yet materialized. And, contrary to agreements, public sector employment had increased and so had the losses of the CNP ... Release of the second tranche proved impossible. Meanwhile, the campaign for the 1986 elections was gathering steam and diverting the attention of policymakers away from economic issues."[25] Beyond a failure to reach full agreement on liberalizing tariffs that proved to be short-lived, the World Bank explicitly highlighted two main areas of failed reform that ultimately doomed the SAL: Rising debts at the agricultural marketing agency, and expanding wages for public sector employees. The role of failed CNP reforms and expanding public wages in driving noncompliance with the IMF is also supported by Nelson (1989, 154). In a period of more general success at economic reform, it is striking the degree to which, in the lead-up to new elections, a democratically elected government proved unwilling to alienate two of its most consistent blocs of voters, even when doing so led to the breakdown of agreements with the international financial institutions. In explaining the failure of these reforms, the Bank's emphasis on electoral considerations is quite straightforward: "first, the SALs got repeatedly caught up in Costa Rica's four-year electoral cycle. Second, the Government was unable to implement some of the measures or was delayed in doing so."[26]

As noted at the beginning of Section 5.2.5, cooperation between the IMF and World Bank in the Costa Rican case meant, effectively, that Costa Rica's failure to control spending on farm support programs and public wages led to a domino-like series of additional financial consequences. Returning to the discussion of Costa Rica's standing with the IMF, the end result of the meeting mentioned earlier was to put Costa Rica's status with the IMF in limbo; given explicit demands by private-sector creditors of successful IMF and WB program implementation, this ultimately led to the collapse of negotiations between the Costa Rican government and its commercial lenders. Faced with an environment in which external creditors demanded reforms to costly programs benefiting electorally crucial supporters, the Costa Rican government ultimately chose to unilaterally suspend payment on commercial bank debt. Without further financing options, the government called for an extraordinary twenty-five-year restructuring of its international financial obligations and a seven-year moratorium on any debt repayment.[27] Thus, rather than face the threat of electoral suicide due to cuts to benefits for farmers and unions, the government instead chose default on its international debt obligations. That this occurred despite a lame-duck president with extraordinary international support helps make clear precisely how important the domestic electoral

---

[25] Bank (1994, 5).   [26] Bank (1994, 4).   [27] IMF (1986b, 14).

dynamics that form the core of my theoretical account are in driving democratic default.[28]

5.3 DEFAULT IN CONTENTIOUS DEMOCRACY

While Costa Rica highlights the importance of agricultural voting blocs in consolidated democracies, unfortunately not all democratic regimes have managed to successfully banish the use of violence as a political tool. Critically, while incumbent survival in such contentious democracies still hinges on the outcome of elections, unlike in the more idealized form of consolidated democracy, the use of violence is accorded a political role. Importantly, this violence is still generally targeted at an electoral aim: it may be used to discourage turnout by opposition voters, or campaign activities by opposition candidates, particularly in areas of "turf" that are considered to be dominated by the party. Depending on the nature of political competition, electoral violence has also been used, for example, to reify ethnic cleavages in order to mobilize voting by a majority-dominant bloc of coethnics (Wilkinson 2006). Finally, under the premise that social stability is an important priority for democratic governments, opposition groups may attempt to discredit the legitimacy of an incumbent regime by staging mass unrest; particularly when occurring in the lead up to elections, popular riots may have the effect of swaying voters' views of the effectiveness of the incumbent ruler.

Of course, as has been discussed at length in earlier chapters, geography is likely to affect the feasibility of organizing mass violence: It is much easier to stage a riot in cities than in the countryside. Additionally, while the use of political violence in rural areas is not impossible, the density of urban areas makes control of political turf through the employment of armed thugs a much more feasible strategy, as compared to the need to travel large distances to intimidate every rural farmer.[29] Each of these advantages of urban collective mobilization suggest that, when political violence is a viable strategy in contentious democracies, the needs of urban dwellers should gain greater relative weight in the decisionmaking process of incumbent rulers.

At a basic level, this suggests that urban interests should receive proportionally greater attention in contentious democracies, as compared against the electoral mobilization advantages of rural areas. Which of these concerns should predominate is, a priori, not necessarily obvious, as politicians in such settings must attempt to counterbalance the need for rural votes against limiting exposure to urban unrest. However, in cases where urban threats to political

---

[28] Largely ineffectual attempts at mass protests by rural agents in the face of subsequent reforms later in the decade help make clear that the political influence of these actors was tied directly to their electoral influence as voters, not to their capacity for revolt, which was especially weak for rural agents. See, e.g., Anderson (1991); Edelman (1990).

[29] As nearly all seats of political power are located in cities, this makes potential exposure of politicians themselves to violence greater in urban than rural settings (Wallace 2014).

rule become particularly acute, I expect to observe similar pressures to those I identify in earlier chapters as arising in closed autocracies: The provision of cheap food policies that, during times of fiscal crisis, may become difficult to reform due to fears of social unrest. Particularly in those cases where democratic incumbents are fearful that urban riots could lead to their ouster from power, and where they face less organized or mobilized rural agents, such pressures may even be so strong as to cause leaders of contentious democracies to renege on their international obligations in order to sustain urban-biased policies, rather than take their chances at the hands of a hungry mob.

5.4 JAMAICA

5.4.1 Case Selection

To investigate the role of democratic elections conducted under the specter of partisan violence, few countries better fit the bill than Jamaica. As regards the necessity of competitive elections as the primary determinant of incumbent survival, Jamaican politics has been characterized by tightly contested elections throughout the postwar period, with regular transfer of control of government between the dominant parties, the Peoples' National Party (PNP) and the Jamaican Labour Party (JLP).

However, particularly since the mid-1960s, Jamaican elections have also been characterized by the routine threat of violence, often organized on behalf of political parties (Stephens and Stephens 1986, 45–46).[30] Over time, this has led to the creation of so-called garrison communities, particularly in the urban areas of the country, with nearly 60 percent of urban constituencies so arranged (Harriott 2008, 20). The manifestation and function of such garrisons is detailed in Lewis (2012, 41), who notes that "[w]ithin a political constituency, a garrison is an area controlled by a leader or don who dispenses scarce benefits and violence in order to keep the constituents aligned to a particular party. This control enables an electoral candidate to win the seat by a large majority and become the Member of Parliament. Garrisons are therefore a central part of the political system because they provide safe political seats. Moreover, garrison constituents may assist in the task of political mobilization in other constituencies." With partisan violence – particularly urban violence – a key component of the nature of political competition, Jamaica fits squarely into the notion of a contentious democracy that I develop in earlier chapters. I have argued that this constitutes a qualitative difference in the type of regime incentives; that the nature of political competition in Jamaica represents a

---

[30] For discussion of the evolution of urban gangs as political tools, see Stone (1980, 18), who argues that "gang leaders became an integral part of the urban power base of the two major parties" in part as a result of the rise of ghetto communities in Kingston and St. Andrew following heavy rural–urban migration in the 1950s and 1960s.

difference in kind is made explicitly in Stone (1980, 108–109)'s extensive account of the political system on the island, arguing that "[Jamaican politics] represents a species of authoritarian democracy the democratic context of which is anchored on the ballot box and competitive elections."

Of central relevance to my theoretical account of urban–rural political biases, Jamaica is of additional interest as a case where rural voters are relatively weak. Unlike the Costa Rican case in the first half of this chapter, where farm votes proved a crucial swing bloc, most accounts of electoral dynamics in Jamaica emphasize the relative passivity of the peasant class. In part, this arguably developed out of the evolution of the two major political parties – the JLP was an explicit outgrowth of a major union, which formed an initial electoral base for the party. As noted by Huber and Stephens (1992, 59), "[w]ith the support of its trade union base and increasing support from the Jamaican upper classes due to JLP red baiting of the PNP, the JLP won the first two elections held under universal suffrage in 1944 and 1949. The PNP responded by organizing its own trade union base ... By the late fifties, both parties had trade union affiliates and multiclass bases of support." Thus, from the beginning of electoral politics in Jamaica, trade unions have formed a crucial role as conduits of votes for both major parties; as suggested by my theory, this should increase the political weight of such (primarily urban) interests.

Despite this mobilization of union workers as an important electoral agent, several works make clear that no major rural organization formed over this period to similarly funnel rural voters into a coherent bloc. For example, Stone (1980, 7) argues that the "relative powerlessness of the lower strata is likely to negatively affect their full integration and incorporation into national political life. This tendency is likely to be greatest within the peripheral rural farming communities." This lack of rural political organizations is echoed by Edie (1989, 19), who notes that there "were no organizations created to isolate the small farmers from the politicians. There were no peasant unions or peasant leagues to lobby collectively for peasant interests. Instead the latter continued to be dependent on bureaucratic and political paternalism." The outcome of a dense network of union organizations, combined with a dearth of agricultural lobbies, was to structure the attention of elected officials in a largely urban direction; as Stone (1980, 206) argues, "where the powerful organized interests are urban based and represent urban class interests, there is often a vacuum of lobbying pressure in the domain of rural and agricultural policies." I note here that my model of urban–rural bias in democracies does not imply that all democracies must exhibit biases towards agricultural producers – instead, I rely on standard accounts from the literature on the greater electoral mobilization capacity of farm votes across many systems to predict that, on average, there should be rural biases in democratic countries. However, Jamaica demonstrates nicely a case where this assumption of greater agricultural mobilization capacity does not hold; in such a situation, the predictions of my model should be for policies structured to benefit the interests of urban workers over the needs of rural farmers, particularly as applies to food pricing.[31]

Importantly, however, the omnipresence of violence in urban areas in Jamaica helps to identify that the political weight of urban citizens did not inhere only in the capacity of unions to mobilize votes. While the standard sources of influence over political leaders came from organized lobbies, not all citizens were linked to party decision making via these channels. As discussed by Stone (1980, 108), "[t]he Jamaican mass public as a heterogeneous body of individuals, classes, and communities ... tends to rely on the representational function of these organized interests to do so on its own behalf. The exception to this general pattern are those infrequent crisis situations in which mass protest action and collective violence are used by sections of the mass public to articulate policy pressures." The potential for violence in urban centers exists not only as a tool for partisan control of geographic areas: In addition, it represents a separate strategy of expressing the popular will to elected politicians. The importance of this additional strategy of political participation for segments of the population is so central to the Jamaican system that Stone (1980, 6) claims that "[s]poradic mass protests are as much a part of the traditions of politics in Jamaica as the constant changing of party governments." Thus, the Jamaican case is well-suited to investigate the hypothesized relationship between urban political pressure, fears of unrest, and pressures to default that I expect from contentious democratic regimes.[32]

5.4.2 Challenges to Jamaican Case

While Jamaica is in many regards an ideal case to investigate the dynamics of contentious democracy, it is important to highlight one set of factors that could potentially limit the relevance of my theory of domestic political pressures: geopolitics. As in the Costa Rican case at the beginning of this chapter, geopolitical alignment with the United States and United Kingdom is emphasized as an important factor in a number of accounts of Jamaican politics over the time

---

[31] Note that Stone (1973, 4) in addition argues that the urban-biased focus of Jamaican politicians also arose from the proximity of urban citizens, stating that the "location of the nerve centers of elite political and economic power in this urban area means that the political behavior of the urban mass public will tend to have disproportionate influence on the overall tactics and strategies by which these elites attempt to control the non-elites ... This clearly adds to the significance of this main urban area in national political life."

[32] Stone (1980, 108) is clear to point out that the capacity for mass unrest is not shared equally by all citizens, which again reduces such citizens to a single source of potential leverage over politicians: voting. For example, while noting that "aggrieved citizens resort sporadically to protest action and demonstrations as a means of articulating demands on the political directorate. Most citizens, however, lack well-developed associational or community groups independent of the party power centers to engage in any organized collective action. The ballot is therefore the only channel for political expression for most citizens who are intimidated by the power of the party machines."

period I consider.³³ This becomes of particular relevance following the switch in leaders from Michael Manley – a candidate who actively attempted to steer the Jamaican state towards a social democratic path and also courted warmer relations with countries in the Soviet sphere of influence – to Edward Seaga, who campaigned against the communist leanings of the PNP and argued for a return to a neoliberal development plan. To the extent that this coincided with a period of fiscal distress for the state and a series of negotiations with the IMF, this geopolitical alignment with the US should have weakened the linkages between international demands for reform in return for continued access to foreign financing. However, as discussed in more detail in the remainder of this chapter, political leaders in Jamaica continued to face trouble in reforming costly policies for influential urban citizens, particularly when faced with mass unrest, leading it to renege on its international obligations despite significant assistance from the United States and the United Kingdom.

5.4.3 Background to the Crisis

Manley's First Term (1972–1976)
After a period of alternating rule between the PNP and JLP through the 1950s and 1960s, the presidential election of 1972 proved a turning point in modern Jamaican politics. The PNP's candidate in these elections, Michael Manley, was the charismatic son of the founder of the party who managed to take on a quasi-religious identity as a father figure to the Jamaican people above the normal fray of politics.³⁴ Upon assuming office – and facing pressure to identify a strategy to limit simmering social tensions as a result of rising economic inequality – Manley set out to radically reorient the Jamaican economy toward a democratic socialist path of heavy state involvement.

Over the course of his first term in office, Manley expanded the reach of government into economic production across a number of areas, while also introducing a host of additional government welfare services to wide swaths of the population. The scale of this expansion was truly impressive; for example, Stephens and Stephens (1986, 70) list forty-six different principal policies and initiatives of the PNP government during its first term from 1972–1976, with programs ranging from literacy initiatives, free secondary and university education, land leasing to rural farmers, public housing, food subsidies, a national minimum wage, rising pensions, and worker participation, among many others. As a strategy for electoral success, expanding provision of state benefits to most major groups (including farmers and union workers) seemed sure to reap electoral gains – assuming, of course, that the state could actually afford such programs.

---

[33] E.g., Edie (1989, 22); Payne (1988, 1222).
[34] For extensive discussion of this campaign, see Stephens and Stephens (1986, 60–68).

The problem with this state expansion was that the Jamaican government was already on tenuous fiscal footing at the start of the 1970s, and the situation was to worsen significantly over the course of the decade. While the prior developmental model (sometimes called "investment by invitation") had generated new growth in Jamaican industry, the investment driving such industrial expansion was largely drawn from foreign financiers. Lacking domestic sources for many critical inputs in manufacturing, the Jamaican economy became particularly dependent upon imports for production. In addition, as many of its industrial products enjoyed protection against foreign competition, the lack of competitiveness on world markets meant that Jamaican manufactured goods did not encounter heavy external demand. Instead, the island remained especially dependent upon extraction and exports of bauxite and sugar; each of these products, however, were largely owned by foreign multinationals, and thus the proceeds recurring to the government from such sales were limited (Stephens and Stephens 1986, 26–28).

The trade imbalance facing the island was further intensified by a growing reliance on imported food, particularly given heavy rural–urban migration over the course of the 1950s and 1960s. As expected in a system in which urban interests were favored over rural ones – and in stark contrast to the Costa Rican case with heavy rural favoritism – "agriculture, which still provided employment for a third of all employed Jamaicans when Michael Manley took office, was, by all accounts, the sick man of the Jamaican economy ... The small farmer was plagued by lack of funds for basic inputs and poor transportation, storage and marketing" (Stephens and Stephens 1986, 28). This lack of developmental programs for farmers resulted in poor overall production of agricultural products, both for export markets but also critically for domestic consumption. For example, Stephens and Stephens (1986, 28) note that demand for food grew at an annual rate of four percent over the 1950s and 1960s, while domestic agriculture grew at a mere 2 percent per year. This growing spread between the domestic food needs of city dwellers and rural food production was only sated by growing imports of food that came to consume an increasingly large share of already scarce foreign exchange – by the late 1970s, Stone (1980, 3) noted that "Jamaica's level of food importation is ten times higher than that found in the typical Third World country." Thus, while sources of external imbalance were not solely the result of urban-biased food policies, secondary accounts make clear that the issue of food policy was a consistent source of financial trouble for the government.

With growing external imbalance, Jamaica had managed to cover its foreign exchange deficit during the 1960s primarily through reliance on inflows of foreign investment. However, shortly after Manley came to power, this shortage of foreign exchange was amplified significantly by the first oil shock in 1973. As a country reliant on oil imports, the spike in import costs in this year turned what was a growing concern over the current account imbalance into a source of actual crisis. While falling oil prices by 1974 helped to ease this pressure somewhat, expansion of government welfare programs created a similar need for increased revenue. The combined pressures of foreign exchange shortages with fiscal weakness seemed to be solved by a radical decision by the government to increase the bauxite levy charged to foreign multinationals in 1974. While heavily criticized by external investors as a form of government expropriation, the move to raise taxes on foreign bauxite firms was initially popular domestically, and in the short term did allow the government to expand its expenditures significantly (Stephens and Stephens 1986, 111). However, these gains were to prove short lived, as spooked foreign investors became increasingly reluctant to continue to fund investments in the Jamaican economy, which also coincided with falling revenue from sugar exports and weakening tourism (another critical source of foreign exchange).

Despite continued weakening on the revenue side of the budget, this did not prevent the Manley government from continuing to expand its welfare programs to the masses. Predictably, with rising expenditures not matched by equal revenue gains, the product was a rapid expansion of sovereign borrowing. Stephens and Stephens (1986, 113) describe that "[a]fter 1974 the government began to rely increasingly on loans to finance the budget ... with borrowing from private banks abroad increasing particularly rapidly. The proportion of Jamaica's total external public debt owed to private banks had risen from 10 percent in 1970 to 44 percent in 1974 and 51 percent in 1975." Thus, the first term under Manley witnessed not only a massive expansion of government involvement in economic activity, but also saw the rise of extensive external government debt. Of course, as these external debts began to come due, repayment to foreign creditors became an additional constraint on dwindling foreign currency available to the government.

By the time of the next round of presidential elections in 1976, the opposition JLP had seized upon a growing sense of pending crisis due to the government's economic policies. The JLP's presidential candidate – Edward Seaga – campaigned extensively on the growing threat to Jamaica's economy due to the mismatch between government expenses and revenues, in addition to concerns over government corruption and rising violence. In contrast, Manley campaigned on the PNP's record of providing expanded welfare development to large segments of the Jamaican population, and downplayed the seriousness of the foreign exchange situation. Despite this apparent lack of concern about the state of the economy in public, Stephens and Stephens (1986, 149) report that Manley had already begun to hold meetings with the IMF in secret to begin discussions on crucial foreign exchange support. As was to be expected, the IMF indicated it would seek a series of reforms to the economy, including a devaluation of the Jamaican currency as well as a dramatic scaling back of government expenditures, to which "Manley responded that this was impossible during the election campaign but agreed that the subject would be taken up again immediately after the elections." More generally, it appears that the depth of the impending crisis for Jamaica was not only hidden from voters in the lead-up to the elections, but even from a number of prominent officials within the PNP leadership itself (Stephens and Stephens 1986, 148).

Beyond issues of economic management, however, the 1976 election also took on a particularly ominous tone as political violence began to escalate. As noted by Stone (1980, 163),

> [d]uring the official campaign at least twelve persons were shot (including two candidates) and over the entire period of the unofficial campaign between late 1975 and election day well over a hundred persons were shot ... Both parties had supporting gangs of youths, some on motorcycles, some on foot, and others in motor cars who terrorized opposing activists, controlled political territory and generally acted as a reserve force backing up the nonviolent campaign arm of the parties. In the urbanized areas and on the main roadways in the rural parishes, citizens were often challenged to declare their party allegiance by shouting the appropriate party slogan or symbol, and violence was used against persons who gave no answers or indicated support for the opposite party.

This use of targeted partisan violence clearly accords with the sorts of political strategies I identify as prominent in contentious democracies. Yet, beyond this employment of violence against clear political targets, Stephens and Stephens (1986, 131–132) describe at length an additional source of concern during the campaign season:

> Early in 1976, a new phenomenon assumed prominence on the political scene, namely political violence accompanied by a series of unexplained violent events which could only be interpreted as part of a campaign of destabilization. Obviously, political violence was by no means new to Jamaica ... In fact, all through 1975 gang warfare with political overtones had been plaguing the Kingston ghetto and the government had initiated joint police-military actions and imposed periodic curfews in an effort to contain them. What was new in early 1976 was a type of violence which was neither of the gang warfare nor partisan terrorization nor ordinary criminal variety, but rather destructive acts without an apparent motive.

In addition to the more standard variant of politically targeted violence, the rise of a series of violent acts arguably meant to destabilize Jamaican society more generally became an area of significant concern for the government.[35] In response, the PNP government declared a State of Emergency on the island, imposing curfews in many central areas and granting security forces additional leeway, which "received virtually universal support in the society, with the notable exception of the JLP" (Stephens and Stephens 1986, 133).

Riding a wave of popular support for both its imposition of the State of Emergency, as well as appreciation of its welfare programs, the PNP secured victory in the presidential elections and won a second term for Manley at the helm. Analysis of the voting results of this period make clear that, while the PNP enjoyed a significant expansion in its electoral support from working

---

[35] Note that Stephens and Stephens (1986, 134–137) argue that this spike in nonpartisan violence may have been linked to an attempt by the CIA to destabilize a prominent left-leaning government in its sphere of influence.

class voters (largely due to its welfare programs), it also witnessed declines in support from business leaders and middle-class voters that were worried about rising social violence as well as the potentially communist leanings of a state heavily involved in economic production. Still, while the overall vote totals only marginally improved for the PNP, their seat share in Parliament improved from thirty-six to forty-seven seats, and the election results were interpreted by the left-wing branch of the PNP as evidence of their ensured electoral success moving forward as a result of their consolidated working class base; these fears were echoed by members of the JLP opposition who feared that the PNP had become unbeatable (Stone 1980, 173).

The Peoples' Production Plan
Almost immediately after securing his second term in office, Manley began to address the brewing balance of payments crisis he had downplayed during the election, with fear that growing shortage of foreign exchange was likely to threaten current and future economic development. However, in a signal of clear unwillingness of elected politicians to seek IMF support in fear of the political losses that could result from austerity programs, Manley instead announced a new "antiimperialist" direction for the Jamaican state, which included an attempt to address the issues plaguing the Jamaican economy outside the approach of the neoliberal international financial institutions.

At the core of this attempt at unorthodox economic reform was the "Peoples' Production Plan," which was the result of a special working group composed of politically sympathetic academics and policymakers who were tasked by the government with coming up with a means of addressing the foreign exchange shortage plaguing the nation. Given relatively poor domestic agricultural production and its heavy reliance on imported food, the Peoples' Production Plan focused centrally on the role of rural development as a means of correcting Jamaican import reliance that consumed large shares of foreign reserves. As noted by Stephens and Stephens (1986, 164), "[i]n reorienting the economy [under the Peoples' Production Plan], agriculture was key: The planners state that the production plan implicitly indicates that the development of a self-reliant national economy must be based on rural development … It was estimated that bringing these new lands into production would provide 37,000 jobs. Most of these would go to the rural unemployed but some would have been reserved for the urban unemployed who would have to be redeployed for the purpose." Thus, a central component of the reform package involved a substantial reorientation of government programs from urban towards rural areas. Beyond this central role for agriculture, the plan additionally targeted expanding exports in the bauxite and aluminum sectors, as well as further encouraging tourism to generate foreign reserves and energy conservation programs to limit the costs of energy imports. Perhaps most controversially, recognizing the heavy import-dependence of a number of Jamaican industries, the plan also called for a significant reduction in manufacturing programs

(Stephens and Stephens 1986, 225). Of course, shuttering these plants would only increase the swelling ranks of urban unemployed.

Despite exerting significant resources early in the period attempting to "educate" the population on the value of this nonorthodox reform plan, as the political consequences of the plan began to become clear, Manley determined that such a reorientation would be politically infeasible. Beyond concerns about the possibility of blowback from owners in the private sector who would lose out from such a reorientation, Stephens and Stephens (1986, 167) emphasize explicitly that Manley also feared "the drastic drop of employment in urban areas, much of which could have been picked up in agriculture only with great difficulty." Lacking a (politically) feasible alternative to the IMF, and given massive foreign exchange shortages, Manley executed an abrupt about-face and turned to the IMF for support.

As expected, this package of international support was conditioned on a series of austerity measures for the island – including emphasis on wage restraint, reduced inflation, limits on imports, and reductions in overall government expenditures – combined with an "Emergency Production Plan" that retained some of the initial emphasis on encouraging domestic food production (Stone 1980, 176). As a result of these austerity programs, living standards began falling for the broad swath of Jamaicans who had become accustomed to government welfare supports, although initially there was more support from rural voters for a series of programs that included expanded access to land for cultivation. For example, in an island-wide survey fielded at the time, Stone (1980, 178) found that "[i]n the case of urban workers fifty-four percent of unionized labor felt that the PNP government's policies were not helping urban workers. This was in contrast to small farmers among whom only thirty-six percent percent expressed the view that farmers were not benefitting from government policies. Clearly, the high profile land lease project continued to keep some of the PNP government's populist credibility and credentials alive among small farmers while its role in relation to other class interests was now viewed mainly in negative terms." More generally, as a result of cuts in government programs, public support for the PNP's approach cratered – while 64 percent of respondents had expressed some degree of satisfaction with the PNP's Production Plan in May of 1977, by September of the same year the number expressing that the Plan had led to good results had dropped to a mere 36 percent (Stone 1980, 219–220).

Despite securing some reforms, the foreign exchange situation in Jamaica was to further deteriorate in 1978 following the second oil crisis. At the time, the government attempted to shield consumers from the spike in oil prices by heavily subsidizing the costs consumers paid at the pump; however, from a perspective of government finances, this only exacerbated an already overburdened budget by generating additional losses. Unsurprisingly, the IMF called for the government to remove oil subsidies in order to remain current on its package of support.

5.4 Jamaica

In response to continued IMF pressure, the government did allow oil prices to appreciate in early 1979. This was met with an almost immediate outpouring of urban unrest via protests. Interestingly, several secondary sources emphasize that – despite maintaining substantial mobilizational capacity over members – antiausterity protests in this period were not linked to union activity (Stone 1980, 214). As argued by Stephens and Stephens (1986, 209),

> [i]ronically, the same economistic trade-union orientation which deprived the PNP of a reliable, ideologically-committed support base among labor, also deprived the opposition of an effective tool to aggravate economic disruptions and social strife in a systematic matter. Whereas organized labor could not be manipulated by the JLP into planned and systematic disruptive action, outbreaks of popular discontent and general labor militancy could be provoked or exploited and escalated into large-scale protests against economic hardship. The most successful such action was the initiation of the demonstrations against the gas-price increases in January 1979, which brought Kingston to a standstill and also affected other towns.

Thus, while unions clearly enjoyed the advantage of political favoritism due to their capacity for electoral mobilization (as well as industrial strikes tied to narrow workplace concerns), the eruption of public unrest in response to austerity programs in this period is quite explicitly not tied to unions, but rather to more general urban unrest by citizens dissatisfied with rising prices on basic goods.

At this point, Manley found himself caught between an inflexible international regime demanding further reforms in order to retain access to international capital, and a fractious and restive body of (particularly urban) citizens willing to take to the streets over pricing policies demanded by the IMF. Especially following failure of the IMF tests of late 1979, and perceiving the government as unable to enforce the austerity measures required, in February of 1980 Manley announced a new set of elections, framing them explicitly as a referendum on the "fundamental choice between different economic strategies."[36] Sadly, given an already restive population, and with the continued rise of partisan threats as an important electoral strategy, the result of renewed political struggle was an orgy of violence. I reproduce here at length Stephens and Stephens (1986, 238)'s account:

> The announcement of early elections in February 1980, then, signaled the beginning of a veritable campaign of violence and terror. People in the ghetto were terrorized by gunmen and arson, the Eventide home for the aged burned down, costing 153 lives (G, 21 May 1980), dances of both political parties were invaded and people killed (G, 21 April and 11 May 1980), party activists killed in their sleep (G, 14 July 1980), and more. Violence started to affect all areas of life; public utilities and services, particularly in Kingston, suffered from disruptions and staff anxiety over surrounding violence. Buses had to be re-routed to avoid areas of frequent shootings, etc. The high level of violence meant that not only party supporters but practically anyone could be hurt by it.

[36] Stephens and Stephens (1986, 223).

The feeling of terror in the population at large was further reinforced by the sound of the guns used which included high-powered weapons like the M16 and others.

The 1980 campaign was peculiar in a further respect. The violence affected more top political leaders directly than ever before. Manley and a touring party were fired on (G, 9 October 1980), Shearer was hurt on his way to a rally (G, 28 July 1980), a PNP MP was shot at and his chauffer was beaten to death (G, 14 October 1980), and two-and-a-half weeks before the election, the Minister of State for National Security, Roy McGann, was shot to death in an incident where the police were on the scene. Despite joint statements issued by Manley and Seaga calling for a halt to violence and warning that any prospective candidate involved in violence would be removed from the election campaign (G, 18 July 1980), despite repeated calls for an end to violence from the churches and various other groups in society, and despite the use of curfews, roadblocks and the like by the security forces, the violence did not stop. The total number of murders reported in 1980 was 889, that is, 538 more than in 1979, a number which has to be attributed primarily to politically-motivated violence.

Despite PNP efforts to campaign on promises of restoring public order as well as greater self-reliance for the Jamaican economy, JLP efforts to discredit the government (both in the streets and in the media) took a heavy toll. This was combined with a successful communication effort by the JLP's Seaga to present himself as a man with deep connections to the international financial community, arguing that Jamaica's current crisis was largely the result of frayed international relations due to Manley's communist leanings as well as broader PNP mismanagement of the economy. The electoral outcome was a resounding success for the JLP, which secured a record 59 percent of the vote, ushering in Seaga to the presidency (Huber and Stephens 1992, 64). Secondary accounts of the 1980 election largely agree that the collapse of support for the PNP derived from both a withdrawal of working class base deprived of access to government resources (Edie 1989, 20), as well as a real loss of legitimacy for an incumbent government that seemed unable to contain the spiral of partisan violence.[37] The election served as a clear example of a democratically elected incumbent that faced direct electoral consequences due to its attempts at implementing economic reform, leading Huber and Stephens (1992, 75) to go so far as to argue that "while it would be an exaggeration to say that principled application of structural adjustment prescriptions is incompatible with democracy, it would appear that the pursuit of such a policy is incompatible with getting re-elected in a democracy."

5.4.4 The Seaga Presidency, 1980–1989

While Seaga had campaigned on a neoliberal reorientation for the Jamaican state, his message was largely interpreted by the voting population not as an

---

[37] For example, drawing on survey data from the period, Stephens and Stephens (1986, 246–247) emphasize that the economy was the number one issue for voters, followed by concerns over violence as the number two issue.

intention to completely withdraw the state from welfare provision. Instead, Seaga's popularity derived in large part from public perceptions that JLP "normalization" of relations with western states would allow the resumption of inflows of foreign capital which would lead to reduced need for government austerity. The ambiguity of the JLP's true reform intentions is highlighted by several secondary sources;[38] while Seaga frequently professed an interest in free market reforms in conversations with international actors such as the IMF, the path of government policy at the beginning of his term followed a somewhat different course.

Thus, while the JLP did impose a series of "reforms" to the Jamaican economy beginning in 1981, none of these primarily involved actual reduction of state involvement in the economy, other than deregulation of import restrictions. Pitched as an attempt to jump-start economic growth by increasing import competition, the initial three-year IMF program agreed to in 1981 did not contain, for example, explicit requirements for wage restraint or details on full decontrol of prices. As noted by Huber and Stephens (1992, 19), in the first year of the new program, "two privatizations were executed, one for a food processing firm, the other for an airline catering company. Both were small enterprises, and the gross proceeds from the two privatizations was only US$1.7m. In the second year of the program, the government acquired an oil refinery from Exxon for US$55m. No further divestments occurred for five years, during which time the government also acquired a sugar estate, a shopping complex, and a rice farm (Stephens and Stephens 1986). Therefore, after the first six years of privatizations, the public sector owned substantially more productive capacity than it did at the start of the program."

Beyond concern by several executive directors at the IMF of the lack of explicit reform demands in several fiscally costly areas, there were also complaints over the slow pace of reform expected in the first year, which was predicted to lead to a large balance of payments and fiscal imbalance for several years, making Jamaica dependent upon continued large inflows of foreign finance.[39] As expected, "with the IMF seal of approval the Seaga government managed to achieve massive borrowing and refinancing targets in its first two years in office. Jamaica's foreign debt increased from an estimated US$1.3bn at the end of 1980 to US$3.1bn (including outstanding debt service) at the end of 1983" (Stephens and Stephens 1986, 255). Beyond this expansion of borrowing, Jamaica also benefited from a geopolitical alignment with the Reagan administration's push for a program to generate an "anti-communist alliance in the region. These ideas were later worked out into the formulation known as the Caribbean Basin Initiative (CBI). Total US government aid to

[38] E.g., Handa and King (1997, 920).
[39] One executive director even argued that renegotiations with international lenders had led to a sense of euphoria regarding Jamaica, which suggests that ideological reorientation under Seaga won Jamaica international support for a program that did not actually touch the most politically sensitive policies (IMF 1981e, 4).

Jamaica during the first year of the Seaga administration climbed from slightly more than US$20 million in 1980 to over US$200 million by the end of 1981" (Edie 1989, 22).

By April of 1982, meetings with the IMF signaled some sense of progress in the first year of the new program, but concern still remained among a number of executive directors that the pace of reforms was too slow, particularly since the Jamaican budget deficit was expected to still be around 10 percent by the end of the program, clearly an unacceptably high level.[40] Lacking further consolidation of the government budget balance, shortfalls were still expected to be financed by (largely concessional) international support; at one point in the meeting, a staff member noted (rather prophetically) that, were this support to fail, Jamaica would be forced to engage in rapid reforms that the current program was trying to avoid. As such, executive directors began to push more heavily for wage restraint and subsidy reductions as important for further fiscal consolidation.[41] Responding to these calls for more direct reduction of government deficit spending, the Jamaican representative to the IMF justified a slower pace of reforms by emphasizing that, "[i]n an economy in which the unemployment rate was running at 25 percent, there were some social constraints that limited the authorities' freedom of action. Similarly, there were social constraints on the degree to which the agricultural sector could be made more efficient. Adjustment measures that caused more unemployment in the short term might not in fact prove tolerable."[42] Assuming that these "social constraints" included heightened sensitivity to mass violence, the defense of the Jamaican authorities at the time explicitly linked an inability to reform agricultural production to concerns about unemployment and its "intolerable" repercussions.

Having witnessed the deleterious consequences for the Jamaican economy of attempts at "shock therapy" at the end of the Manley administration, it is understandable that policymakers at the time might have preferred more gradual reforms that might have been consistent with renewed economic progress, even if this required additional international financial support to sustain (given the lack of broader fiscal reforms by the government). In addition, given the relatively easy access to private market lending for developing countries that had ballooned over the 1970s, expectations that such access would continue to be forthcoming might not have seemed a crazy prospect at the time. Unfortunately, in hindsight the timing of these plans could not have been worse, given the impending shockwave to the international financial system that was to arise from the Mexican sovereign default late in 1982.

By early 1983, private international tolerance for lending to developing countries had largely collapsed. In January, the foreign exchange situation had become so dire in Jamaica that Seaga was forced to establish a two-tier exchange rate program, despite repeated concern by the IMF over the distor-

[40] IMF (1982).   [41] IMF (1982, 18).   [42] IMF (1982, 23).

tionary consequences of such a multiple-rate policy (Stephens and Stephens 1986, 256). Of central relevance to my own emphasis on the political sensitivity of food prices in contentious democracies, it is important to note that the "official" stronger exchange rate was reserved for a small number of critical functions, which included government debt servicing as well as imports of food and oil, suggesting that these were high political priorities for the government. Of course, the consequence of this overvaluation of the Jamaican dollar was to heighten the balance of payments issues that the government faced by further weakening the competitiveness of Jamaican exports.

When the price of many goods not on the official rate began to increase due to devaluation pressures on the second exchange tier, the government – facing pressure from unions over declining purchasing power for their workers – also responded via a program of wage expansion. In explaining the causes of this policy, the IMF was remarkably direct in attributing this to political pressure, noting that "the labor union movement in Jamaica was relatively strong. There were two large federations, each linked with one of the two major political parties, and it was difficult for any government to exercise strong leadership in wage negotiation. If a government tried to restrain wages, workers tended to shift their allegiance to the union supporting the political opposition, thereby eroding the political base of the government in power."[43] As expected by my formal theory in Chapter 2, when particular social groups are capable of swinging large blocs of voters in response to unfavorable policy, reform of the programs such groups favor should prove difficult. Yet, beyond this electoral inability to reform union wages, the Jamaican representative to the IMF again emphasized a secondary set of nonelectoral concerns over reform progress, stating that the "high rate of unemployment in Jamaica as a whole and in Kingston in particular, where many unemployed persons tended to congregate, was creating social tensions and was clearly a cause for concern ... The implementation of stringent adjustment measures was certainly difficult in an economy characterized by considerable unemployment."[44] Facing both the prospect of electoral defection and renewed urban violence, the Seaga regime was clearly hesitant to engage in more wide-ranging reforms to those programs seen as beneficial to core political supporters.

The combination of a dual exchange rate policy and wage expansion only increased the difficulty of successful implementation of the IMF program. The end result, as described by Payne (1988, 1225), was that "[t]he moment of failure came in March 1983 when the deficit reached the figure of US$150 million: the Fund promptly suspended further disbursements and Seaga had no alternative but to plead for a waiver. In order to impress the IMF, he introduced a series of austerity measures which included new taxes, public spending cuts, reduced foreign exchange allocations for imports and the shift of many more items to the more expensive parallel market rate ... The IMF generously

[43] IMF (1983a, 20).   [44] IMF (1983a, 22).

granted the waiver, the World Bank produced two more loans, and the US government offered US$25 million in emergency balance-of-payments assistance as well as agreeing to make a further purchase of bauxite for its strategic reserve."

Despite these initial waivers on project nonperformance, by late 1983 the IMF made unification of the dual exchange rates (and the implied devaluation that would result) a condition for provision of new standby credits. As discussed by Payne (1988, 1226), as conditions continued to deteriorate the IMF increasingly began to stiffen its demands for concrete evidence of reforms. This led to the announcement by the JLP in November 1983 that it was unifying the official and parallel exchange rates for the Jamaican dollar, and pegging it to the US dollar at a rate of J$3.15, which corresponded to an approximate 40 percent devaluation for any item that had been traded at the official rate (Payne 1988, 1226).

Crucially, given extreme sensitivity of the government to the potential for rising food prices to trigger unrest, the government responded to this devaluation by introducing explicit subsidies on the cost of food; these subsidies alone were anticipated to cost nearly 1.5 percent of GDP.[45] In effect, the government replaced an implicit subsidy on the cost of food (financed via scarce foreign exchange) for an explicit subsidy (financed via direct budgetary support). As these food imports were conducted largely by the Jamaican state-owned enterprise JCTC, this involved purchase of food goods from foreign producers at the prevailing world market price, then reselling these goods at a loss to domestic (and primarily urban) consumers, precisely as I model in Chapter 2. In fact, in its summary of unscheduled expansions in nonprogram government expenditure, the IMF noted that "[t]otal expenditure exceeded program targets by 10 percent reflecting higher current outlays due mainly to new subsidies and the higher cost of debt servicing."[46]

While this devaluation might have been expected to lead to electoral losses for the JLP, the US invasion of Grenada in late 1983 proved perfect political cover for Seaga to induce a "rally around the flag" effect. With an invasion largely portrayed as necessary to restore the sovereignty of Grenada following a military coup, Seaga played up Jamaican support for the US military action as an important means of helping a regional neighbor facing instability. With public support for the JLP temporarily spiking due to its intervention in the Grenada situation, Seaga availed himself of the opportunity to cement his political control by calling snap elections in December 1983. This came despite an explicit inter-party agreement reached between the JLP and PNP to not call for new elections until certain issues pertaining to the electoral system itself had been resolved (Huber and Stephens 1992, 68). Central among these changes was the generation of a new roll for the electorate, which would have significantly increased the number of young voters who were presumed

---

[45] IMF (1984e, 16).   [46] IMF (1984e, 16).

to be PNP supporters. Worried that, absent these updates to the electorate, the outcome of the election might still favor the JLP, the PNP responded by boycotting the election entirely, arguing that the elections were illegitimate absent agreed-upon reforms to the electoral system. With no major opposition party to face, the response was universal dominance by the JLP, which won all legislative seats (although with very low voter turnout).

Having cleared the decks of any remaining political opposition, and facing continual pressure from international financial actors to make meaningful progress on gaping fiscal and balance of payments gaps, Seaga undertook a major attempt at reforming the Jamaican economy. This included, critically, a reduction in food subsidies by 50 percent, although this policy change was accompanied by a rise in food aid from the US (Edie 1989, 24). While these austerity measures did improve Jamaican balance sheets somewhat, external pressures for continued belt-tightening became even more stringent as the price of bauxite – Jamaica's primary source of foreign reserves – continued to fall, dragging down government revenue even further. This collapse in bauxite prices led one of the major international firms in operation on the island, Alcoa, to announce its intention to shutter its bauxite plant entirely in 1984; absent the tax duties on Alcoan exports, the consequences for Jamaican government revenue were dire. The government managed to convince the corporation to transfer ownership of the plant to the government, which would take over operations and ensure that the doors remained open. While hailed as a political victory of sorts, it is important to remember that Alcoa had taken this action in order to avoid additional profit losses, which shifted in effect an additional loss-making enterprise onto the government's books.

In the face of mounting budgetary woes, in late 1984 the IMF recommended additional need for government austerity. This included explicit concerns by the IMF of deteriorating budget consequences of subsidized imports of food; one executive director noted that "[a]s for the rest of the public sector, the improvement in the overall balance of the parastatals was encouraging but it had been largely due to cuts in capital expenditure. The operating balance had worsened significantly, as a result of the maintenance of the prices of imported foods at pre-devaluation levels. While the political difficulties were understandable, it was essential that the pressure on the fiscal deficit and on the current account should be reduced; he welcomed the authorities' commitment to phase out subsidies by 1985/86."[47] Under extreme external pressure, the Jamaican government responded by deregulating the price of oil (although, crucially, not food) in January of 1985.

With rising unemployment and weakened purchasing power, the consequences of spiking oil prices was an eruption of unrest. Payne (1988, 1228) captures the central dilemma for the Jamaican government well, arguing that "Seaga's problem was that he had not only to satisfy the IMF's demands but also

[47] IMF (1984d, 41).

to manage the domestic political situation in Jamaica, which by the beginning of 1985 was becoming increasingly tense ... In the circumstances [of devaluation and rising unemployment], riots and protests which followed the gas price increases in January 1985 were, if anything, overdue. Even so, the government was shaken by the extent of the anger obviously felt by ordinary working-class Jamaicans at its economic policies." This outpouring of mass unrest was again sparked in June, after the government again attempted to raise fuel prices under fierce external pressure.

Facing the real prospect of sustained societal violence as a result of austerity measures demanded by the IMF, Seaga ultimately concluded that the political consequences of reform were too high, as emphasized explicitly in Huber and Stephens (1992, 70)'s account: "the popular protests of 1985 and the failure of the September 1985 IMF test prompted Seaga to change his policies. In presenting the 1986–1987 budget, he publicly rejected IMF prescriptions and instead announced that there would be no further devaluation, that the prices of some essential goods would be lowered, that price controls would be reinstated on a temporary basis, that interest rates would be lowered, and that government funds would be allocated for road construction." In short, caught between the demands of the international financial community and the specter of mass violence in the streets of Kingston, Seaga chose to renege on the policy prescriptions necessary to keep Jamaica current on its repayment obligations, including specific emphasis on the need to keep basic costs constrained. This framing was not hidden behind closed doors; indeed, as noted in Walton, Shefner, and Seddon (1994, 97–98), "Mr. Seaga concluded 'We have gone to the maximum as far as the social costs of devaluation are concerned.' Before long, the Prime Minister was echoing the sentiments of his predecessor and principal antagonist, Michael Manley of the PNP, when Seaga proclaimed 'I don't intend to let [the IMF] add Jamaica to their tombstone of failures.'" This linkage between domestic political survival and the pressures to abstain from austerity is captured perhaps most directly by Wilson (1996, 71), who notes that "[t]he JLP government, then, implemented some neoliberal reforms, but chose to depart from the reforms when the political cost increased and jeopardized its political survival strategy. For example, in response to devaluations and austerity measures introduced in late 1984 and early 1985, social unrest increased ... Seaga, then, although committed to significantly reducing the role of the state and increasing the role of market forces in the allocation of resources, had to back off from some of his economic reforms for political survival reasons."

In addition to the reinstatement of price controls, in October 1985 – facing rapid devaluation on the Jamaican dollar – the government reintervened in the foreign exchange market to prop up the value of the currency. Internal discussion at the IMF notes that this was done explicitly in the fear that further price effects on food and oil would lead to the eruption of additional civil unrest. Indeed, the summary of the situation at the time in Jamaica by the IMF's own staff read as follows: "[a]s Directors were aware, increases in gasoline prices implemented in mid-January had triggered social disturbances that had adversely affected the tourist season and had led to a considerable reluctance by the authorities to push forward rapidly with the remaining adjustments, which had covered mostly basic food commodities."[48] That this suggested a willingness on the part of the authorities to forestall program reforms – even to the point of default – out of fear of revolt is made directly apparent by the fact that in this same month, Jamaica not only continued to accumulate arrears on its sovereign debt, but engaged in the most damning of sins in the international financial community: Default on IMF borrowing. As noted by Payne (1988, 1231–1232), "[t]hese were high stakes, since the running-up of arrears with the IMF unquestionably meant a moratorium on any other new loans or debt rescheduling agreements."

Critically, across the secondary accounts of default highlighted here, and supported by primary documentation of discussions at the IMF itself, the concerns of the government over reforms centered around the dangers posed by unrest; while such unrest might likely have had subsequent electoral consequences,[49] as presidential elections were not slated for several more years, the most direct concern about the consequences of austerity were framed in terms of the danger of revolt itself, not simply in terms of loss of future voters. This pressure against reform to costly domestic policies, including explicit reference to sensitive food subsidies, formed a core component of the Jamaican government's decision to default on its external debt in late 1985 and throughout 1986, precisely as I would expect in an urban-biased contentious democracy.

5.5 DISCUSSION

In consolidated democracies where winning votes is all that matters, I expect rural electoral mobilization advantages to suggest that, on average, democratic rulers should favor farming blocs with costly support policies that may become difficult to reform during times of fiscal crisis. The Costa Rican case helps highlight precisely these dynamics, despite better capacity at reforming other programs, even to the point of driving default on international financial obligations. Yet violence still plays a role in many democracies today. While often initially intended for electoral aims, this also likely raises fears among incumbents of the possibility that more widespread unrest could lead to social instability. In such scenarios, concerns about minimizing urban unrest should suggest that incumbent rulers may place greater emphasis on urban interests, particularly in minimizing the cost of food. Yet, if such programs are also accompanied by food imports, the fiscal burden of such policies can be difficult to unwind without leading to spiking food prices and an outpouring of unrest. The Jamaican case – where partisan gangs were often

[48] IMF (1985g). [49] Indeed, regional elections in 1986 resulted in heavy losses for the JLP.

employed to stir up violence against electoral opponents – fits this scenario almost perfectly. Yet, after cheap food policies were called out explicitly by the IMF as contributing to budget troubles, the Jamaican government ultimately defaulted not only on its private creditors, but on the IMF itself, rather than face additional unrest as a result of attempts to increase the price of food.

6

Urban–Rural Pressures across Regime Types
The Case of Turkey

> At least one-third of the votes belong to the farmers in Turkey. This high percentage is quite critical for the politicians. The potential power of the farm vote in Turkey seems obvious. The electoral cycle seems to largely determine the timing of decisions related to the granting of farm subsidies.
> A. Halis Akder (2007) "Policy formation in the process of implementing agricultural reform in Turkey"

> The bulk of the 1980–1985 program coincided with transitional military rule in Turkey, such rule having been instigated essentially on non-economic grounds...the prevailing restrictions on political participation and contestation were clearly instrumental in providing the technocrats with the requisite autonomy to introduce a wide range of radical reforms and the ability to withstand the distributional consequences.
> Merih Celasun and Dani Rodrik (1989) "Debt, adjustment, and growth: Turkey"

6.1 INTRODUCTION

In the preceding several chapters, I have demonstrated that, on average, more rural democracies are more likely to renege on their international borrowing obligations, whereas more urban autocracies are more likely to default. Chapters 4 and 5 demonstrate, through detailed historical cases, that the importance of urban or rural bases of support to autocratic or democratic leaders has been associated with different biases in food policy; these food policies have also led to fiscal trouble for regimes reliant on external markets. The cases I discuss vary in terms of the relative importance of rural voters versus urban protesters in ways that are in concert with my theoretical predictions. Yet, as is true with nearly all historical comparisons across countries, the cases may vary as well along other potentially important dimensions for which I cannot control directly. In many ways, the ideal test of my theoretical predictions over the relative importance of urban or rural citizens to incumbent survival would be to consider the same leader in the same country, with all other potential explanations held constant, competing for power under democratic or autocratic rule. Of course, such cases are likely to be extremely rare historically.

Fortuitously, the case of Turkey in the late 1970s and 1980s offers exactly this sort of "natural experiment": Following a period of military intervention, competitive elections were restored in the country. In a rare historical accident, the man who served as Minister of Finance under military rule – Turgut Ozal – also ran for Prime Minister following the restoration of elections. Of particular importance to my theory linking urban–rural biases to varying food price policies, Ozal was directly in control of overseeing reforms to agricultural subsidies while working for the military, and so had a public record of his views about the costs associated with such programs. However, once forced to compete in elections, Ozal learned a crucial rule of electoral survival in developing democracies like Turkey: It is difficult to win an election without rural support, and one of the most straightforward ways to earn the support of farmers is through favorable agricultural pricing policies. Thus, the Turkish case provides an ideal "within-case" example of variation in the institutions of executive survival that I argue crucially structure the relative importance of urban and rural actors. If my theory is correct, under periods of electoral competition farm support programs should be an important campaign tool that is fiscally burdensome when paired with agricultural overproduction. Conversely, when military officers run the country without the need for electoral support, the importance of such farm support programs should be radically diminished. By considering the approach of the same individual leader, in the same country at approximately the same time, I hold fixed nearly all of the alternative sets of explanations that could pollute the interpretation I provide of earlier historical cases, and investigate directly the relationship between regime institutions, urban–rural biases, and the resultant pressures for sovereign default that arise from attempting to appease crucial political supporters.

In this chapter, I provide a detailed discussion of sovereign default in Turkey, demonstrating that the rising fiscal burden of agricultural subsidies was identified as a primary concern in original internal IMF documents from the time, and that the inability of democratically elected governments in Turkey to reduce these rural-biased policies arose precisely in an electoral environment in which losing the rural vote was viewed as politically suicidal. In addition, I show that, following default under democratic rule, a military intervention was successful in reducing or removing these agricultural support policies, revealing that the political influence of rural voters in Turkey was highly contingent on regime characteristics of executive replacement. Finally, I also provide historical accounts that document that an identical ruling incumbent – who had previously opposed agricultural support prices while backed by the military – subsequently restored fiscally costly farmer subsidies once competitive elections were reintroduced to Turkish politics.

6.2 CASE SELECTION

For investigating a theory of the relative political influence of urban and rural groups under different political regimes, few countries could be of greater interest than Turkey. Turkey's modern political history has seen extended spells of democratic rule punctuated by several military interventions. In addition, it is a country where the needs of rapidly developing urban industries have often been pitted against a large agricultural sector responsible for employing much of the population. And finally, it has been confronted with the need for structural adjustment in the face of fiscal crisis several times. Thus, Turkey is an excellent case for testing the relationship between rural electoral support and democratic default that I highlight as being an important driver of such decisions, as well as the changing political importance of such farm support programs under nonelectoral rule. In what follows, after briefly describing Turkey's initial experience with democratic elections, I detail Turkish experiences with adjustment and fiscal crises over the past 35 years, beginning with the build up to the major crisis experienced by the economy during the late 1970s and then turning to its subsequent financial meltdown in 2000–2001.

6.3 INITIAL TRANSITION TO DEMOCRACY

In response to growing sentiment against single-party states that swept the globe in the aftermath of World War II, the leader of Turkey's ruling Republican People's Party (RPP), Ismet Inonu, encouraged the development of opposition political parties beginning in 1946. This culminated in the first democratic change of power in Turkey in 1950 when the Democrat Party (DP) rode a tidal wave of populist support into office. The source of this electoral support was clear: As noted in the summary of this period by Celasun and Rodrik (1989, 620), the "mass basis of the DP was rural conservatives," which was secured in large part through heavy subsidization of agricultural production, often at great fiscal cost to the state. The DP was able to maintain this successful electoral strategy for nearly a decade, although rising macroeconomic distortions from government agricultural purchasing schemes, coupled with policies meant to discriminate against an opposing urban elite, eventually led to military intervention and the removal of the DP from power. While brief, this autocratic interlude was motivated by a desire to introduce constitutional limits on the ability of political parties in Turkey to pander so heavily to the electorally crucial rural majority. In discussing this initial period of democratic rule, Celasun and Rodrik (1989, 621) highlights explicitly the rural–urban dimension as a critical divide in Turkish politics:

> To the students of Turkey's recent history, a balanced reassessment of the Democratic Party administrations represents, in our view, a continuing research challenge. On the one hand, DP rule in the 1950s stimulated broader political participation and improved the political status of the rural population. On the other hand, the DP governments became increasingly repressive in the face of mounting economic difficulties and rising political dissent by the urban elite. The end result was a tragic one for the top party leaders and came in the form of a complete military takeover in May 1960. Military rule was transitional and ended quickly after the adoption of a socially progressive constitution in 1961, which provided more checks and balances in the overall political process.

Thus, in its first flirtations with electoral competition, distortionary agricultural subsidies quickly emerged as a powerful tool to win rural support in Turkey. Yet did the subsequent attempt by the military to limit populist practices reduce this sort of rural-biased electoral strategy? Did costly agricultural support policies reemerge, and if so, were democratically elected governments willing to remove them in times of fiscal crisis?

6.4 BUILD-UP TO THE FIRST CRISIS

By the 1960s, Turkey began to experience sporadic current account and balance of payments problems that would continue to trouble it periodically for the next forty years. As in many developing countries, such problems usually necessitated turning to the IMF for a standby arrangement to make available temporary funds intended to help Turkey bridge financing gaps during times of difficulty. The Turkish government initially tried to present its troubles as due primarily to world market forces outside of its control; however, over time it became increasingly clear that Turkey faced serious structural imbalances.

While the workings of many international organizations often remain hidden behind doors closed to researchers, declassified internal documents from the IMF help make clear precisely what the Fund thought about the situation in Turkey. For example, in the minutes from an executive board discussion at the IMF in 1965 of a recent request by Turkey for a new stand-by agreement, one of the executive directors argued that "the Turkish problem at present was less that of establishing and maintaining monetary stability," as had been argued by the Turkish authorities, "and more of remedying the structural weaknesses" of the Turkish economy.[1] The executive director went on to elaborate on some of the specific details of the policies that were considered to be troubling: "[I]n particular, the taxation of agriculture was still deficient, and tax collection generally presented a serious problem. Another structural weakness was the high dependence of TOPRAK (the Soil Products Marketing

[1] IMF (1965a, 10).

6.4 Build-Up to the First Crisis

Organization) and the State Economic Enterprises and the Monopolies Administration on direct financial assistance from the Central Bank Government. This was partly a result of a shortage of working capital, but was also partly connected with certain price policies, which should be reconsidered."[2]

The Soil Products Marketing Organization (TOPRAK) was an arm of the central government responsible for purchasing, at established prices, specified agricultural products from rural Turkish farmers; this institution matches nearly perfectly with the formalized structure of a democratic government capable of increasing agricultural prices through producer subsidies that I describe in Chapter 2. In addition to TOPRAK, there also existed a number of other marketing institutions charged with a similar role in securing rural production at government-mandated prices, including several State Economic Enterprises (SEEs) as well as Monopoly Administrations. Thus, when forced to seek external financing in 1965, Turkey was specifically reprimanded by an executive director of the IMF for pursuing a costly project of agricultural price supports. Nor was this dissatisfaction with the agricultural pricing policies of the Turkish government a unique position – statements by the next three executive directors in the meeting all return to a similar critique of the way that rural producer price supports were funded by central government funds.[3]

Upon closer consideration of the actual text of the letter of intent sent by Turkey to the IMF explaining its need for additional financing, it is made apparent that (in describing strains on the Treasury from the previous year) "[i]n 1964 owing to the record 1963 crops it was necessary to make special adjustments to the amount of Central Bank credit which the Soil Products Marketing Organization (TOPRAK) could use to help finance its purchases of domestically grown cereals."[4] Additionally, in a proposal submitted later in 1965 to modify the standby agreement with Turkey discussed earlier, Turkish authorities again explained their violation of previous terms by noting that the "increase from LT 250 million to LT 450 million requested in the letter dated June 8, 1965 ... is necessary to finance a larger volume of purchases entailed by a much better crop. In a decree of June 10, 1965 the Council of Ministers raised the buying price of cereals by 6–10 percent."[5] One of the main justifications offered by Turkey for needing external financing was the strain placed on the central government's budget by purchases of exceptionally large cereal crops.

Yet, why should these purchases have merited a loss to the government at all? Shouldn't it simply have been able to resell these commodities, thereby reducing

---

[2] IMF (1965a, 10).
[3] Beyond the statements by Mr. Lieftinck on the previous page, see subsequent similar worries expressed by Mr. Kirbyshire (11–12), Mr. Handfield-Jones (13), and the director of the Exchange Restrictions Department (14).
[4] IMF (1965c, 5).
[5] See IMF (1965b, 4). Note that this letter also highlights additional financial pressures arising from subsidized purchases of sugar and tobacco (see 5).

any fiscal impact of such producer support policies? As I discuss in Chapter 2, the cost of such a policy should come only when the government is unable to resell these goods, or is forced to do so for less than the price it paid. In fact, as made clear in a letter from Turkey's Minister of Finance to the IMF in June of 1965, this was precisely the position in which TOPRAK found itself. While it expected to need LT 795 million for crop purchases and operating expenses, it expected to recoup only about a quarter of this (LT 215 million) from domestic sales, and amazingly lists expected revenue from exports at a mere LT 1 million!

Later reports make clear that this lack of crop exports was a direct result of the producer price paid by the government being so high as to make Turkish grains noncompetitive on the world market.[6] This led to a build-up in Turkish grain stocks that were only reduced in subsequent years when the mandated selling price for exports was lowered to become closer to the going world market price. Of course, by lowering the selling price below that which was paid to purchase this agricultural produce, the government incurred an additional fiscal loss. Thus, even accounting for subsidies from the Treasury, TOPRAK's crop purchasing scheme was expected to result in a loss of nearly LT 500 million.

However, while internal IMF documents make clear that the executive directors were unhappy with this arrangement, at the end of the day the Fund still approved the SBA for Turkey, arguing that "the increases in the two limits mentioned above, in the staff's view, are warranted in the particular circumstances of the Soil Products Marketing Organization."[7] Perhaps this case of unexpectedly large agricultural harvests placing undue stress on government finances was a one-off situation. Nor did this case lead to an extended fiscal crisis for Turkey – this was not to come until the late 1970s.

6.5 THE CRISIS OF 1978–1979

By the time Turkey turned to the IMF for emergency financing in 1978, it was clear that the Turkish economy was in a state of serious fiscal disequilibrium.[8] I expect democratic rulers reliant on agricultural price subsidies for political support to be particularly unwilling to remove these subsidies in the face

---

[6] See, for example, discussion of build up in export stocks due to supra-market pricing in Turkey in IMF (1979d, 49).

[7] IMF (1965b, 7).

[8] The sources of this fiscal crisis emphasized in the secondary literature are many, including rising energy prices, high dollar interest rates, a downswing in volumes of trade, as well as the "Convertible Lira Deposit Scheme" (CTLD) in which the Turkish government guaranteed foreign investors the value of funds deposited in Turkish domestic banks at a time when interest rates in Turkey were far above LIBOR. While initially hailed as a success for attracting large flows of foreign capital into domestic financial institutions, when these accounts became due one or two years later, this constituted an additional fiscal burden on the Central Bank as the foreign funds quickly exited the country.

6.5 The Crisis of 1978-1979

of fiscal crisis. Given the centrality of agricultural subsidies in general, and producer price supports in particular, to my theory of democratic default, a brief discussion of the structure of Turkish agricultural policy is in order. Thankfully, one year prior to the eruption of economic crisis in 1978, the IMF prepared for the GATT background material on the state of the Turkish economy, including detailed discussion of agricultural policy, which I quote at length given its relevance:

> In Turkey agricultural support prices are set for a number of products each year. Government agencies and sales cooperatives are obliged to purchase at the officially set support price any amount of these agricultural products offered to them by the farmers. The Government provides funds for the support purchases through the Central Bank, and absorbs any losses incurred by the intervening agencies in purchasing, storing, and selling the commodities in question. This system, which aims at preventing large fluctuations in agricultural incomes from year to year, is often a burden on public finances, particularly at times when unrealistic pricing vis-à-vis developments in international markets leads to export bottlenecks. In 1977 support prices were adjusted marginally...especially for important agricultural commodities such as wheat and cotton, which were also export items. This was done with the purpose of not aggravating the discrepancies between domestic and foreign prices for these products, since prices of wheat and cotton had exceeded world market prices since late 1976.[9]

The Turkish case in the lead-up to its crisis in 1978 fits the theoretical model I detail earlier almost perfectly: It was a democracy that made costly government interventions into agricultural producer prices, often setting these above the world price. In addition, this policy represented a drain on public coffers specifically when these products were prominent export items, precisely as predicted by my formal model. Yet perhaps these interventions were small in scale, or not considered to be particularly distorting to the broader macroeconomy?

In addressing this concern, the Turkish letter of intent to the IMF in 1978 is of particular interest. It begins by noting that "[t]he purpose of the stand-by arrangement is to support the policies that have been and are to be adopted by the Government of Turkey to strengthen to balance of payments position ... The key element of the adjustment program is to reduce the borrowing requirement of the public sector."[10] This sort of introduction is standard for countries turning to the IMF while facing fiscal troubles – it says that the country understands that imbalances that have placed it in jeopardy are generally related to public sector overspending. What is of particular importance, however, are the suggestions that the letter offers for ways that the government can address these imbalances. In this case, the *very first* specific policy recommendation is that "[i]t is the intention of the Government to establish support prices for agricultural export commodities at levels consistent with world prices"; the second policy proposal notes that "[t]he Government has traditionally provided subsidies through the consolidated budget. The Government realizes that a

---

[9] IMF (1977a, 9).   [10] IMF (1978b, 1).

sustainable policy for the future requires SEEs to adjust prices and fees ... to ensure that planned public sector investment can be carried out without undue recourse being made to the Central Bank."[11] In other words, the first two policy proposals made by the government, in attempting to address its fiscal imbalances, both relate to government intervention in pricing policies, especially in the agricultural market.

This proposal was sufficient to win IMF backing of a stand-by arrangement in early 1978. Yet, by the middle of the year, it was clear that the Turkish government was unable to follow through on a number of the conditions set as terms for emergency financing, and it was forced to request a waiver of several performance criteria. In evaluating this request, the IMF noted that despite some progress in addressing fiscal imbalances, "the immediate prospect is for erosion in some areas. The Government has made efforts to avoid excessive increases in agricultural support prices ... As a result, the fiscal position is likely to deteriorate and the objective stated in the Letter of Intent ... is not now attainable."[12] Note, in particular, that instead of *lowering* agricultural price supports, Turkish authorities had managed merely to limit "excessive increases"; indeed, across the fourteen agricultural commodities with support prices reported to the IMF in this year, thirteen saw price increases ranging from 13 percent in the case of wheat to 45 percent in the case of raisins, at an estimated cost to the budget from support purchases of LT 67.6 billion.[13] In a fiscal environment that demanded reducing the budgetary imbalance of these subsidization policies, this clearly did not comport with the government's stated aims of limiting the burden of state economic enterprises.

While the IMF was willing to allow suspension of the performance criteria requested in September, by December compliance had deteriorated so much that "the IMF's monitors in Turkey reported that the Turks were not complying to the conditions attached to its standby credit, and suspended further disbursements in the absence of more stringent austerity measures ... While the amount of IMF funds withheld was not a critical element in Turkey's overall restructuring, the Fund's judgment that Turkey's adjustment program was not sufficient had a crucial impact on OECD creditors, who refused to furnish the Turks with new loans if a second IMF adjustment package was not approved" (Carvounis 1984, 91). Unable to apply the structural adjustments stipulated as conditions to further emergency funding, the IMF withdrew its support from Turkey, effectively cutting off all other sources of outside finance and moving Turkey into default.

6.6 RURAL ELECTORAL ADVANTAGES

What explains this inability to adjust, especially on costly agricultural subsidies, by the Turkish government? On this point the secondary literature is largely

[11] IMF (1978b, 1).   [12] IMF (1978a, 8).   [13] IMF (1979d, 25).

6.6 Rural Electoral Advantages

in agreement: Operating in an extremely fragmented political environment, Turkish politicians were unwilling to suffer the electoral consequences of alienating their voter base. Previous parliamentary elections in 1973 had resulted in a razor-thin margin of victory for the Republican People's Party over the Justice Party of 33 percent to 30 percent; an initial coalition government with the minority National Salvation Party lasted a mere ten months before being reconstituted around an alliance of strange bedfellows between the RPP and DP.

Reluctance to engage in structural reforms in this uncertain political environment was apparent at the outset of negotiations in 1977, as highlighted in Carvounis (1984, 91): "the Turkish government met with IMF officials to arrange a conditional emergency loan to assist it in meeting balance of payments deficits. With DP and the RPP maintaining a shaky hold on the Turkish government, the discussions between the Turks and the Fund 'started off with governmental reluctance to make policy changes on the scale the Fund considered necessary.'" Given heavy fragmentation of the governing coalition, any loss of voter support was likely to spell electoral doom. Precisely as my theory would expect under such circumstances, "reduction in government spending was only half-hearted ... The governments in power were too cautious of political support to administer radical shock treatment and too divided to implement any feasible alternative" (Celasun and Rodrik 1989, 656).

An electoral reshuffling in mid-1977 found the ruling Republican People's Party still with a majority of seats but shy of an outright parliamentary majority; forming a government involved bringing a new party member – the Justice Party (JP) – into the governing coalition. However, a core part of the JP's electoral base was rural landowning interests, and removal of agricultural support prices would have been seen as a betrayal of this crucial constituency. In summarizing the failure of democratically elected leaders to implement necessary structural reforms, Carvounis (1984, 95) notes that, with "the Turkish polity and parliament split down the middle, neither the RPP nor the JP was able to reduce growth rates or current consumption without fear of undermining their popular support, and both solved the problem by borrowing abroad. As debt service on these loans became more burdensome, neither [leader of the two political parties] ever enjoyed sufficient parliamentary support to put through unpopular stabilization measures." Thus, in a fragmented political environment in which loss of key voters spelled almost certain loss of office, no party was willing to enact the structural reforms seen as necessary to remain constant on Turkey's foreign borrowing. Yet these accounts merely highlight that politicians were unwilling to hurt their support base generally – this does not prove that agricultural support was afforded any special electoral position.

In this regard, Akder (2007, 522)'s description of the electoral environment in Turkey is particularly straightforward: "[a]t least one-third of the votes belong to the farmers in Turkey. This high percentage is quite critical for the politicians. The potential power of the farm vote in Turkey seems obvious.

The electoral cycle seems to largely determine the timing of decisions related to the granting of farm subsidies." Turkey resembles many other developing democracies in having a demographic distribution of the population that favors rural farmers numerically – it is hard to win elections without the support of at least a third of the overall population. Beyond this simple mathematical edge, however, agricultural interests enjoy particular advantages in mobilizing votes over farm policies as well.

At an institutional level, the infrastructural requirements of enacting government purchases of agricultural produce necessitated the construction of many chambers of agriculture around the country. An account by the OECD (2011, 43) notes that these "[c]hambers of agriculture, through which the government's consultations and contacts with different professions are conducted, have a broad mandate, which includes providing farmers with vocational services and representation, and assisting the government in the formulation and implementation of agricultural policies." The report continues by noting that there "are over 700 chambers of agriculture in Turkey, with a total membership of approximately 5 million." By providing rural farmers a focal location for their economic activity that is explicitly tied to government, these chambers help facilitate precisely the sort of electoral mobilization advantages discussed in my theory in Chapter 2: They bring farmers together as an economic class, and help link their well-being as a class directly to government-provided benefits. In doing so, they mobilize large blocs of farmers in response to rural-biased agricultural policies.

In accordance with theories of the "swingness" of rural voters, there do not appear to be similar electoral mobilization advantages for voters that might be opposed to high farm prices. Indeed, Akder (2007, 521) goes so far as to claim that "[c]onsumer (and taxpayer) interests are also weakly organized ... The consumers, in return, are not particularly critical about the high support price of agriculture, even if it results in higher food and fiber prices." This seemingly incoherent set of preferences is reconciled by arguing that the "urban population does not consider itself just as consumer of food but they are concerned about their cousins in the village and politically they do not support necessarily more liberal views that favor more liberalization in agriculture." Not only are (mostly urban) consumers poorly mobilized in opposition to agricultural support, but there exists a social norm of supporting farmers more generally. While certainly external to my theory, this additional source of "rural bias" in democratic policymaking is not necessarily unique to the Turkish case – indeed, the philosophical roots of American democracy are deeply entwined with a Jeffersonian conception of the ideal republic as one made up of independent farming communities. Beyond these structural advantages of rural mobilization, this normative appeal of rural society only serves to further deepen the electoral advantages to be gained from providing farmers with agricultural support: If farming interests are likely to mobilize heavily around the issue, whereas urban consumers are much more dispersed in their preferences over agricultural policy, this suggests precisely the sort of rural electoral mobilization advantage that is demonstrated in my formal theory to be linked to democratic sovereign default.[14]

In explaining the thrust of Turkish agricultural policy, Ilkkaracan and Tunali (2010, 107) provide several motives for continued producer support prices, including food self-sufficiency and containment of urban–rural migration. Yet "an equally important motive was a hard-learned lesson in politics: rural voters with strong ties to land have had a say in election outcomes ever since multiparty politics began." Later analysis of the failure of Turkish structural reform by Moghadam (2005, 14–15) is especially specific on this point: "[a]t the same time, weak governments consisting of multiparty coalitions and facing frequent elections also had the incentive to patronize their electoral supporters and abandon fiscal discipline. In particular, the agricultural sector...had to be repeatedly compensated for electoral advantage." Thus, Turkey in 1978 seems a clear case in which democratically elected rulers, paralyzed by fear of losing key rural electoral support in a highly fragmented environment, were unable to implement reforms in costly agricultural pricing policy as demanded by the IMF, and therefore were forced to default on international loans.

6.7 MILITARY INTERVENTION, 1980–1985

Yet Turkey was able, just a few short years later, to implement several sweeping structural adjustment programs, including removal or substantial reduction of agricultural support prices. What had changed? Most obvious, of course, was a military coup which suspended electoral competition in Turkey beginning in late 1980, and which lasted effectively until freely contested elections were fully reintroduced in 1985. Where democratically elected governments were unable to reform Turkey's system of agricultural subsidization, an autocratic military regime managed to do away with many of the costly and inefficient State Economic Enterprises plaguing the Turkish economy. As suggested by my theory, however, there were a handful of goods in which subsidized prices controlled by the government were retained, "in particular, bread, coal, fertilizer, and sugar," precisely the sorts of goods that would be favored by urban consumers (Kopits 1987, 9).

In their summary of Turkey's "successful" reforms during this period, Celasun and Rodrik (1989, 678–679) ask "whether the 1980–1985 policy episode had any missing element in an important sense. Our answer is an affirmative one, and we suggest that broad political participation and contestation were crucial elements missing in this important national experience."

---

[14] Recent work in Japan by Naoi and Kume (2011) finds a similar lack of consumer opposition to policies that protect agricultural producers, although this paper suggests the effect may have more to do with consumers' projection of job fears onto rural producers rather than an argument based on rural "sympathies" per se.

More specifically, they note that the "bulk of the 1980–1985 program coincided with transitional military rule in Turkey, such rule having been instigated essentially on non-economic grounds [and that] the prevailing restrictions on political participation and contestation were clearly instrumental in providing the technocrats with the requisite autonomy to introduce a wide range of radical reforms and the ability to withstand the distributional consequences." Note, firstly, that this suggests that autocratic elites were able to do away with agricultural transfers because they did not perceive rural actors to be a political threat. This substantiates the distinction developed in earlier chapters that non-democratic leaders should generally favor urban interests – particularly when not facing the need to mobilize electoral supporters – as the capacity for collective revolt in rural areas is low. In addition, the rapid about-face in Turkish agricultural policy following a dramatic change in political institutions again suggests that, while rural actors may be particularly potent electoral agents, this political influence is not universal.

This is made most explicitly clear by considering the evolution of Turkish agricultural policy following reinstitution of competitive elections in 1985. At the time, the sitting Prime Minister in Turkey was Turgut Ozal, a man who as finance minister under the military had promoted and implemented an extremely hawkish budget policy, including explicitly denouncing the distortionary costs of agricultural subsidies. The account in Ilkkaracan and Tunali (2010, 107, emphasis added) of Ozal's response to change in the political institutions dictating executive survival is worth repeating in full:

After decades of [agricultural] protection, the macroeconomic policy reorientation unleashed in 1980 *under the mantle of a military regime* dismantled price supports and introduced the agricultural sector to the whims of the global market. As imported agricultural commodities flooded the market, local agricultural prices fell and aggregate output increased, giving Prime Minister Turgut Ozal an early opportunity to boast of the virtues of the liberal stance he championed. Following the restoration of freely contested elections, however, Ozal discovered that his liberal policies *did not provide the best election platform*. As his second term as Prime Minister came to an end, the third looked more and more elusive. He desperately revived the policies he had vehemently opposed, *in an effort to win back the rural vote*. This ushered in a new era of agricultural supports as his victorious competitors followed suit. According to the OECD, supports to the agricultural sector, which claimed 3.5 percent of GDP in 1988, crept up and reached their peak of 6.7 percent during 1997–1999 ... Agricultural supports *contributed to the large budget deficits* and high inflation that marked the 1990s.

Thus, an identical individual ruler, who had been a fierce critic of agricultural support prices while backed by nondemocratic military rule, changed his position to favor costly agricultural subsidies as soon as democratic competition returned to Turkish politics.

Following restoration of competitive elections, the use of agricultural support prices as a means of earning rural support returned to Turkey with a vengeance. And, as the use of these policies became increasingly ubiquitous,

6.8 Discussion

so too did the fiscal burden. In discussing the resurgence of agricultural state enterprises, the OECD (2011, 43) notes that the "trading losses and capital needs of these organizations were regularly met from public funds. For the years 1991–1995, the average annual duty loss of TMO [grains], TEKEL [tobacco] and TSFAS [sugar], taken together, were USD 622 million, rising to an annual average of over USD 1.7 billion during 1996–2001. In addition, the government began writing off the debt of agricultural SEEs in the mid-1990s. The average annual debt write-off for TMO, TEKEL, TSFAS and CAYKUR during 1996–2001 was USD 550 million, whilst equity injections from the Treasury to agricultural SEEs averaged USD 150 million during the same period." With fiscal losses running into the billions of dollars annually, it was only a matter of time before this had knock-on effects to the macroeconomy.

In a political environment that continued to be characterized by fragmented ruling coalitions incapable of enacting reforms damaging to rural voters, Turkey gradually crept back closer to serious fiscal crisis. The OECD (2011, 10) summarizes clearly the effect that a resurgence in agricultural price supports had on the broader Turkish economy: "[b]esides affecting price formation, weak budget constraints on agricultural SEEs and ASCUs have led to poor financial discipline. Financial losses due to intervention purchasing by ASCUs, the Turkish Grain Board, the State-owned Tobacco Enterprise and the State-owned Sugar enterprise, coupled with borrowing by the SEEs from commercial banks at relatively high interest rates, were key factors in the country's economic turbulence in the 1980s and 1990s." In accordance with my broader theory of the fiscal burdens of rural-biased programs under democracy, the end result of such turbulence came in 2001 as Turkey again approached the brink of financial ruin, and triggered another external sovereign debt crisis.

6.8 DISCUSSION

The case of sovereign default in Turkey helps to highlight the political paralysis that can result in democratic systems characterized by heavy reliance on rural voters to secure electoral success. From its very first flirtations with competitive elections, pandering to rural farmers through the provision of agricultural support policies has proved a strong component of populist platforms. In a country where farming has been the dominant source of employment for much of its modern history, the simple numerical advantages of pandering to rural voters are obvious. Beyond this absolute mathematical edge, rural voters have enjoyed a number of other electoral mobilization advantages, ranging from government marketing boards throughout rural communities serving as a conduit of votes in exchange for policy benefits, to profarmer norms held by urban consumers that limit their ability to organize against higher food prices.

In a political environment where a dominant electoral mandate has been a rarity, Turkish parties have proven reluctant to reform rural support policies, in fear of angering critical rural voters. This has proven particularly important during times of fiscal crisis, when external pressure for reform of supramarket agricultural pricing has been clear and consistent. Indeed, reducing or removing government interference in the agricultural market has often been made an important term in conditional support packages from the international financial institutions, which recognize that farmer subsidies have constituted an increasingly severe fiscal burden for the Turkish government. In spite of this external pressure, and knowing that failure to enact structural reforms would eventually lead to default, democratically elected incumbents have been unwilling to do away with rural support policies. In the end, they have frequently chosen the long-run economic consequences of default over short-run threats to their tenure.

And yet periods of military intervention in Turkish politics help make clear that this rural political influence is linked intimately to existing institutions of executive replacement. When not subject to electoral pressure, the military was able to reform many of the most burdensome agricultural support policies – indeed, it was heralded (for a time) as a poster child of successful reform by the international financial institutions throughout the early 1980s. That the military felt insulated from popular pressures against adjustment helps highlight that citizen political influence does indeed vary across regime settings: While paper stones may turn the tide of democratic politics, if they cannot be exchanged for real stones to throw in autocracies, in the end they may be only so many names on paper, and be stripped of power.

7

Conclusion

Political survival is costly. The promise of foreign borrowing allows spending today that does not require repayment until the distant future; for short-sighted politicians facing pressing political challenges, the temptation to leverage future economic resources is often too great to resist. Access to international debt is therefore a crucial component of politics for the majority of governments around the globe that engage in sovereign borrowing, often excessively so, in some cases bringing their country to the brink of financial ruin. Eventually, as private lenders recognize the growing risk of over-burdened sovereigns, international lending runs dry – and, as countries are forced to bring their spending priorities in line with their revenue capacity, incumbents must engage in the dangerous and difficult task of weighing the political support of one group against another. These times of fiscal crisis can be extremely socially wrenching, as waves of antiausterity protests across the globe in recent years have made clear. When facing these stuggles over fiscal politics, some countries manage to adjust successfully; others prove incapable of doing so, and end up in default on their sovereign debt.

The decision to default is ultimately made by political actors, yet our understanding of specific features likely to drive default have been limited in prior work. In this book, I provide a comprehensive theory linking particular strategies of common citizens to the survival incentives of incumbents in different regime settings. In so doing, I help highlight precisely those areas where reform should be most difficult for politicians and default should be most likely. By focusing on the ways that voting power and mass unrest vary across democracies and non-democracies, I provide in Chapter 2 a unified conceptual framework to explain starkly varying default outcomes across regime types. Importantly, I highlight that different types of political rule bias leaders toward appeasing either urban or rural citizens – while the capacity for unrest in cities makes autocrats more worried about the needs of urban masses, the electoral importance of farming blocs drives democrats to prioritize the rural vote.

In focusing on the urban–rural divide, my theoretical account enjoys wide applicability, as all countries have urban centers and rural hinterlands. In addition, the geographic association of rurality with agricultural production also suggests a natural issue area to explore the economic preferences of differing social groups, focusing around food price politics. In Chapter 3 I demonstrate robust quantitative support for my main claims that urban and food importing autocracies will default more often, whereas rural democracies are more likely to renege on their financial obligations to international markets, especially when they are food exporters. A series of detailed historical cases spanning Chapters 4–6 demonstrate strong qualitative support for my proposed emphasis on food price politics as a key component of the survival strategy of varied incumbents, although I also demonstrate important variation in these core predictions in autocracies that rely on rural voters, and in democracies that fear urban violence. Important in its own right as the first unified theory of domestic political determinants of sovereign default across regime settings, these findings also contribute to a number of related bodies of work and suggest several avenues of future research.

7.1 INTERRELATIONSHIP BETWEEN DOMESTIC POLITICS AND INTERNATIONAL MARKETS

By honing in on a specific issue area through which to explore the importance of urban–rural pressures on politicians, my theory helps highlight that concerns over the price of food should play an important role in the survival considerations of incumbents. Yet, more careful attention to the market dynamics surrounding pricing policy suggests that the fiscal burden to the state of such programs – and therefore also the likely difficulty of reforming these policies – depends crucially on the extent of integration of these products into global markets. While dictators can intervene in domestic food markets to keep prices low, the implied costs of such a policy for the state depend on the amount of food that must be imported from abroad at prevailing world prices (and then resold at subsidized rates to consumers). Likewise, for democratic leaders that provide above-market prices to rural farmers, the costs of buying domestic food production depend on how difficult it will be to offload excess food to export markets.

While in this book I have generally focused on the ways that these costs arise due to food pricing policy, the broader theoretical implications should apply to essentially any government attempt to affect market prices for goods that can also be traded freely on international markets. One obvious extension of this theory could apply to the costs consumers pay for oil: indeed, several of my case studies make clear that – beyond subsidizing food costs for urban dwellers – many states have imposed subsidies on fuel. Yet, particularly for oil-importing countries, such a price-setting policy is likely to be a substantial burden on the government's budget, as was clearly true in the Jamaican instance discussed in Chapter 5. In prior work, I have shown that oil-importing autocracies are also significantly more likely to default on their sovereign loans (Ballard-Rosa 2016). These findings help substantiate the more general validity of an approach that considers precise policy areas where government attempts to alter prices may ultimately be undermined by the movement of goods across borders. This book therefore helps contribute – through careful attention to the interplay between domestic and international pricing – a novel theoretical framework that can be applied to a much wider set of policy areas.

7.2 URBAN–RURAL POLITICS

Much of my account of politics on around citizen strategies for voting and violence. I build on existing accounts of mass mobilization that note that protests have historically been an overwhelmingly urban affair, suggesting that leaders sensitive to citizen unrest should cater to city dwellers. Conversely, in democracies where votes are all that matter to incumbents, I highlight a common thread from work on electoral mobilization that identifies agricultural blocs as electorally crucial. In doing so, this work helps to draw together two bodies of work on geographic biases across differing political settings that have not always been in dialogue with one another. In addition, I help clarify that the average expectation of urban bias in autocracies, and rural bias in democracies, may actually be undone in cases where voting plays an important stabilizing role for autocrats, or where violence poses a serious threat to social stability for democrats.

This framework for identifying the relative political weight of urban or rural interests across regime constellations could be extended to a host of additional issue areas. In addition, this work helps emphasize the continued importance of considering the urban–rural divide as a crucial source of political division. This accords well with recent accounts, for example, of American elections, which have noted that political preferences of rural Americans are often in strict competition with urban ones. Nor is this political salience unique to studies of American partisanship – indeed, several of the most momentous political events of recent memory – including the Brexit referendum in the United Kingdom and the rise of right-wing nationalist parties across much of Europe – have all shared a common fact that urban–rural location was one of the strongest predictors of citizen political behavior. My book suggests that attention to competing interests across regional economies is likely to prove relevant for understanding mobilization of mass action. While I focus on food policies as one important policy lens, the rise of regional economies with wildly varying economic prospects in vibrant urban hubs versus dying rural hinterlands is likely to prove politically consequential for the coming generation.

7.3 LOOMING FISCAL CRISES IN THE DEVELOPED WORLD

This book demonstrates that food pricing politics have been of crucial political importance across a wide range of historical cases, and that the difficulty of reforming costly food support programs has driven political leaders to the brink of sovereign default. However, it is important to recognize that such issues may be of lesser importance in the developed world. In part this is likely to arise from a natural consequence of Engel's law: While low-income individuals spend a large fraction of their income acquiring food, wealthier citizens generally spend a smaller fraction of their economic resources on food, suggesting that the relative salience of such issues should be lessened. If true, this suggests that a reasonable scope condition for a more narrow interpretation of my theory is that it should be most likely to hold in the developing world; given that the lion's share of sovereign defaults have occurred outside the wealthiest countries, this is a reasonable limit to apply.

More generally, my theory of the politics of sovereign default suggests that politicians should favor those groups that are central to their continued survival in office. When such policies become a burden on the budget, however, politicians will be faced with the same core dilemma that I describe theoretically in this work: Remove costly policies and face the threat of removal from power, or continue placating support groups and potentially lose access to important sources of international lending? In this regard, the core of my theoretical work can be used to identify likely sources of fiscal friction in the years to come, especially in the developed world, where fiscal crises arising from the need for reform of so-called entitlement programs loom large. For example, my theory would predict that in developed democracies like the United States, highly mobilized voter groups should be provided with large (and costly) government transfers. Of course, one of the most active identities of voters in the US today is the elderly, who can be counted to turn out in droves and are particularly likely to emphasize protection of the social benefits they enjoy, like Social Security and Medicare.

Yet, turning from the national level to more local levels of government, with state and municipal pension plans vastly underfunded, it can be only a matter of time until local political leaders must face the choice between scaling back costly pension benefits, or instead reneging on existing borrowing obligations. In fact, precisely this kind of dynamic has been at play in the spate of municipal-level defaults that have occurred in places like Stockton, California, or Detroit, Michigan, where private bondholders have often been subjected to large haircuts on their outstanding loans while state pension plans have gone largely untouched. If my general theory of political default is correct, then looming fiscal crises over pension reform are likely to herald a new wave of government defaults across developed countries in the coming years.

7.4 CONCLUDING REMARKS

This work has focused on times when concerns for political survival trump attempts at economic reform. Yet, in investigating those factors that make structural adjustment politically unpalatable, I have also brushed up against cases where political and economic incentives were aligned. While democratically elected parties were unwilling to remove agricultural subsidies for fear of losing crucial rural votes, a military intervention did away with costly farm supports. And when autocratic rulers proved unable to reform cheap food policies, leaders selected in a competitive electoral environment were more successful. This suggests that greater attention to specific survival dynamics across political regimes may help us not only understand when reform will fail, but may also help us understand what changes can be made to help it succeed. In a world where the fiscal footprint of prior generations' over-borrowing is likely to take center stage, comprehension of the political determinants of sovereign default will be crucial.

Bibliography

Acemoglu, Daron and James Robinson. 2006. *Economic Origins of Dictatorship and Democracy*. Cambridge: Cambridge University Press.
Akder, A. Halis. 2007. "Policy formation in the process of implementing agricultural reform in Turkey." *International Journal of Agricultural Resources, Governance and Ecology* 6(4):514–532.
Alesina, Alberto and Enrico Spolaore. 2005. *The Size of Nations*. Cambridge, MA: MIT Press.
Ameringer, Charles D. 1982. *Democracy in Costa Rica*. Stanford, CA: Hoover Institution Press.
Anderson, Leslie. 1991. "Mixed blessings: Disruption and organization among peasant unions in Costa Rica." *Latin American Research Review* 26(1):111–143.
Arias Sánchez, Oscar. 1971. *Grupos de presión en Costa Rica*. San José: Edit. Costa Rica, 1987.
Athukorala, Prema-Chandra. 2013. "The Malaysian economy during three crises." In *Malaysia's Development Challenges*. Hal Hill, Tham Siew Yean, and Ragayah Haji Mat Zin (eds.). Singapore: Routledge, pp. 109–131.
Aziz, Rahimah Abdul. 2012. "New economic policy and the Malaysian multiethnic middle class." *Asian Ethnicity* 13(1):29–46.
Ballard-Rosa, Cameron. 2016. "Hungry for change: Urban bias and autocratic sovereign default." *International Organization* 70(2):313–346.
Ballard-Rosa, Cameron, Bryan Schonfeld, and Allison Carnegie. 2018. "Collapsing support for democracy and the urban–rural divide." Unpublished Working Paper, University of North Carolina at Chapel Hill.
Bandiera, Luca, Jesus Cuaresma, and Gallina Vincelette. 2010. "Unpleasant surprises: Sovereign default determinants and prospects." World Bank Policy Research Working Paper 5401.
Barari, Soubhik, Song Kim, and Weihuang Wong. 2019. "Trade liberalization and regime type: Evidence from a new tariff-line dataset." Unpublished Working Paper, Cambridge, MA: MIT.

Bates, Robert H. 1982. *Markets and States in Tropical Africa: The Political Basis of Agricultural Policies*. Berkeley, CA: University of California Press.

Bates, Robert H. and Paul Collier. 1993. "The politics and economics of economic reforms in Zambia." In Robert H. Bates and Anne O. Krueger, *Political and Economic Interactions in Economic Policy Reform*, Blackwell, Oxford, 334:807–824.

Bates, Robert H., and Steven Block. 2011. "Political institutions and agricultural trade interventions in Africa." *American Journal of Agricultural Economics* 93(2):317–323.

Baumgartner, Frank R., and Bryan D. Jones. 2010. *Agendas and Instability in American Politics*. Chicago, IL: University of Chicago Press.

Beaulieu, Emily, Gary W. Cox, and Sebastian Saiegh. 2012. "Sovereign debt and regime type: Reconsidering the democratic advantage." *International Organization* 66(4):709–738.

Beazer, Quintin H., and Byungwon Woo. 2016. "IMF conditionality, government partisanship, and the progress of economic reforms." *American Journal of Political Science* 60(2):304–321.

Beramendi, Pablo. 2012. *The Political Geography of Inequality: Regions and Redistribution*. Cambridge: Cambridge University Press.

Blaydes, Lisa. 2010. *Elections and Distributive Politics in Mubarak's Egypt*. Cambridge: Cambridge University Press.

Booth, John A. and Mitchell A. Seligson. 1979. "Peasants as activists: A reevaluation of political participation in the countryside." *Comparative Political Studies* 12(1):29–59.

Borensztein, E. and U. Panizza. 2009. "The costs of sovereign default." *IMF Staff Papers* 56(4):683–741.

Bulow, J. and K. Rogoff. 1989. "Sovereign debt: Is to forgive to forget?" *The American Economic Review* 79(1):43–50.

Callaghy, Thomas M. 1990. "Lost between state and market: The politics of economic adjustment in Ghana, Zambia, and Nigeria." In *Economic Crisis and Policy Choice* Joan M. Nelson (ed.). Princeton, NJ: Princeton University Press, pp. 257–319.

Carter, David B. and Curtis S. Signorino. 2010. "Back to the future: Modeling time dependence in binary data." *Political Analysis* 18(3):271–292.

Carvounis, Chris C. 1984. *The Debt Dilemma of Developing Nations: Issues and Cases*. Westport, CT: Quorum Books.

Celasun, Merih and Dani Rodrik. 1989. "Book IV: Debt, adjustment, and growth: Turkey." In *Developing Country Debt and Economic Performance, Volume 3: Country Studies–Indonesia, Korea, Philippines, Turkey*. Chicago, IL: University of Chicago Press, pp. 615–616.

Chaudoin, Stephen, Helen V. Milner, and Xun Pang. 2015. "International systems and domestic politics: Linking complex interactions with empirical models in international relations." *International Organization* 69(02):275–309.

Cheibub, Jose, Jennifer Gandhi and James Vreeland. 2010. "Democracy and dictatorship revisited." *Public Choice* 143(1):67–101.

Chen, Jowei and Jonathan Rodden. 2013. "Unintentional gerrymandering: Political geography and electoral bias in legislatures." *Quarterly Journal of Political Science* 8(3):239–269.

Chinn, Menzie D. and Hiro Ito. 2008. "A new measure of financial openness." *Journal of Comparative Policy Analysis* 10(3):309–322.

Chinn, Menzie D. and Jeffry A. Frieden. 2011. *Lost Decades: The Making of America's Debt Crisis and the Long Recovery.* New York, NY: W.W. Norton.

Clark, John and Caroline Allison. 1989. *Zambia Debt & Poverty.* Oxford: Oxfam.

Cole, Shawn. 2009. "Fixing market failures or fixing elections? Agricultural credit in India." *American Economic Journal: Applied Economics* 1(1):219–250.

Copelovitch, Mark S. 2010. *The International Monetary Fund in the Global Economy: Banks, Bonds, and Bailouts.* Cambridge: Cambridge University Press.

Cox, Gary W. 2011. "Sovereign debt, political stability and bargaining efficiency." Unpublished typescript, Stanford University.

Cruces, Juan J. and Christoph Trebesch. 2013. "Sovereign defaults: The price of haircuts." *American Economic Journal: Macroeconomics* 5(3):85–117.

Curtis, K. Amber, Joseph Jupille, and David Leblang. 2014. "Iceland on the rocks: The mass political economy of sovereign debt resettlement." *International Organization* 68(03):721–740.

Davis, Christina L. 2003. *Food Fights over Free Trade: How International Institutions Promote Agricultural Trade Liberalization.* Princeton, NJ: Princeton University Press.

De Paoli, Bianca and Glenn Hoggarth. 2006. "Costs of sovereign default." *Bank of England Quarterly Bulletin, Fall 2006, Bank of England Financial Stability Paper No. 1.*

Diamond, Larry J. 2002. "Thinking about hybrid regimes." *Journal of Democracy* 13(2):21–35.

DiGiuseppe, Matthew and Patrick E. Shea. 2015. "Sovereign credit and the fate of leaders: Reassessing the democratic advantage." *International Studies Quarterly* 59(3):557–570.

Dixit, Avinash and John Londregan. 1996. "The determinants of success of special interests in redistributive politics." *Journal of Politics* 58:1132–1155.

Dreher, Axel. 2006. "IMF and economic growth: The effects of programs, loans, and compliance with conditionality." *World Development* 34(5):769–788.

Drury, Bruce. 1988. "The limits of conservative reform: Agricultural policy in Malaysia." *ASEAN Economic Bulletin* 4(3):287–301.

Dunning, Thad. 2008. *Crude Democracy: Natural Resource Wealth and Political Regimes.* Cambridge: Cambridge University Press.

Eaton, Jonathan and Mark Gersovitz. 1981. "Debt with potential repudiation: Theoretical and empirical analysis." *The Review of Economic Studies* 48(2):289–309.

Edelman, Marc. 1990. "When they took the muni: Political culture and anti-austerity protest in rural northwestern Costa Rica." *American Ethnologist* 17(4):736–757.

Edelman, Marc. 1999. *Peasants against Globalization: Rural Social Movements in Costa Rica.* Stanford, CA: Stanford University Press.

Edie, Carlene J. 1989. "From Manley to Seaga: The persistence of clientelist politics in Jamaica." *Social and Economic Studies* 38(1):1–35.

Eichengreen, Barry and Peter H. Lindert. 1992. *The International Debt Crisis in Historical Perspective.* Cambridge, MA: MIT Press.

Eichengreen, Barry, Ricardo Hausmann, and Ugo Panizza. 2007. "Currency mismatches, debt intolerance, and the original sin: Why they are not the same and why it matters." In *Capital Controls and Capital Flows in Emerging Economies: Policies, Practices and Consequences.* Chicago, IL: University of Chicago Press, 121–170.

Frankel, Francine R. 1978. *India's Political Economy, 1947–1977: The Gradual Revolution.* Princeton, NJ: Princeton University Press.

Frieden, Jeffry A. 1991. *Debt, Development, and Democracy: Modern Political Economy and Latin America, 1965–1985*. Princeton, NJ: Princeton University Press.
Funston, John. 1988. "Challenge and response in Malaysia: The UMNO crisis and the Mahathir style." *The Pacific Review* 1(4):363–373.
Gandhi, Jennifer. 2008. *Political Institutions under Dictatorship*. Cambridge: Cambridge University Press.
Gelvin, James L. 2015. *The Arab Uprisings: What Everyone Needs to Know*. Oxford: Oxford University Press.
Golden, Miriam and Brian Min. 2012. Theft and loss of electricity in an Indian state. Technical report Working Paper 12/0060, International Growth Centre.
González Vega, Claudio. 1984. "Fear of adjusting: The social costs of economic policies in Costa Rica in the 1970s." In *Revolution and Counter-Revolution in Central America and the Caribbean*, Donald Schulz and Douglas H. Graham (eds.). Boulder, CO: Westview Press.
Gourevitch, Peter. 1986. *Politics in Hard Times: Comparative Responses to International Economic Crises*. Ithaca, NY: Cornell University Press.
Grossman, Gene M. and Elhanan Helpman. 1994. "Protection for sale." *The American Economic Review* 84(4):833–850.
Hafner-Burton, Emilie M., Susan D. Hyde, and Ryan S. Jablonski. 2014. "When do governments resort to election violence?" *British Journal of Political Science* 44(1):149–179.
Haggard, Stephan. 1985. "The politics of adjustment: Lessons from the IMF's Extended Fund Facility." *International Organization* 39(3):505–534.
Handa, Sudhanshu and Damien King. 1997. "Structural adjustment policies, income distribution and poverty: A review of the Jamaican experience." *World Development* 25(6):915–930.
Hansen-Kuhn, Karen. 1993. *Structural Adjustment in Central America: The Case of Costa Rica*. Development GAP (Group for Alternative Policies).
Harding, Robin. 2012. "Democracy, Urbanization, and Rural Bias: Explaining Urban/Rural Differences in Incumbent Support Across Africa." Working paper, "Afrobarometer Working Paper Series."
Harriott, Anthony. 2008. *Organized Crime and Politics in Jamaica: Breaking the Nexus*. Kingston: University of West Indies Press.
Hawkins, Jeffrey J. 1991. "Understanding the failure of IMF reform: The Zambian case." *World Development* 19(7):839–849.
Hazell, Peter B. R. 1992. "The appropriate role of agricultural insurance in developing countries." *Journal of International Development* 4(6):567–581.
Hendrix, Cullen and Stephan Haggard. 2014. "International Food Prices, Regime Type, and Protest in the Developing World." *Unpublished Working Paper, UCSD, La Jolla, CA*.
Hendrix, Cullen and Stephan Haggard. 2015. "Global food prices, regime type, and urban unrest in the developing world." *Journal of Peace Research* 52(2):143–157.
Hollyer, James R., B. Peter Rosendorff, and James R. Vreeland. 2011. "Democracy and transparency." *The Journal of Politics* 73(4):1191–1205.
Hollyer, James R., B. Peter Rosendorff and James R. Vreeland. 2015. "Transparency, protest, and autocratic instability." *American Political Science Review* 109(4):764–784.

Hollyer, James R., B. Peter Rosendorff, and James R. Vreeland. 2018. "Transparency, protest and democratic stability." *British Journal of Political Science* 49(4):1–27.
Horowitz, Donald L. 2001. *The Deadly Ethnic Riot*. Berkeley, CA: University of California Press.
Huber, Evelyne and John D. Stephens. 1992. "Changing development models in small economies: The case of Jamaica from the 1950s to the 1990s." *Studies in Comparative International Development* 27(3):57–92.
Hugo, Gustav R. 1819. *Lehrbuch des Naturrechts*. Berlin: Mylius.
Hyde, Susan D. 2011. *The Pseudo-Democrat's Dilemma: Why Election Monitoring Became an International Norm*. Ithaca, NY: Cornell University Press.
Ilkkaracan, Ipek and Insan Tunali. 2010. "Agricultural transformation and the rural labor market in turkey." In *Rethinking Structural Reform in Turkish Agriculture: Beyond the World Bank's Strategy*, Baris Karapinar, Fikret Adaman, and Gokhan Ozertan (eds.). New York: Nova Science, 105–48.
IMF. 1965a. "Minutes of Executive Board Meeting 65/7 (January 29)." https://archivescatalog.imf.org/Details/archive/125046995. Accessed: August 14, 2013.
IMF. 1965b. "Turkey – Modification of Stand-by Arrangement (July 30)." https://archivescatalog.imf.org/Details/archive/125046289. Accessed: August 14, 2013.
IMF. 1965c. "Turkey – Stand-by Arrangement (January 29)." https://archivescatalog.imf.org/Details/archive/125046986. Accessed: August 14, 2013.
IMF. 1970a. "Malaysia – Staff Report for the 1970 Article VIII Consultation." https://archivescatalog.imf.org/Details/archive/125034760. Accessed: June 23, 2015.
IMF. 1970b. "Minutes of Executive Board Meeting 70/86 (September 9)." https://archivescatalog.imf.org/Details/archive/125034556. Accessed: June 23, 2015.
IMF. 1970c. "Mr. Merican's Statement on Malaysia (EBM/70/76)." https://archivescatalog.imf.org/Details/archive/125034568. Accessed: June 23, 2015.
IMF. 1971a. "Malaysia – Staff Report for the 1971 Article VIII Consultation." https://archivescatalog.imf.org/Details/archive/125032920. Accessed: June 23, 2015.
IMF. 1971b. "Minutes of Executive Board Meeting 71/79 (July 30)." https://archivescatalog.imf.org/Details/archive/125032545. Accessed: June 23, 2015.
IMF. 1972. "Malaysia – Recent Economic Developments." https://archivescatalog.imf.org/Details/archive/125016663. Accessed: June 23, 2015.
IMF. 1973a. "Malaysia – Staff Report for the 1973 Article VIII Consultation." https://archivescatalog.imf.org/Details/archive/125014102. Accessed: June 23, 2015.
IMF. 1973b. "Minutes of Executive Board Meeting 73/89 (August 31)." https://archivescatalog.imf.org/Details/archive/125013832. Accessed: June 23, 2015.
IMF. 1974a. "Malaysia – Recent Economic Developments." https://archivescatalog.imf.org/Details/archive/125011020. Accessed: June 23, 2015.
IMF. 1974b. "Malaysia – Staff Report on the 1974 Article VIII Consultation." https://archivescatalog.imf.org/Details/archive/125011160. Accessed: June 23, 2015.
IMF. 1975. "Malaysia – Staff Report for the 1975 Article VIII Consultation." https://archivescatalog.imf.org/Details/archive/125008192. Accessed: July 8, 2015.
IMF. 1976a. "Malaysia – Recent Economic Developments." https://archivescatalog.imf.org/Details/archive/125005354. Accessed: July 8, 2015.
IMF. 1976b. "Minutes of Executive Board Meeting 76/4 (January 16)." https://archivescatalog.imf.org/Details/archive/125007671. Accessed: July 8, 2015.
IMF. 1976c. "Zambia – Request for Stand-By Arrangement (July 12)." https://archivescatalog.imf.org/Details/archive/125006185. Accessed: January 16, 2014.

IMF. 1977a. "Turkey – Supplementary Background Material for GATT (October 12)." https://archivescatalog.imf.org/Details/archive/125027188.. Accessed: August 15, 2013.
IMF. 1977b. "Zambia – Recent Economic Developments (February 15)." https://archivescatalog.imf.org/Details/archive/125028990. Accessed: February 5, 2014.
IMF. 1978a. "Turkey – Request for Modification and Waiver of Performance Criteria Under Stand-by Arrangement (September 15)." https://archivescatalog.imf.org/Details/archive/125024456. Accessed: August 15, 2013.
IMF. 1978b. "Turkey – Request for Stand-By Arrangement (March 27)." https://archivescatalog.imf.org/Details/archive/125025993. Accessed: August 14, 2013.
IMF. 1979a. "Malaysia – Recent Economic Developments." https://archivescatalog.imf.org/Details/archive/125022822. Accessed: July 8, 2015.
IMF. 1979b. "Malaysia – Staff Report for the 1979 Article IV Consultation." https://archivescatalog.imf.org/Details/archive/125022948. Accessed: July 8, 2015.
IMF. 1979c. "Minutes of Executive Board Meeting 79/166 (October 29)." https://archivescatalog.imf.org/Details/archive/125021006. Accessed: February 11, 2014.
IMF. 1979d. "Turkey – Recent Economic Developments (February 21)." https://archivescatalog.imf.org/Details/archive/125023171. Accessed: August 14, 2013.
IMF. 1980. "Malaysia – Recent Economic Developments." https://archivescatalog.imf.org/Details/archive/125019314. Accessed: July 8, 2015.
IMF. 1981a. "Costa Rica – Request for Extended Arrangement (June 4)." https://archivescatalog.imf.org/Details/archive/125003880. Accessed: June 5, 2015.
IMF. 1981b. "Malaysia – Recent Economic Developments." https://archivescatalog.imf.org/Details/archive/125003859. Accessed: July 8, 2015.
IMF. 1981c. "Malaysia – Staff Report for the 1981 Article IV Consultation." https://archivescatalog.imf.org/Details/archive/125003983. Accessed: July 8, 2015.
IMF. 1981d. "Minutes of Executive Board Meeting 81/143 (November 18)." https://archivescatalog.imf.org/Details/archive/125002852. Accessed: February 12, 2014.
IMF. 1981e. "Minutes of Executive Board Meeting 81/56." https://archivescatalog.imf.org/Details/archive/125004304. Accessed: July 23, 2015.
IMF. 1982. "Minutes of Executive Board Meeting 82/56." https://archivescatalog.imf.org/Details/archive/125001850. Accessed: July 23, 2015.
IMF. 1983a. "Jamaica – 1982 Article IV Consultation, and Review of Extended Arrangement." https://archivescatalog.imf.org/Details/archive/125070013. Accessed: July 23, 2015.
IMF. 1983b. "Malaysia – 1983 Article IV Consultation." https://archivescatalog.imf.org/Details/archive/125067734. Accessed: July 8, 2015.
IMF. 1983c. "Malaysia – Recent Economic Developments." https://archivescatalog.imf.org/Details/archive/125067894. Accessed: July 8, 2015.
IMF. 1983d. "Minutes of Executive Board Meeting 83/63 (April 18)." https://archivescatalog.imf.org/Details/archive/125068767. Accessed: February 13, 2014.
IMF. 1983e. "Staff Report for the 1983 Article IV Consultation." https://archivescatalog.imf.org/Details/archive/125068105. Accessed: July 8, 2015.
IMF. 1984a. "Costa Rica – 1984 Article IV Consultation." https://archivescatalog.imf.org/Details/archive/125071532. Accessed: June 5, 2015.
IMF. 1984b. "Costa Rica – Recent Economic Developments." https://archivescatalog.imf.org/Details/archive/125071626. Accessed: June 5, 2015.

IMF. 1984c. "Costa Rica – Staff Report for the 1984 Article IV Consultation." https://archivescatalog.imf.org/Details/archive/125071625. Accessed: June 5, 2015.
IMF. 1984d. "Jamaica – 1984 Article IV Consultation; Stand-By Arrangement; and Purchase Transaction." https://archivescatalog.imf.org/Details/archive/125072137. Accessed: April 4, 2017.
IMF. 1984e. "Jamaica – Staff Report for the 1984 Article IV Consultation and Request for Stand-By Arrangement." https://archivescatalog.imf.org/Details/archive/125072167. Accessed: April 4, 2017.
IMF. 1984f. "Malaysia – 1984 Article IV Consultation." https://archivescatalog.imf.org/Details/archive/125071787. Accessed: July 8, 2015.
IMF. 1984g. "Malaysia – Recent Economic Developments." https://archivescatalog.imf.org/Details/archive/125071995. Accessed: July 8, 2015.
IMF. 1984h. "Minutes of Executive Board Meeting 84/169 (November 26)." https://archivescatalog.imf.org/Details/archive/125070420. Accessed: February 14, 2014.
IMF. 1985a. "Costa Rica – 1985 Article IV Consultation (1st session)." https://archivescatalog.imf.org/Details/archive/125075106. Accessed: June 5, 2015.
IMF. 1985b. "Costa Rica – 1985 Article IV Consultation (2nd session)." https://archivescatalog.imf.org/Details/archive/125075109. Accessed: June 5, 2015.
IMF. 1985c. "Costa Rica – Recent Economic Developments." https://archivescatalog.imf.org/Details/archive/125075266. Accessed: June 5, 2015.
IMF. 1985d. "Costa Rica – Request for Stand-By Arrangement." https://archivescatalog.imf.org/Details/archive/125077189. Accessed: June 5, 2015.
IMF. 1985e. "Costa Rica – Staff Report for the 1985 Article IV Consultation." https://archivescatalog.imf.org/Details/archive/125075133. Accessed: June 5, 2015.
IMF. 1985f. "Costa Rica – Stand-By Arrangement." https://archivescatalog.imf.org/Details/archive/125077149. Accessed: June 5, 2015.
IMF. 1985g. "Jamaica – Review Under Stand-By Arrangement and Waiver of Performance Criteria; and Exchange System." https://archivescatalog.imf.org/Details/archive/125076436. Accessed: May 20, 2017.
IMF. 1985h. "Malaysia – 1985 Article IV Consultation." https://archivescatalog.imf.org/Details/archive/125075662. Accessed: July 8, 2015.
IMF. 1985i. "Malaysia - Recent Economic Developments." https://archivescatalog.imf.org/Details/archive/125075851. Accessed: July 8, 2015.
IMF. 1985j. "Minutes of Executive Board Meeting 85/158 (October 30)." https://archivescatalog.imf.org/Details/archive/125074611. Accessed: February 14, 2014.
IMF. 1985k. "Report on Costa Rica's External Debt Renegotiation." https://archivescatalog.imf.org/Details/archive/125076510. Accessed: June 5, 2015.
IMF. 1986a. "Costa Rica – Recent Economic Developments." https://archivescatalog.imf.org/Details/archive/125079040. Accessed: June 5, 2015.
IMF. 1986b. "Costa Rica – Staff Report for the 1986 Article IV Consultation." https://archivescatalog.imf.org/Details/archive/125078744. Accessed: June 5, 2015.
IMF. 1986c. "Malaysia – 1986 Article IV Consultation." https://archivescatalog.imf.org/Details/archive/125079480. Accessed: July 8, 2015.
IMF. 1986d. "Malaysia – Recent Economic Developments." https://archivescatalog.imf.org/Details/archive/125080007. Accessed: July 8, 2015.
IMF. 1986e. "Minutes of Executive Board Meeting 86/187 (November 24)." https://archivescatalog.imf.org/Details/archive/125078433. Accessed: February 14, 2014.

IMF. 1987. "Minutes of Executive Board Meeting 87/14 (January 23)." https://archivescatalog.imf.org/Details/archive/125086176. Accessed: February 14, 2014.
IMF. 1988. "Costa Rica – Recent Economic Developments." https://archivescatalog.imf.org/Details/archive/125089678. Accessed: June 5, 2015.
Jorgensen, Erika and Jeffrey D. Sachs. 1988. "Default and renegotiation of Latin American foreign bonds in the interwar period." NBER Working Paper Series No. 2636.
Kahler, Miles. 1989. "International financial institutions and the politics of adjustment." In *Fragile Coalitions: The Politics of Economic Adjustment*. Valeriana Kallab and Richard E. Feinberg (eds.). New Brunswick: Transaction Books, 139–159.
Kaplan, Stephen B. 2013. *Globalization and Austerity Politics in Latin America*. Cambridge: Cambridge University Press.
Kaplan, Stephen B. and Kaj Thomsson. 2017. "The political economy of sovereign debt: Global finance and electoral cycles." *The Journal of Politics* 79(2):605–623.
Kasara, Kimuli. 2007. "Tax me if you can: Ethnic geography, democracy, and the taxation of agriculture in Africa." *American Political Science Review* 101(1):159–172.
King, Gary, James Honaker, Anne Joseph, and Kenneth Scheve. 2001. "Analyzing incomplete political science data: An alternative algorithm for multiple imputation." *American Political Science Review* 95(1):49–70.
Kohlscheen, E. 2010. "Sovereign risk: Constitutions rule." *Oxford Economic Papers* 62(1):62–85.
Kopits, George. 1987. *Structural Reform, Stabilization, and Growth in Turkey*. Vol. 52. Washington, DC: International Monetary Fund.
Kraay, Aart and Vikram Nehru. 2006. "When is external debt sustainable?" *The World Bank Economic Review* 20(3):341–365.
Krueger, Anne O. 1996. "Political economy of agricultural policy." *Public Choice* 87(1):163–175.
Krueger, Anne O., Maurice Schiff, and Alberto Valdes. 1988. "Agricultural incentives in developing countries: Measuring the effect of sectoral and economywide policies." *The World Bank Economic Review* 2(3):255–271.
Krueger, Anne O., Maurice Schiff, and Alberto Valdes et al. 1991. *The Political Economy of Agricultural Pricing Policy. Vol 1: Latin America. Vol 2: Asia*. Baltimore, MD: Johns Hopkins University Press.
Lall, Ranjit. 2016. "How multiple imputation makes a difference." *Political Analysis* 24(4):414–433.
Lee, David R. and Muna B. Ndulo. 2011. *The Food and Financial Crises in Sub-Saharan Africa: Origins, Impacts and Policy Implications*. Cambridge, MA: CABI Publishing.
Levi, M. 1989. *Of Rule and Revenue*. Berkeley, CA: University of California Press
Levitsky, Steven and Lucan A. Way. 2010. *Competitive Authoritarianism: Hybrid Regimes after the Cold War*. Cambridge: Cambridge University Press.
Lewis, Rupert. 2012. "Party politics in Jamaica and the extradition of Christopher 'Dudus' Coke." *The Global South* 6(1):38–54.
Lipton, Michael 1977. *Why Poor People Stay Poor: A Study of Urban Bias in World Development*. London: Temple Smith.
Lombard, C. Stephen and Alex H. C. Tweedie. 1974. *Agriculture in Zambia since Independence*. Lusaka: Neczam.

Loxley, John 1990. "Structural adjustment in Africa: Reflections on Ghana and Zambia." *Review of African Political Economy* 17(47):8–27.
Magaloni, Beatriz. 2006. *Voting for Autocracy: Hegemonic Party Survival and Its Demise in Mexico.* Cambridge: Cambridge University Press.
McAdam, Doug, Sidney Tarrow, and Charles Tilly. 2003. "Dynamics of contention." *Social Movement Studies* 2(1):99–102.
Meyer, David S. and Sidney G. Tarrow. 1998. *The Social Movement Society: Contentious Politics for a New Century.* New York, NY: Rowman & Littlefield.
Milne, Robert Stephen 1986. "Malaysia: beyond the new economic policy." *Asian Survey* 26(12):1364–1382.
Moghadam, Reza. 2005. *Turkey at the Crossroads: From Crisis Resolution to EU Accession.* Vol. 242. Washington, DC: International Monetary Fund.
Moravcsik, Andrew. 2010. "Active citation: A precondition for replicable qualitative research." *PS: Political Science & Politics* 43(1):29–35.
Mosley, Layna. 2000. "Room to move: International financial markets and national welfare states." *International Organization* 54(04):737–773.
Mosley, Layna. 2003. *Global Capital and National Governments.* Cambridge: Cambridge University Press.
Mulgan, Aurelia George. 1997. "Electoral determinants of agrarian power: Measuring rural decline in Japan." *Political Studies* 45(5):875–899.
Naoi, Megumi and Ikuo Kume. 2011. "Explaining mass support for agricultural protectionism: Evidence from a survey experiment during the global recession." *International Organization* 65(04):771–795.
Narayanan, Suresh. 1996. "Fiscal reform in Malaysia: Behind a successful experience." *Asian Survey* 36(9):869–881.
Nelson, Joan. 1989. "Crisis management, economic reform and Costa Rican democracy." In *Debt and Democracy in Latin America.* Barbara Stallings and Robert Kaufman (eds.). Boulder, CO: Westview Press, 143–162.
Nelson, Joan. 1992. "Poverty, equity, and the politics of adjustment." In *The Politics of Economic Adjustment.* Stephan Haggard and Robert R. Kaufman (eds.). Princeton, NJ: Princeton University Press, 221–269.
Nelson, Joan M. 1990. *Economic Crisis and Policy Choice: The Politics of Adjustment in the Third World.* Princeton, NJ: Princeton University Press.
Nelson, Stephen C. and David A. Steinberg. 2018. "Default positions: What shapes public attitudes about international debt disputes?" *International Studies Quarterly* 62(3):520–533.
Nooruddin, Irfan and James Raymond Vreeland. 2010. "The Effect of IMF Programs on Public Wages and Salaries." *Global Governance, Poverty and Inequality* p. 90.
Nooruddin, Irfan and Joel W. Simmons. 2006. "The politics of hard choices: IMF programs and government spending." *International Organization* 60(04):1001–1033.
Oatley, Thomas. 2004. "Why is stabilization sometimes delayed? Reevaluating the regime-type hypothesis." *Comparative Political Studies* 37(3):286–312.
Oatley, Thomas. 2010. "Political institutions and foreign debt in the developing world." *International Studies Quarterly* 54(1):175–195.
Oatley, Thomas. 2011. "The reductionist gamble: Open economy politics in the global economy." *International Organization* 65(02):311–341.

OECD. 2011. *Evaluation of Agricultural Policy Reforms in Turkey*. Organization for Economic Cooperation and Development.
Olson, Mancur. 1965. *The Logic of Collective Action*. Vol. 124. Cambridge, MA: Harvard University Press.
Panizza, Ugo, Federico Sturzenegger, and Jeromin Zettelmeyer. 2009. "The economics and law of sovereign debt and default." *Journal of Economic Literature* 47(3):651–698.
Pathmanathan, Murugesu. 1985. "Malaysia in 1984: A political and economic survey." *Southeast Asian Affairs* pp. 211–234.
Payne, Anthony J. 1988. "Orthodox liberal development in Jamaica: Theory and practice." *Third World Quarterly* 10(3):1217–1238.
Pepinsky, Thomas. 2007. "Autocracy, elections, and fiscal policy: Evidence from Malaysia." *Studies in Comparative International Development* 42(1–2):136–163.
Pepinsky, Thomas B. 2008. "Capital mobility and coalitional politics: Authoritarian regimes and economic adjustment in Southeast Asia." *World Politics* 60(03):438–474.
Pepinsky, Thomas B. 2009. *Economic Crises and the Breakdown of Authoritarian Regimes: Indonesia and Malaysia in Comparative Perspective*. Cambridge: Cambridge University Press.
Persson, Torsten and Guido Tabellini. 2000. *Political Economics: Explaining Economic Policy*. Cambridge, MA: MIT Press.
Pierskalla, Jan H. 2016. "The politics of urban bias: Rural threats and the dual dilemma of political survival." *Studies in Comparative International Development* 51(3):286–307.
Przeworski, Adam. 1991. *Democracy and the Market: Political and Economic Reforms in Eastern Europe and Latin America*. Cambridge: Cambridge University Press.
Przeworski, Adam, Antonio Cheibub, Fernando Limongi, and Michael Alvarez. 2000. *Democracy and Development: Political Institutions and Material Well-Being in the World, 1950–1990*. Cambridge: Cambridge University Press.
Putnam, Robert D. 1988. "Diplomacy and domestic politics: The logic of two-level games." *International organization* 42(3):427–460.
Rakner, Lise. 2003. *Political and Economic Liberalisation in Zambia 1991–2001*. Uppsala: Nordic Africa Institute.
Rasiah, Rajah and Ishak Shari. 2001. "Market, government and Malaysia's new economic policy." *Cambridge Journal of Economics* 25(1):57–78.
Reinhart, Carmen and Kenneth Rogoff. 2009. *This Time Is Different: Eight Centuries of Financial Folly*. Princeton, NJ: Princeton University Press.
Reinhart, Carmen and Kenneth Rogoff. 2010. Growth in a Time of Debt. Technical Report, National Bureau of Economic Research.
Reinhart, Carmen, Kenneth Rogoff, and Miguel Savastano. 2003. Debt Intolerance. Technical Report, National Bureau of Economic Research.
Rickard, Stephanie J. 2018. *Spending to Win: Political Institutions, Economic Geography, and Government Subsidies*. Cambridge: Cambridge University Press.
Riker, William H. 1962. *The Theory of Political Coalitions*. New Haven, CT: Yale University Press.
Robertson, Graeme B. 2007. "Strikes and labor organization in hybrid regimes." *American Political Science Review* 101(04):781–798.

Robertson, Graeme B. 2010. *The Politics of Protest in Hybrid Regimes: Managing Dissent in Post-Communist Russia.* Cambridge: Cambridge University Press.
Roos, Jerome E. 2019. *Why Not Default?: The Political Economy of Sovereign Debt.* Princeton, NJ: Princeton University Press.
Rose, Andrew K. 2005. "One reason countries pay their debts: Renegotiation and international trade." *Journal of Development Economics* 77(1):189–206.
Saasa, Oliver S. 1996. "Policy reforms and structural adjustment in Zambia: The case of agriculture and trade." *Technical Paper.*
Saiegh, Sebastian M. 2009. "Coalition governments and sovereign debt crises." *Economics & Politics* 21(2):232–254.
Sano, Hans-Otto. 1988. "The IMF and Zambia: The contradictions of exchange rate auctioning and de-subsidization of agriculture." *African Affairs* 87(349):563–577.
Schultz, Kenneth A. and Barry R. Weingast. 2003. "The democratic advantage: Institutional foundations of financial power in international competition." *International Organization* 57(1):3–42.
Schultz, Theodore W. 1978. *Distortions of Agricultural Incentives.* Bloomington, IN: Indiana University Press.
Scott, James C. 1985. *Weapons of the Weak: Everyday Forms of Peasant Resistance.* New Haven, CT: Yale University Press.
Seligson, Mitchell A. and Edward N. Muller. 1987. "Democratic stability and economic crisis: Costa Rica, 1978–1983." *International Studies Quarterly* 31(3):301–326.
Sen, Amartya. 1999. *Development as Freedom.* Oxford: Oxford University Press.
Sheng, Andrew. 1996. *Bank Restructuring: Lessons from the 1980s.* Washington, DC: World Bank Publications.
Simmons, Beth A. 1997. *Who Adjusts?: Domestic Sources of Foreign Economic Policy during the Interwar Years.* Princeton, NJ: Princeton University Press.
Stasavage, David. 2003. *Public Debt and the Birth of the Democratic State: France and Great Britain, 1688–1789.* Cambridge: Cambridge University Press.
Stasavage, David. 2005. "Democracy and education spending in Africa." *American Journal of Political Science* 49(2):343–358.
Stephens, Evelyne Huber, and John D. Stephens. 1986. *Democratic Socialism in Jamaica: The Political Movement and Social Transformation in Dependent Capitalism.* Princeton, NJ: Princeton University Press.
Stone, Carl. 1973. *Class, Race, and Political Behaviour in Urban Jamaica.* Mona: Institute of Social and Economic Research, University of the West Indies.
Stone, Carl. 1980. *Democracy and Clientelism in Jamaica.* New Brunswick, NJ: Transaction Books.
Stone, Randall W. 2004. "The political economy of IMF lending in Africa." *American Political Science Review* 98(04):577–591.
Stone, Randall W. 2008. "The scope of IMF conditionality." *International Organization* 62(4):589–620.
Sturzenegger, Federico and Jeromin Zettelmeyer. 2006. *Debt Defaults and Lessons from a Decade of Crises.* Cambridge, MA: MIT Press.
Svolik, Milan W. 2012. *The Politics of Authoritarian Rule.* Cambridge: Cambridge University Press.
Tilly, Charles. 2004. *Contention and Democracy in Europe, 1650–2000.* Cambridge: Cambridge University Press.

Tomz, Michael 2002. "Democratic default: Domestic audiences and compliance with international agreements." In *Paper delivered at the 2002 Annual Meeting of the American Political Science Association, Boston, August*. Stanford Working Paper.

Tomz, Michael 2004. "Voter sophistication and domestic preferences regarding debt default." Unpublished Working Paper, Stanford University, Palo Alto, CA.

Tomz, Michael. 2007. *Reputation and International Cooperation: Sovereign Debt across Three Centuries*. Princeton, NJ: Princeton University Press.

Tomz, Michael, Jason Wittenberg, and Gary King. 2003. "CLARIFY: Software for interpreting and presenting statistical results." *Journal of Statistical Software* 8(1):1–30.

Tomz, Michael and Mark L. J. Wright. 2013. "Empirical research on sovereign debt and default." *Annual Review of Economics* 5(1):247–272.

Van de Walle, Nicolas. 2001. *African Economies and the Politics of Permanent Crisis, 1979–1999*. Cambridge: Cambridge University Press.

Van Rijckeghem, Caroline and Beatrice Weder. 2009. "Political institutions and debt crises." *Public Choice* 138(3):387–408.

Varshney, Ashutosh. 1998. *Democracy, Development, and the Countryside: Urban-Rural Struggles in India*. Cambridge: Cambridge University Press.

Voeten, Erik and Adis Merdzanovic. 2009. "United Nations General Assembly Voting Data." *Washington, DC, United States: Georgetown University*. http://dvn.iq.harvard.edu/dvn/dv/Voeten/faces/study/StudyPage.xhtml.

Vogel, Robert C. 1984. "The effect of subsidized agricultural credit on income distribution in Costa Rica." In Undermining Rural Development with Cheap Credit. Dale W. Adams, Douglas H. Graham, and John D. Von Pischke (eds.). Boulder, CO: Westview Press.

Vreeland, James R. 2006. *The International Monetary Fund (IMF): Politics of Conditional Lending*. London: Routledge.

Wallace, Jeremy L. 2010. "Political economy of crisis: Exogenous shocks and Redistribution in Autocracies."

Wallace, Jeremy L. 2014. *Cities and Stability: Urbanization, Redistribution, and Regime Survival in China*. Oxford: Oxford University Press.

Walter, Stefanie. 2013. *Financial Crises and the Politics of Macroeconomic Adjustments*. Cambridge: Cambridge University Press.

Walter, Stefanie. 2016. "Crisis politics in Europe: Why austerity is easier to implement in some countries than in others." *Comparative Political Studies* 49(7):841–873.

Walton, John and David Seddon. 2008. *Free Markets and Food Riots: The Politics of Global Adjustment*. Cambridge, MA: Wiley-Blackwell.

Walton, John, Jonathan Shefner, and David Seddon. 1994. "Latin America: Popular protest and the state." In *Free Markets and Food Riots: The Politics of Global Adjustment*. John Walton and David Seddon (eds.). Cambridge, MA: Wiley-Blackwell 97–134.

Weinberg, Joe and Ryan Bakker. 2014. "Let them eat cake: Food prices, domestic policy and social unrest." *Conflict Management and Peace Science* 32(3): 309–326.

Weiss, Jessica C. 2013. "Authoritarian signaling, mass audiences, and nationalist protest in China." *International Organization* 67(1):1–35.

Weiss, Jessica C. 2014. *Powerful Patriots: Nationalist Protest in China's Foreign Relations*. Oxford: Oxford University Press.

Wibbels, Erik. 2006. "Dependency revisited: International markets, business cycles, and social spending in the developing world." *International Organization* 60(2):433–468.

Widner, Jennifer A. 1994. "Single party states and agricultural policies: The cases of Ivory Coast and Kenya." *Comparative Politics* 26(2):127–147.
Wilkinson, Steven I. 2006. *Votes and Violence: Electoral Competition and Ethnic Riots in India*. Cambridge: Cambridge University Press.
Wilson, Bruce M. 1994. "When social democrats choose neoliberal economic policies: The case of Costa Rica." *Comparative Politics* 26(2):149–168.
Wilson, Bruce M. 1996. "From democratic socialism to neoliberalism: The metamorphoses of the people's national party in Jamaica." *Studies in Comparative International Development* 31(2):58–82.
Wilson, Bruce M. 1998. *Costa Rica: Politics, Economics, and Democracy*. Boulder, CO: Lynne Rienner Publishers.
Wilson, Bruce M. 1999. "Leftist parties, neoliberal policies, and reelection strategies: The case of the PLN in Costa Rica." *Comparative Political Studies* 32(6):752–779.
World Bank. 1994. "Performance audit report: Republic of Costa Rica, structural adjustment loans I and II." Document of World Bank, http://documents.worldbank.org/curated/pt/766661468914965146/pdf/13263-PAR-REVISED-PUBLIC.pdf.
Yaakob, Usman, Tarmiji Masron, and Fujimaki Masami. 2010. "Ninety years of urbanization in Malaysia: A geographical investigation of its trends and characteristics." *Journal of Ritsumeikan Social Sciences and Humanities* 4(3):79–101.
Yusof, Zainal Aznam and Deepak Bhattasali. 2008. *Economic Growth and Development in Malaysia: Policy Making and Leadership*. Washington, DC: International Bank for Reconstruction and Development/The World Bank.

Index

African National Congress (ANC), 82
agricultural biases, 12–13
Akder, 157, 165–166
Allison, 80, 84, 90
Ameringer, 119
ANC, see African National Congress
Arab Spring, 22
Argentina, 7n6
  democratic default, 9, 37, 70
Arias Sanchez, Oscar, 116, 120
aura of invincibility, 44, 97
autocracies/autocrats, see also closed autocracies; competitive autocracies
  autocratic game proof, 48
  democracy compared to, 32
  food subsidy cost equations, 49–50
  future borrowing and, 24–25
  mass politics and, 24–26
  political limits of, 4
  political power of, 24
  voting and, 44–45
autocratic default, 9
  dilemma of, 30–31
  hypothesis 1 for, 31
  hypothesis 2 for, 31
  1960–2009 data, 60t
  proof for decision, 50–51
  urban bias and, 26–27
Aziz, 98

Bates, 19, 29, 33, 84, 85, 89, 92
Block, 33
block mobilization, 116–117

bondholder behavior, 7, 9
Borensztein, 7
bread riots, 2, 22–23
Brexit, 173
Bulow, J., 6–7
Bumiputera, 95, 106–109, 112

CACM, see Central American Common Market
Callaghy, 91, 92
Cañas, Alberto, 119
capital openness, 70
Carazo Odio, Rodrigo, 126–128
Caribbean Basin Initiative (CBI), 149
Carter, 71
Carvounis, 165
CBI, see Caribbean Basin Initiative
Celasun, 157, 159–160, 167
Central American Common Market (CACM), 125–126
Central Bank, Costa Rica, 131–133
Chinn, 29
citizen indirect utility equations, 49
citizen preferences, 21–22
Clark, 80, 84, 90
closed autocracies, 15, 26, see also Zambia
  case study, 43
  revolt in, 22–24
  urban bias and, 10–11
  urban bias/imported food and, 57–58
CODESA, see Costa Rican Development Corporation
Cole, 33

collective action, 18, 23
  age and gender in, 85
  of urban areas, 10
Collier, 84, 85, 89, 92
competitive autocracies
  legislature and, 11
  urban bias limits, 11–12, 43–45
conditional loan programs, 25
consolidated democracy, *see also* Costa Rica case study, 43
  agricultural electoral biases and, 12–13
  protest in, 35
  voting in, 35–38
contentious democracy, *see also* Jamaica case study
  agricultural biases and, 13
  default in, 137–138
  rural bias limits, 45–46
  violence in, 45–46, 172
  voting in, 46
Copelovitch, 70
Costa Rica case study, 14, 41, 116
  autonomous institution deficits in, 131
  case selection, 119–121
  Central Bank losses in, 131–133
  discussion, 155–156
  employment in, 124, 127, 130, 136
  farmers in, 119
  GDP in, 125, 127, 132
  geopolitics as challenge, 122–123
  IMF reform conditions in, 127–129
  institutional cross-conditionality/1986 elections and, 133
  Monge presidency in, 128–133
  pressure groups in Costa Rica, 120–121
  public sector wages in, 130–131
  rise of PLN in, 123–128
  term limits as challenge in, 121–122
  urbanization in, 120
Costa Rican Development Corporation (CODESA), 128, 131, 135
credit rationing, 8, 10n9, 25
Cruces, J. J., 7
Curtis, 37

DAI, *see* Distortions to Agricultural Incentives
debt, 1, *see also* sovereign debt
  debt restructuring, 7
  debt-to-GDP, 60, 62, 65, 72t
  repayment, 8
  shock triggers, 61
  sovereign default, 3

default, *see specific topics*
democracy, 10, *see also* consolidated democracy; contentious democracy
  autocracy compared to, 32
  rural-based agriculture in, 12, 33
  swingness in, 33, 35
  transition in Turkey, 159–160
  voting in, 32, 42, 44
democratic default
  in Argentina, 9, 37, 70
  citizen view on, 37–38
  dilemma of, 38–43
  in equilibrium, 40
  food exports and, 75t
  food price policies and, 38–40
  hypothesis 3 for, 41–42
  hypothesis 4 for, 42–43
  international influences, 46–48
  1960–2009 data, 61t
  rates of, 55–56
  rural bias and, 32–54, 57–58
  theoretical predictions for, 116–118
  urbanization and, 56, 70
  voting in consolidated democracy and, 35–38
democratic game
  derivation of food subsidy cost, 52–53
  party vote share proof, 54
  probability of electoral victory function, 53
  proof for timing of, 51–52
Democratic Party, Turkey (DP), 159
dictatorships, 10, *see also* Malaysia case study; Zambia case study
  elections and, 43–45
  food trade and, 57–58, 69, 104, 172
  pure, 11
  revolt and, 18, 27, 30, 68
  urban-biased, 13
  urbanization and, 56–57, 67
Distortions to Agricultural Incentives (DAI), 76–77
Dixit, 33
DP, *see* Democratic Party, Turkey
Dreher, 63
Drury, 80, 97, 99

Eaton, J., 6–7
economic crisis, 59–61, *see also* fiscal crisis
  political reform and, 4–6
economic reform, politics of, 4–6
economies
  IMF on Turkish, 162–164

Index

macroeconomics, 59–65
SEEs, 161, 167, 169
urbanization and, 62
Economist, 2
Edelman, 125
Edie, 116, 139
Egypt
  bakeries, 26
  bread riots, 2
  electoral system, 44n27
  food subsidies in, 1–2
elections, *see also* voting
  agricultural electoral biases, 12–13
  citizen revolts and, 13
  Costa Rica institutional cross-conditionality and, 133–137
  Costa Rican term limits, 121–122
  dictatorships and, 43–45
  Egypt, 44n27
  Malaysia, 96–98
  median voters, 36, 116–117, 119
  probability of electoral victory function in democratic game, 53
  pseudo-democratic elections, 44n26
  UMNO, 110–111
electoral autocracies, *see also* Malaysia case study
  characteristics of, 12, 43, 45
  voter mobilization and, 81
employment, 4, 85, 102, *see also* unemployment
  in Costa Rica case study, 124, 127, 130, 136
  in Jamaica case study, 142, 146
  in Malaysia case study, 107–108
Engel's Law, 10, 20, 174
equilibrium behavior, in mass politics, 30–31

farmers, 4, 28
  Costa Rica, 14, 119
  empowerment of, 32
  farming blocs, 63
  GSE, 77
  rural, 10, 21, 114, 119, 137, 166, 169, 172
Faustian Bargain of urban bias, 29
Federal Land Development Agency (FELDA), 100, 102
fiscal crisis
  1978 in Turkey, 162–164
  in developed world, 174
  Jamaica case study background, 141–148
  in Malaysia case study, 107–115
  Turkey case study buildup, 160–162
  in Zambia case study, 88–93

fiscal footprint, 91, 142, 175
food consumption, 21–22, 29–30, 49, 90
food trade
  agricultural pricing policies, 19–20
  cost of subsidy program and status, 27–30
  democratic default and food exports, 75t
  democratic default and food price policies, 38–40
  derivation of subsidy cost in democratic game, 52–53
  dictatorships and, 57, 69, 104, 172
  equations for subsidy costs in autocracy, 49–50
  farming blocs, 63
  food subsidies, 1–2, 26, 30, 173
  food subsidy costs, 74–78
  generalizability of, 15
  IMF on subsidies, 88, 92
  Malaysian food subsidies, 104
  Malaysian rice production, 99–100
  revolt and food crises, 22–23
  rural-biased export cost regime, 28
  rural-biased import cost regime, 28–29
  sovereign default and, 172
  urban bias and, 10–11
  urban bias/imported food in closed autocracy, 57–58
  urban-biased export cost regime, 28
  urban-biased import cost regime, 28–29
  urbanization and, 14, 66t
  urbanization/sovereign default and, 66t
  in Zambia case study, 85–89, 91–92
foreign reserves/months of imports, 68
Frankel, 34, 97
French Revolution, 22
Frieden, Jeffry A., 4, 34

garrison communities, 138
GATT, 163
GDP
  change in, 61–62
  in Costa Rica case study, 125, 127, 132
  debt-to-GDP, 60, 62, 67, 72t, 79t
  food imports over, 63, 66, 72t, 75t
  GDP per capita, 60, 62, 79t
  in Jamaica case study, 152
  in Malaysia case study, 114
  in Turkey case study, 168
  in Zambia case study, 88
Gerakan, *see* Parti Gerakan Rakyat Malaysia
Gersovitz, M., 6–7

GNP, in Malaysia case study, 107, 108, 112, 114
Gold Standard, 4
Golden, 33
González Vega, 126, 130
Gourevitch, Peter, 4, 19
government monopsony, 27n12
Great Leap Forward, 29
gross subsidy equivalent to farmers (GSE), 78

Hafner-Burton, 13, 46
Haggard, 33
Harding, 34
Hawkins, 85, 89
Hendrix, 33
Hollyer, 64
Huber, 139, 148–149, 154
Hyde, 13, 46

ICA, see Industrial Coordination Act, Malaysia
Ilkkaracan, 167–168
IMF, see International Monetary Fund
India, rural bias in, 32–33
Industrial Coordination Act, Malaysia (ICA), 106
International Monetary Fund (IMF), 47, 63
  Costa Rica reform conditions, 127–130
  cross-conditionality of, 133–134, 136
  documents, 81
  on fiscal imbalance, 108
  on food subsidies, 88, 92
  Jamaica reform demands, 149–150, 152, 154–155
  on Malaysian policies, 98–99, 102, 107, 112–114
  pricing policies, 147
  on public wage restraint, 131
  reform demands of, 89–90
  on Turkish economy, 162–164
Ito, 70

Jablonski, 13, 46
Jamaica case study, 14–15, 116
  case selection, 138–140
  challenges to, 140–141
  discussion, 155–156
  employment in, 142, 146
  fiscal crisis background, 141–148
  garrison communities in, 138
  GDP in, 152
  IMF pricing policies in, 147
  IMF reform demands, 149–150, 152, 154–155
  labor unions and, 151
  oil prices and, 142
  People's Production Plan in, 145–148
  Seaga presidency in, 148–155
  unemployment in, 150, 151, 153–154
Jamaican Labour Party (JLP), 138–139, 141, 143–144, 148–149, 152–153
Japan, rural-based agriculture in, 34
Jeffersonian ideal republic, 166
JLP, see Jamaican Labour Party
JP, see Justice Party, Turkey
Jupille, 37
Justice Party, Turkey (JP), 165

Kasara, 33
Kaunda, Kenneth, 55, 82, 91
  ouster of, 93
  reforms of, 89, 93
  urban bias under, 83–88
Kohlscheen, 9
Kraay, 8, 33, 61

Lall, 64
Leblang, 37
Lewis, 138
Londregan, 33

Magaloni, 11, 44
Mahathir bin Mohamad, 108, 110, 112–113
Malay party of the Alliance bloc (UMNO), 95–102, 104, 106–107
  coalition members, 113
  elections, 110–111
  support base, 115
Malaysia case study, 14
  Bumiputera in, 95, 106–109, 112
  case selection, 94
  directed credit requirement, 105
  discussion, 115
  employment in, 107–108
  fiscal crisis/reform in, 107–115
  food subsidies in, 104
  GDP in, 114
  GNP in, 107, 108, 112, 114
  growth of urban base in Malaysia, 106–107
  IMF on Malaysian policies, 98–99, 102, 107, 111–112, 114
  Malaysian early history, 94–96
  Malaysian elections and political geography, 96–98

Index

May 13 Incident, 96, 98
NEP in, 98–101, 106, 109, 111, 113
OBAs in, 109
privatization in, 113
rice production in, 99–100
SMP in, 99–100
Third Malaysian Plan in, 103
unemployment in, 98–99, 102
urban counter pressure in Malaysia, 101–106
Manley, Michael, 141, 154
first term of, 141–145
second term of, 145–148
mass politics, 14, 173, *see also* collective action
autocrats and, 24–26
cost of subsidy program and food trade status, 27–30
equilibrium behavior in, 30–31
formalization of citizen preferences in, 21–22
political survival and, 17–31
revolt in closed autocracy, 22–24
theory, 35
urban bias and autocratic default, 26–27
urban–rural divide and, 18–20
May 13 Incident, 96, 101
median voters, 36, 116, 119
Medicare, 37, 174
Merdzanovic, 63
Meyer, 35
Milne, 110, 112
Min, 33
Moghadam, 167
Monge, Luis Alberto, 128–133
Mosley, Paul, 5, 60
Mulgan, 34

NAMBOARD, *see* National Agricultural Marketing Board, Zambia
Narayanan, 113
National Agricultural Marketing Board, Zambia (NAMBOARD), 85–86
National Elections Across Democracy and Autocracy (NELDA), 68
National Salvation Party, Turkey, 165
Nehru, 8, 61
NELDA, *see* National Elections Across Democracy and Autocracy
Nelson, 38, 121, 136
New Economic Policy, Malaysia (NEP), 98–101, 106, 109, 111, 113

Nokyo, 34
Nooruddin, Irfan, 4

OBAs, *see* off-budget agencies
OECD, *see* Organisation for Economic Co-operation and Development
off-budget agencies (OBAs), 109
oil rents per capita, 68
Olson, 18
OPEC crisis of 1979, 107
Organisation for Economic Co-operation and Development (OECD), 5, 164, 166, 169
Ozal, Turgut, 158, 168

Panizza, 7
Parti Gerakan Rakyat Malaysia (Gerakan), 95
Party of National Liberation, Costa Rica (PLN), 123–128
Pathmanathan, 110–112
Paul, Rand, 1
Payne, 151, 153–155
Peoples' National Party, Jamaica (PNP), 138–139, 141, 143–148
supporters, 153
People's Production Plan, Jamaica, 145–148
Pepinsky, Thomas B., 5, 45, 97, 101, 113
Persson, 20
PLN, *see* Party of National Liberation, Costa Rica
PNG, *see* private non-guaranteed
PNP, *see* Peoples' National Party, Jamaica
political reform, 4–6
political survival, 171
mass politics and, 17–31
sovereign default and, 16–17
politics
Costa Rica geopolitics, 122–123
domestic and international markets, 172–173
of economic reform, 4–6
as fiscal, 2
political survival, 16–17
of sovereign default, 3, 9–10
urban–rural, 173
PPG, *see* public and publicly guaranteed
Pressure Groups in Costa Rica (Arias Sanchez), 120
private non-guaranteed (PNG), 70
privatization, 113
problem of authoritarian control, 27n14
pseudo-democratic elections, 44n26
public and publicly guaranteed (PPG), 70

Rakner, 91
Rasiah, 106, 108
regime-contingent theory of sovereign default, 3, 13, 32–33, 35, 42
　alternate accounts in, 67–69
　data and estimation for, 59
　discussion, 78
　food subsidy costs in, 74–78
　macroeconomic explanations in, 59–65
　motivation in, 55–57
　reform and, 123
　results from baseline specifications, 65–67
　rural bias and democratic default, 58
　temporal/systemic factors in, 70–74
　urban bias/imported food in closed autocracy, 57–58
Reinhart, Carmen M., 3, 8, 59, 62
relative rate of assistance to agriculture (RRA), 76–77
Republican People's Party, Turkey (RPP), 159, 165
revolt, 18
　in closed autocracies, 22–24
　dictatorship and, 18, 27, 30, 68
　elections and, 13
　food crises and, 22–24
risk premia, 5, 8
Robertson, 35
Rodrik, 157, 159–160, 167
Rogoff, Kenneth S., 3, 6–8, 59, 62
Rose, A., 7
Rosendorff, 64
RPP, *see* Republican People's Party, Turkey
RRA, *see* relative rate of assistance to agriculture
rural bias
　democratic default and, 32–48, 58
　food export cost regime, 28
　food import cost regime, 28–29
　in India, 32–33
　limits, in contentious democracy, 11–12
　in Turkey case study, 166
rural citizens, *see* urban–rural divide
rural-based agriculture
　in democracies, 12, 33
　in Japan, 34
　in Turkey, 15
Russian Revolution, 22

Sadat, Anwar, 1
Saiegh, 9
Sano, 88
Savastano, 8
Seaga, Edward, 141, 143
　presidency of, 148–155
Second Malaysia Plan (SMP), 99–100
Seddon, 22
SEEs, *see* State Economic Enterprises
Sen, 32
serial default, 71
Shari, 106, 108
Sheng, 107
Signorino, 71
Simmons, Beth, 4
Simmons, Joel W., 4
Singh, Charan, 32
SMP, *see* Second Malaysia Plan
Social Security, 37, 174
Soil Products Marketing Organization (TOPRAK), 161–162
sovereign borrowing, 5, 62
　over-borrowing, 175
　reputation-based arguments for, 7–8
sovereign debt, 3, 6
　enforceability in, 16
　as puzzle, 15
sovereign default, *see also* autocratic default; democratic default; regime-contingent theory of sovereign default
　causes and consequences of, 6–9
　conditions for, 6
　in contentious democracy, 137–138
　of Costa Rica, 14
　debt and, 3
　decision to, 171–172
　in developing countries, 9–10
　food imports/urbanization and, 66t
　food trade and, 172
　future borrowing and, 7–8
　of Jamaica, 14–15
　political survival and, 16–17
　politics of, 4, 9–10
　reputation damage with, 16
　serial default, 71
Stasavage, 9, 27
State Economic Enterprises (SEEs), 161, 167, 169
Steinberg, 38
Stephens, 139, 141, 143–144, 146–149, 154
Stone, 139–140, 144
Stone-Geary utility function, 21
Svolik, 11, 27n14, 69
swingness, 151
　in democracy, 35
　in rural and urban voters, 41, 166

Index

Tabellini, 33
Tarrow, 35
Tilly, 35
Tomz, 7–9, 37
TOPRAK, *see* Soil Products Marketing Organization
Trebesch, C., 7
Tunali, 167–168
Turkey case study, 101
  case selection, 159
  conclusion, 169–170
  first fiscal crisis buildup in, 160–162
  fiscal crisis of 1978 in, 162–164
  GDP in, 168
  IMF on Turkish economy, 162–164
  military invention of 1980–1985 in, 167–169
  rural bias in, 166
  rural electoral advantage in, 164–167
  rural-based agriculture in, 15
  TOPRAK in, 161–162
  transition to democracy in, 159–160

UMNO, *see* Malay party of the Alliance bloc
unemployment, 25, 90
  in Jamaica case study, 150, 151, 153
  in Malaysia case study, 98–99, 101–102
unionized labor, 19, 151
United National Independence Party, Malaysia (UNIP), 82–85, 87, 93
urban bias
  autocratic default and, 26–27
  closed autocracies and, 10–11
  Faustian Bargain of, 29
  food export cost regime, 29
  food import cost regime, 30
  food trade and, 10–11
  imported food in closed autocracy, 57–58
  under Kaunda, Zambia case study, 83–88
  limits, in competitive autocracies, 11–12, 43–45
  urban-biased dictatorship, 13
urbanization, 14, 31, 117
  in Costa Rica case study, 120
  democratic default and, 56, 70
  dictatorship and, 56–57, 67
  economies and, 62
  food trade/sovereign default and, 66t
  measures for, 63–64

urban–rural divide, 18–20, 173
urban–rural politics, 173
US Agency for International Development (USAID), 123, 129, 135

Van de Walle, Nicolas, 4
Van Rijckeghem, 9
Varshney, 32
violence, 45–46, 172
Voeten, 63
Vogel, 132
voting, 14, 18
  autocracies and, 44–45
  in consolidated democracy, 35–38
  in contentious democracy, 46
  in democracy, 32, 42, 44
  mass unrest and, 171
Vreeland, 64
vulnerability profiles, 5

Wallace, 29
Walter, S., 5–6
Walton, 22
WDI, *see* World Development Indicators
Weder, 9
Wilkinson, 46
Wilson, 119, 122, 124–125, 128, 154
World Bank, 1, 47, 60, 74, 123
  cross-conditionality of, 133–137
  loans from, 127, 152
  reform conditions, 130
World Development Indicators (WDI), 60
World Trade Organization (WTO), 63

Yang Di Pertuan Agong, 110

Zambia case study, 14
  case selection, 82
  copper revenues in, 84
  discussion, 115
  food policies in, 85–89, 91–92
  GDP in, 88
  post-electoral reforms, 93
  urban bias under Kaunda, 83–88
  Zambian early history, 82–83
  Zambian response to fiscal crisis, 88–93
Zambia Congress of Trade Unions (ZCTU), 83

For EU product safety concerns, contact us at Calle de José Abascal, 56–1°, 28003 Madrid, Spain or eugpsr@cambridge.org

www.ingramcontent.com/pod-product-compliance
Ingram Content Group UK Ltd.
Pitfield, Milton Keynes, MK11 3LW, UK
UKHW020403060825
461487UK00009B/790